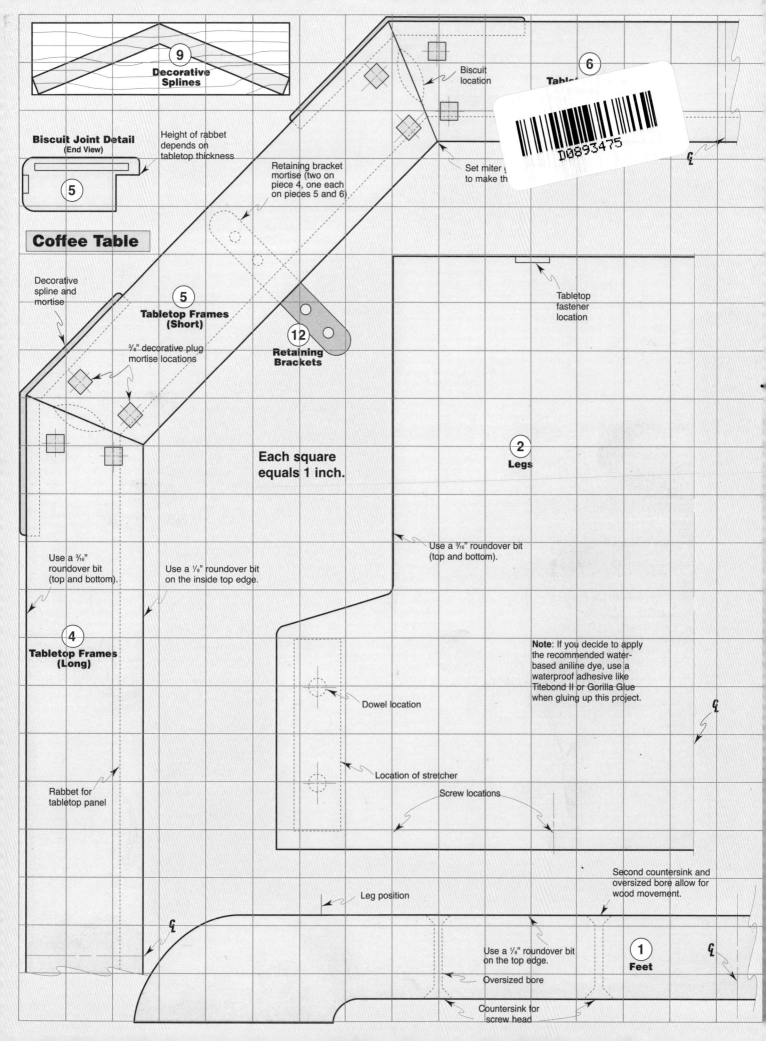

Coffee Table

Decorative Splines
9

Biscuit Joint Detail
(End View)
5

Height of rabbet depends on tabletop thickness

Decorative spline and mortise

Retaining bracket mortise (two on piece 4, one each on pieces 5 and 6)

Biscuit location

6

Tablet...

Set miter g...
to make th...

Tabletop Frames (Short)
5

³⁄₈" decorative plug mortise locations

Retaining Brackets
12

Tabletop fastener location

Legs
2

Use a ³⁄₁₆" roundover bit (top and bottom).

Each square equals 1 inch.

Note: If you decide to apply the recommended water-based aniline dye, use a waterproof adhesive like Titebond II or Gorilla Glue when gluing up this project.

Use a ³⁄₁₆" roundover bit (top and bottom).

Use a ¹⁄₈" roundover bit on the inside top edge.

Tabletop Frames (Long)
4

Rabbet for tabletop panel

Dowel location

Location of stretcher

Screw locations

Second countersink and oversized bore allow for wood movement.

Leg position

Feet
1

Use a ¹⁄₈" roundover bit on the top edge.

Oversized bore

Countersink for screw head

From the Editors of

WOODWORKER'S JOURNAL®

Home Woodworking:
Classic Projects for Your Home and Shop

Safety First: Learning how to operate power and hand tools is essential for developing safe woodworking practices. For purposes of clarity, necessary guards have been removed from equipment shown in our book. We do not recommend using this equipment without safety guards and urge readers to follow manufacturers' instruction and safety precautions.

Home Woodworking:
Classic Projects for Your Home and Shop

Produced by Woodworker's Journal with Hylas Publishing

Hylas Publishing®
129 Main Street, Ste. C
Irvington, NY 10533
www.hylaspublishing.com

4365 Willow Drive • Medina, MN 55340

Hylas Publishing
Publisher: Sean Moore
Creative Director: Karen Prince
Art Director: Gus Yoo
Editorial Director: Gail Greiner
Production Managers: Sarah Reilly, Wayne Ellis
Designer: Marian Purcell

Woodworker's Journal
Editor in Chief: Larry N. Stoiaken
Senior Editor: Chris Marshall
Contributing Writers: Rob Johnstone, Rick White, Jeff Jacobson, Len Urban, Rick Christoperson, Dick Dorn, Mike McGlynn, Dick Coers, Jim Jacobson, David Larson
Illustrators: Jeff Jacobson, John Kelliher

ISBN: 1-59258-208-7

Library of Congress Cataloging-in-Publication Data available upon request.
Printed and bound in China
Distributed in the United States by National Book Network
Distributed in Canada by Kate Walker & Company, Ltd.
First American Edition published in 2006
10 9 8 7 6 5 4 3 2 1

Hard-To-Find Hardware: Our friends at Rockler Woodworking and Hardware supplied us with most of the hardware used in this book. We highly recommend them as a source. Visit rockler.com or call them at 800-279-4441.

TABLE OF CONTENTS

INTRODUCTION

Sometimes the hours you spend out of the shop and under a reading lamp studying a good woodworking book can be as rewarding as actually making the sawdust. Building from published plans can save you time as well as some of the headaches that come from designing a new, untested project. At the very least, you'll probably learn a few new and clever ways of doing things or take elements from these projects and transform them into your own unique furniture. Good design doesn't have to be a secret; we all learn from sharing our shop successes (and hard knocks!) along the way.

Woodworker's Journal has always advocated this "community" approach to woodworking. You'll see the evidence in this new book, "Home Woodworking: Classic Projects for Your Home and Shop". If it's a good technique article you're after, be sure to read "Avoiding Kickback" on page 52 or the Journal's approach to creating keen cutting edges (page 8). Maybe some shop organization or an improvement in workflow is in order. Find options for storing lumber and plywood on page 30, or build the Sharpening Station, Downdraft Workbench, Mobile Clamp Cart or Sandpaper Caddy. These sensible shop projects will help you get down to business faster so you can build more projects with less effort.

If you'd rather jump straight into making furniture, we've selected some gems in this book. For the bedroom, consider building contributing editor Rick White's matching ash-and-walnut Bowfront Bureau and Bed for Reader's. Need a signature piece for the den or home office? For a good challenge, try your hand at the Federal Secretary Desk, and to compliment your other favorite hobby, build the Angler's Cabinet. We also tip our hats to the Greene brothers and the Arts and Crafts movement with classic serving and coffee table plans. The handsome Trestle Table on page 112 will get rave reviews at your next holiday meal, and so will the butcher-block style Kitchen Island, where everyone usually gathers anyway.

Maybe your shop time is limited to Saturday afternoons, and you need projects with shorter material lists. No problem: The Entry Bench, Portable Folding Bench and One-board Hall Table should help scratch that weekend woodworking itch.

Each of the 19 projects in this book includes a complete materials list, construction drawings, how-to photographs and informative directions that helps you every step of the way. There's even Pinup Shop Drawings included on the inside covers that you can copy and post right in the shop to provide some full-size patterns and helpful technical details when you're in the thick of things.

So, by all means study these projects and techniques carefully, but then get out there and make some chips fly. We hope this book will inspire you to keep on reading— and of course, making sawdust.

Larry Stoiaken
Editor in Chief,
Woodworker's Journal Magazine
www.woodworkersjournal.com

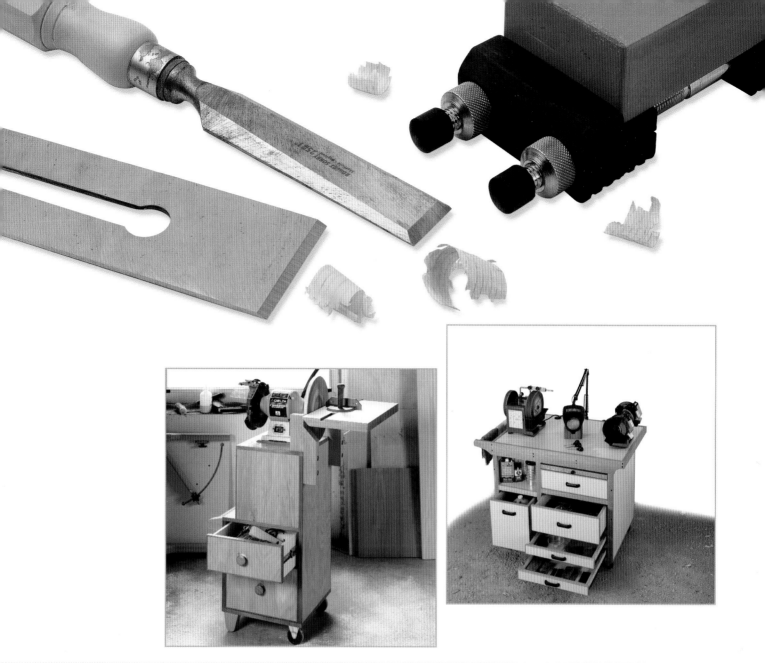

Shop Projects

Nine proven shop techniques, jigs and fixtures
that add safety and convenience to your woodworking.

Thin, Smooth and Strong

As editor Rob Johnstone's luthiery instructor once explained, "The perfect cutting edge would be infinitely thin, infinitely smooth and infinitely strong — anything else is a compromise of one sort or another." With that as gospel, every cutting edge we use must be an appropriately designed compromise. When you sharpen a knife, a gouge or a chisel, your goal will be to create the smoothest, thinnest edge that will remain strong enough to perform its task. This isn't as tricky as it may sound, since most tools have the manufacturer's best guess for the optimum cutting edge already ground and polished.

Provided you keep the factory bevel when you sharpen your tools, in most circumstances you'll end up with serviceable cutting edges. But as soon as you start changing bevels and regrinding willy-nilly, that's when you'll run into trouble. This sort of significant grinding should be reserved for dire situations — badly nicked or seriously deformed edges.

Grinding

Grinding and honing are the two basic steps in sharpening any knife-edged tool. Grinding removes a significant amount of metal and sets you up for honing success. It is also the step where danger lurks. Improper grinding will generate excessive heat and change the metal's temper — the official term for the strength component of our perfect cutting edge. Using a lubricated grinding wheel run at a slow speed and removing the minimum amount of material are keys to keeping your tool's temper ... and yours, too. The wheel also must be the correct coarseness — just coarse enough to cut metal without compromising your ability to control the process.

The first important detail in any single-beveled edge is that the back of the blade must be perfectly flat. Another general principle for those of us who don't do a lot of grinding is to avoid changing the angle of the existing bevel. The bevel of an edge is the compromise of a steel tool relative to our goal of infinite thinness. Most cutting bevels will be within the 25° to 35° range. Unless your expertise exceeds that of the manufacturer, make every effort to keep the existing bevel of the tool — even when you need to remove a good deal of metal (as when eliminating a large nick). This is true if it is a regular chisel, double-beveled knife or a curved gouge. Also, with the aid of an appropriate guide or jig, do your best not to grind out of square or change the shape of the curved or shaped edge you are grinding.

Dull and damaged cutting edges are dangerous and unnecessary. Follow these guidelines and step-by-step instructions to create sharp, clean cutting edges.

STEP 1 *Flatten the back and remove milling marks on a lapping plate. Use emery paper mounted to a flat surface and a figure-eight stroke.*

STEP 2 *Next, use a bench-top grinder to create a proper, hollow-ground cutting bevel. Grind with a light hand!*

STEP 3 *Move through a series of ever finer-grained stones to polish the bevel and back to mirror smoothness.*

Honing

Honing starts where grinding ends. After you have successfully ground the edge to the proper angle (thinness), while retaining the temper (strength), you must hone the edge to a mirror finish (infinitely smooth). Compared to the grinding operation, honing can be a pleasurable, somewhat meditative experience … which is good, as it is a process not to be hurried. Begin with a coarser stone (a diamond "stone" is a good choice) to remove the grinding marks and establish the honing bevel. When the primary bevel is smooth, many sharpeners add five to ten degrees of bevel to the very tip of the ground edge. This "microbevel" makes the edge a little thinner while smoothing the actual cutting edge.

Move from coarse to ever finer-grained stones, making the same number of strokes on both faces of the tool. Don't skip a grit level as you hone. Missing a degree of coarseness will not save you time, and will negatively affect your edge. The smoother you hone, the sharper your tool. You may even choose to continue past the point where you can use stones effectively. If so, you'll need a polishing wheel or a leather strop.

Tools with curved or shaped edges are sharpened in the exact same way as flat-edged tools. Their shapes just present more complicated challenges. Slip stones and shaped grinding accessories provide solutions for grinding and honing curved edges effectively.

Infinitely thin, smooth and strong cutting edges are beyond what we woodworkers are able to produce, but by following these basic guidelines, you will have tools of exceptional sharpness. And that's the gospel truth.

SURROUNDED BY STONES

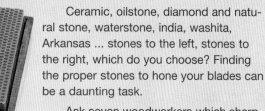

Diamond Stones: fast cutting, low build-up.

Oilstones: the workhorses for honing.

Ceramic, oilstone, diamond and natural stone, waterstone, india, washita, Arkansas ... stones to the left, stones to the right, which do you choose? Finding the proper stones to hone your blades can be a daunting task.

Ask seven woodworkers which sharpening stones they prefer and you'll get seven different answers. And that's exactly the point. Used properly and regularly, all the popular choices will do the job of keeping your edges sharp.

Rob Johnstone's personal preference runs in the direction of diamond and hard Arkansas stones; he likes to get done in a hurry. The slip stones that keep his gouges keen are also from a variety of materials. The stone's composition isn't nearly as important as how you use it. Using proper lubricants (water for waterstones and whet stones, oil for oilstones), storing your stones properly and using them regularly is far more important.

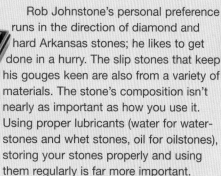

Ceramic: efficient and clean.

Select stones and sharpening systems to suit your budget. If you're just getting started, try the stones a woodworking friend uses and see how they work for you.

Waterstones from Asia have helped to spark renewed interest in sharpening.

The Ultimate Sharpening Station

There seems to be a strong correlation between the amount of time woodworkers spend in the shop and the shape of their tools. Novices rarely sharpen, while the pros are almost fanatical about slurries, grits and bevel angles. During editor Rob Johnstone's quarter of a century as a professional woodworker, he's accumulated most of the elements of a great sharpening station. Trouble was, the tools and supplies were so widely scattered around the shop that an otherwise calming activity — sharpening — was becoming more and more of a headache. Then the resolve came: Time to stop searching for stuff and start building them a proper home.

Starting with the Carcass

Melamine-coated particleboard is a great choice for the carcass of this station because it's durable, inexpensive and resistant to the fluids involved in sharpening. It's heavy, too, and this extra weight doesn't hurt; the station needs to be solid to absorb the vibrations of machines and the elbow grease of a determined woodworker.

Begin construction by cutting parts to the dimensions shown in the Material List on the next page. After counterboring and predrilling for the screws (see the Technical Drawings on page 14 for locations), glue and screw the bottom trim (pieces 1) to the bottom edge of two of the sides (pieces 2). Use three 2" screws (pieces 3) to secure each piece of trim.

The remaining side serves as a center divider and is attached to the bottom (piece 4) with screws. Lay out and predrill the countersunk holes in the bottom as shown in the Technical Drawings. Before attaching it, bore countersunk holes through two faces of the divider cleat (piece 5) and mount it to the back end of the divider, as shown in the Carcass Exploded View on page 13. Attach the center divider to the bottom, using care to keep the pieces square.

Next, glue and clamp trim (pieces 6 and 7) to the side and bottom edges of the back (piece 8). Now, with the T-shaped subassembly on a large flat surface, glue and clamp both sides to the bottom.

After the glue cures, glue and clamp the back to the sides and the bottom. Next, make sure the center divider is perfectly square within the cabinet cavity and drive

screws into the back through the remaining holes in the divider cleat. To keep the assembly from moving, tack a temporary cleat across the top of the three sides with short brads. You can remove it once the face frame is in place.

The left-hand bay of your new carcass receives a shelf (piece 9) supported by four cleats (pieces 10 and 11). Predrill three of the cleats for 1¼" screws (pieces 12) at the locations shown on the *Technical Drawings*, then fasten the cleats in place. Drive screws up through the cleats to secure the shelf. The last cleat will be attached to the face frame later.

Making the Face Frame

With the rough treatment this sharpening station will receive over the years, it

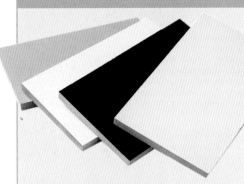

MELAMINE

If you happen to have a chemistry lab attached to your shop, heat up a bucket of dicyandiamide and you'll have the chief component for making melamine resin. Add formaldehyde and you're on your way to a nice laminated plastic. Now all you have to do is impregnate some Kraft paper with phenolic resin and bond it to your melamine layer.

Too much? The alternative is to walk into a building supply center and ask for melamine board. They'll show you a stack of particleboard with a plastic covering that works great for projects like this sharpening center. Melamine comes in several colors and is sold oversized at 49" x 97" to allow for trimming.

Four Steps to Chip-free Cutting

1. Use a zero-clearance insert.
2. Cut pieces slightly oversized.
3. Use a straightedge and a sharp knife to score the material at the exact size you need.
4. Put a carbide plywood-cutting blade (very slight set on the teeth) in your table saw and cut to exact size.

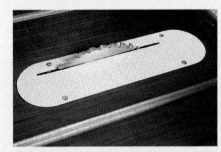

A zero-clearance insert is the real key to creating clean, chip-free edges when cutting melamine-coated materials on a table saw.

MATERIAL LIST—*CARCASS & DRAWERS*

#		T x W x L
1	Bottom Trim, Sides (2)	3/4" x 1 1/2" x 24"
2	Sides (3)	3/4" x 24" x 28 1/2"
3	Large Screws (50)	#8 x 2"
4	Bottom (1)	3/4" x 24" x 35 1/2"
5	Divider Cleat (1)	3/4" x 3/4" x 28 1/2"
6	Back Trim, Sides (2)	3/4" x 3/4" x 29 1/4"
7	Back Trim, Bottom (1)	3/4" x 3/4" x 37"
8	Back (1)	3/4" x 28 1/2" x 37"
9	Shelf (1)	3/4" x 14 1/2" x 24"
10	Shelf Cleats, Sides (2)	3/4" x 3/4" x 22 1/2"
11	Shelf Cleats, Front and Back (2)	3/4" x 3/4" x 14 1/2"
12	Small Screws (50)	#6 x 1 1/4"
13	Frame Top & Bottom Rails (2)	3/4" x 1 1/2" x 35 1/2"
14	Frame Side Stiles (2)	3/4" x 1 1/2" x 29 1/4"
15	Frame Middle Stile (1)	3/4" x 1 1/2" x 26 1/4"
16	Frame Left Rail (1)	3/4" x 1 1/2" x 13"
17	Frame Right Rails (3)	3/4" x 1 1/2" x 21"
18	Frame Dowels (26)	3/8" *Dia. Fluted*
19	Trim Plugs (26)	3/8" *Oak face grain*
20	Drawer Spacers (7)	3/4" x 2 1/2" x 20 5/8"
21	Drawer Slides (6 pairs)	22" *Blum 3/4 extension*
22	Tray (1)	3/4" x 20" x 23 1/4"
23	Tray Liner (1)	1/4" x 20" x 23 1/4"
24	Tray Front (1)	3/4" x 1 1/2" x 20 7/8"
25	Left Drawer Front & Back (2)	3/4" x 14" x 10 1/2"
26	Left Drawer Sides (2)	3/4" x 14" x 22"
27	Left Drawer Bottom (1)	1/4" x 12" x 22"
28	Left Drawer Face (1)	3/4" x 12 1/2" x 14 1/2"
29	Upper Drawer Front & Back (2)	3/4" x 4 1/2" x 18 1/2"
30	Upper Drawer Sides (2)	3/4" x 4 1/2" x 22"
31	Upper Drawer Bottom (1)	1/4" x 20" x 22"
32	Upper Drawer Face (1)	3/4" x 5 3/4" x 20 1/2"
33	Large Drawer Front & Back (2)	3/4" x 6 1/4" x 18 1/2"
34	Large Drawer Sides (2)	3/4" x 6 1/4" x 22"
35	Large Drawer Bottom (1)	1/4" x 20" x 22"
36	Large Drawer Face (1)	3/4" x 7 1/2" x 20 1/2"
37	Small Drawer Fronts, Backs (4)	3/4" x 1 3/4" x 18 1/2"
38	Small Drawer Sides (4)	3/4" x 1 3/4" x 22"
39	Small Drawer Bottoms (2)	1/4" x 20" x 22"

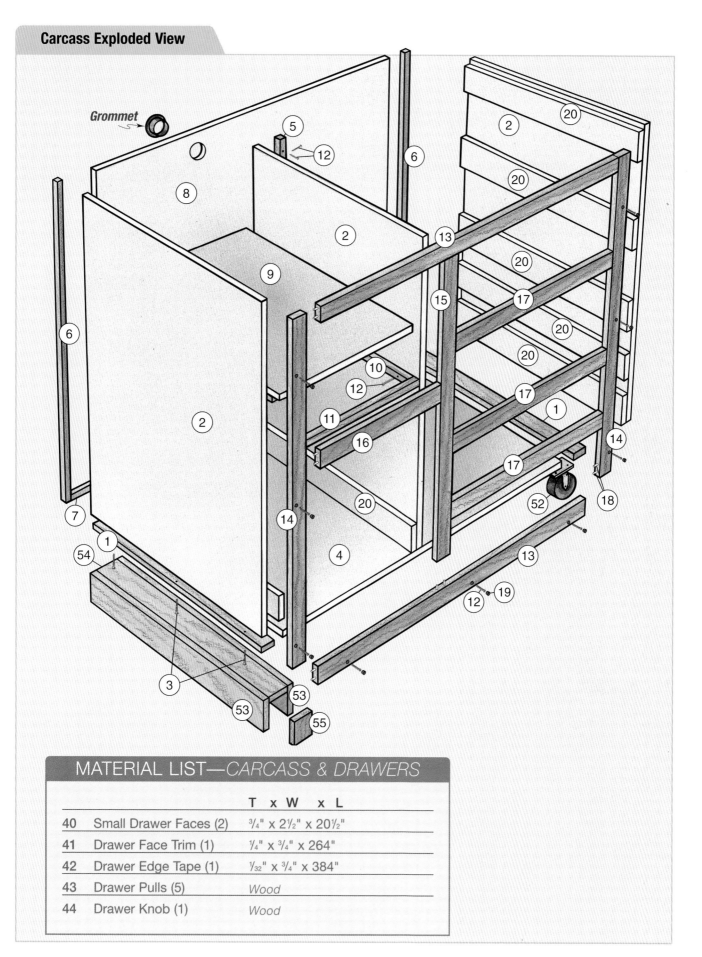

Grommet

MATERIAL LIST—*CARCASS & DRAWERS*

		T x W x L
40	Small Drawer Faces (2)	³⁄₄" x 2¹⁄₂" x 20¹⁄₂"
41	Drawer Face Trim (1)	¹⁄₄" x ³⁄₄" x 264"
42	Drawer Edge Tape (1)	¹⁄₃₂" x ³⁄₄" x 384"
43	Drawer Pulls (5)	Wood
44	Drawer Knob (1)	Wood

Carcass Joinery: Cleat and Spacer Locations
(Front View)

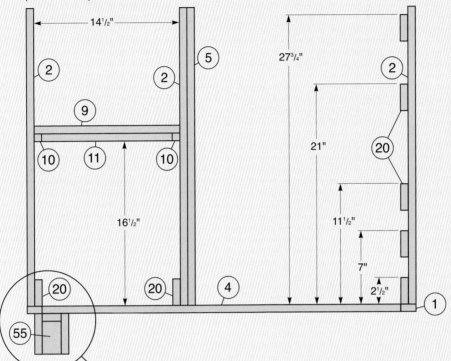

14¹/₂"

② ⑤

② ⑨

⑩ ⑪ ⑩

27³/₄"

② ⑳

21"

16¹/₂"

11¹/₂"

⑳ ⑳ ④

7"

2¹/₂"

① ①

⑳

55

Foot Detail
(Section View)

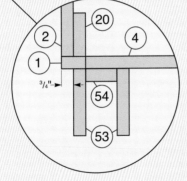

⑳

② ④

①

³/₄"

54

53

Chamfer the front
edges of the tray front.

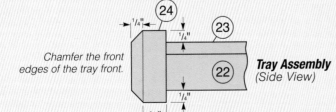

24

¹/₄"

¹/₄"

23

22

¹/₄"

¹/₂"

Tray Assembly
(Side View)

Face Frame Layout
(Front View)

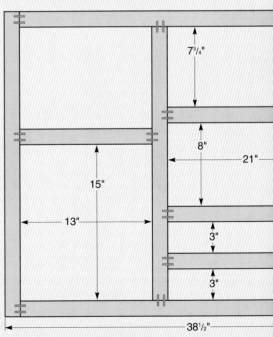

7³/₄"

8"

21"

15"

13"

3"

3"

38¹/₂"

The work top frame fits outside of
the carcass and rests on the work
frame supports.

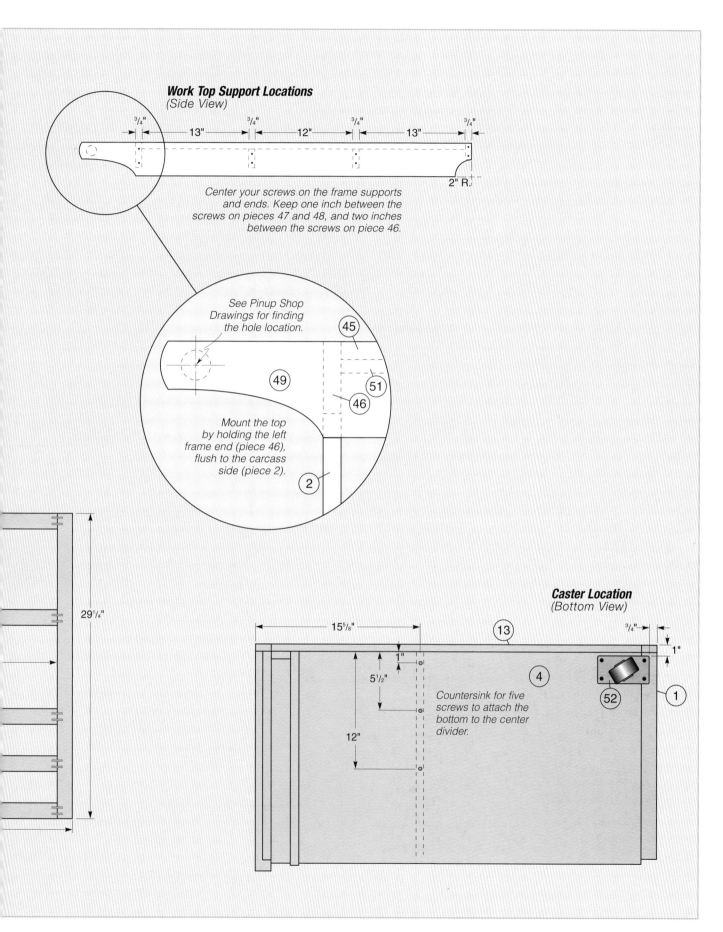

Work Top Support Locations
(Side View)

3/4" ⊢13"⊣ 3/4" ⊢12"⊣ 3/4" ⊢13"⊣ 3/4"

2" R.

Center your screws on the frame supports
and ends. Keep one inch between the
screws on pieces 47 and 48, and two inches
between the screws on piece 46.

See Pinup Shop
Drawings for finding
the hole location.

(45)

(49)

(51)

(46)

Mount the top
by holding the left
frame end (piece 46),
flush to the carcass
side (piece 2).

(2)

29¹/₄"

Caster Location
(Bottom View)

⊢15⁵/₈"⊣   (13)   3/4"

1"

1"

5¹/₂"

(4)

Countersink for five
screws to attach the
bottom to the center
divider.

12"

(52)

(1)

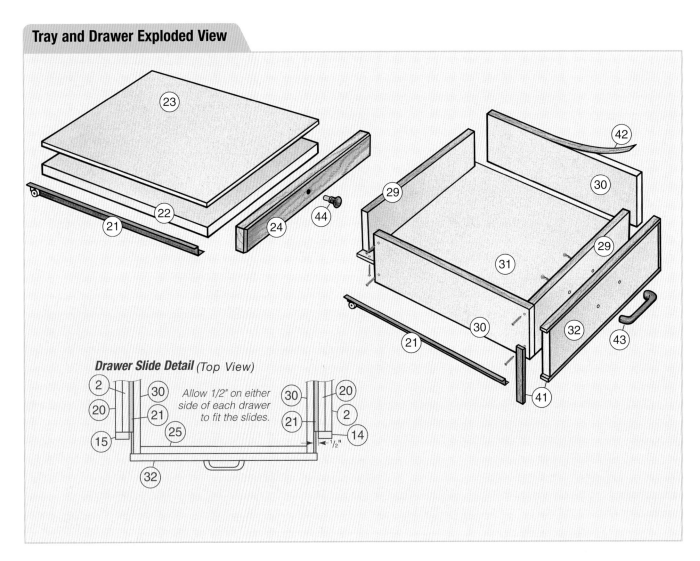

Drawer Slide Detail (Top View)

Allow 1/2" on either side of each drawer to fit the slides.

made sense to construct the face frame (pieces 13 through 17) out of a tough hardwood. We chose white oak because of its durability and good looks. All the joints are simple butts, each kept in line with a pair of 3⁄8" fluted dowels (pieces 18). Dry-fit all the parts according to the *Face Frame Layout* on the *Technical Drawings*, test their fit on your assembled carcass, and, when everything looks right, glue and clamp your frame together. Note: The right edge of the center stile lines up flush with the right face of the center divider. Make sure the frame remains flat and square during clamping.

Let the glue dry overnight, then remove the clamps and sand the frame smooth. Chisel out any excess glue in the inside corners. Make sure the lower edge of the face frame is flush with the bottom of the carcass, then predrill for countersunk screws

(pieces 3) and join the subassemblies. Glue 3⁄8" oak plugs (pieces 19) in all the counterbored screw holes in the carcass, and sand them flush.

Adding Some Inside Details

The face frame is flush with the left side of the large carcass opening, but you'll need to build out the right side before installing the drawer slides. Glue and screw these spacers (pieces 20) in place now, following the locations on the *Technical Drawings*. Attach the remaining shelf cleat to the face frame at this time.

Building the Drawers

Storage is a primary concern with sharpening supplies, so this station features five drawers and a slide-out tray. All six units are mounted on 22" drawer slides (pieces

21). The tray (piece 22) is 3⁄4"-thick melamine with a 1⁄4" melamine liner (piece 23) glued to its top face. Place a heavy weight on it while the glue dries. Chamfer the front edges of the tray front (piece 24) with a chamfering bit chucked in your router, as shown in the *Technical Drawings*. Attach the front to the tray with glue and finish nails, predrilling pilot holes for the nails, then setting and filling their heads.

All five drawers (pieces 25 through 40) are built alike, and all are flush-mounted (that is, they don't overlay the frame). This is a workshop project, so the construction process was kept simple. Butt the fronts and backs to the sides, securing them with glue and screws. Attach the bottoms with glue and screws, then trim all four edges of each face with 1⁄4" hardwood stock (piece 41). Attach this trim with glue and 3d finish nails driven through predrilled pilot holes, setting and filling the heads as you go. Center the drawer faces on the drawers (See *Drawing* and *Sidebar* on these two pages) and attach them from the inside, predrilling the screw holes first. Wrap up the drawers by sealing the exposed top edges of the sides, fronts and backs with iron-on hardwood tape (piece 42), then drill holes in each drawer face for the pulls (pieces 43). Install the pulls and tray knob (piece 44), slide the drawers in place, and you're all set to start building the work top.

Constructing the Work Top

The work top (piece 45) is a slab of ¾" thick melamine-coated particleboard surrounded by a hardwood frame. The frame is composed of two ends (pieces 46 and 47), a pair of supports (pieces 48), two shaped sides (pieces 49), a handle and towel bar (piece 50).

Transfer the profile of the sides from the full-size pattern found on the *inside back cover*, then band-saw them to shape. Clean up the saw cuts with a drum sander and drill the stopped holes on their insides for the handle. The work top is surrounded by the hardwood frame and held securely by glue blocks (pieces 51) and screws, as shown in the Exploded View on page 18.

Building the Frame Assembly

The white oak frame is held together with screwed butt joints. Temporarily clamp the frame elements together, then counterbore and predrill for the large screws. You'll find all the locations on the *Technical Drawings*. While you have the frame clamped, dry-fit it to the carcass. A half inch of the face frame's top rail should be peeking out below the bottom of the shaped sides. When everything fits, glue and screw

HOW TO INSTALL DRAWER SLIDES

This sharpening station uses Blum's low profile 3/4 extension slides. This all-purpose, bottom mounted steel slide features an epoxy coating and is self-closing, a nice feature on a project like this. Rated at up to 100 pounds per drawer, this is one of the easiest slides on the market to mount—just follow the four steps below. Remember, you'll need 1/2" on each side of the drawer to accommodate your slides.

1. In the case of this sharpening center (and many other cabinet projects), spacer blocks are installed to provide a mounting surface flush with the face frame.

2. Once the spacers are installed, use your drill to mount the inside slide component to the bottom edge of your drawer bottoms. Be sure to drill pilot holes first.

3. With the drawer components in place, move on to the casework components and mount them to the spacer blocks or cabinet sides, predrilling your pilot holes.

4. Locate the drawer fronts on the drawers. An old trick is to use double-sided tape to tack the drawer face in place before you secure it with screws.

the top frame together, trapping the handle as you do. Plug the screw holes as you did earlier and make sure the handle remains free to turn.

Place the frame on top of the carcass, locating it as shown on the *Drawings*. Then glue and screw it in place, driving the screws from the inside of the cabinet into the frame.

Wrapping Up the Final Details

While you won't be moving this station around too much, it's always nice to be able to rearrange the workshop to accommodate new tools or big projects. Have a friend help you lift the project onto a couple of sawhorses, then bolt a pair of swivel casters (pieces 52) to one end of the bottom, at the loca-

tions shown in the *Technical Drawings*.

Bolt a matching foot on the other end: this is a simple hollow box made up of two sides, a top and two ends (pieces 53, 54 and 55). Butt joint, glue and clamp the foot together, then glue and screw it in place to complete the footings.

There isn't a lot of finishing to this project. Start by filling any nail holes you missed, then glue hardwood plugs over the tops of all the counterbored screws. Mask the melamine along all the hardwood edges, then clamp a square or a metal ruler along these same edges while you lightly sand the wood. Apply three coats of clear satin varnish to the hardwood, then install the drawers, adding the pulls and knob. If you have a

MATERIAL LIST—*TOP SUBASSEMBLY*

		T x W x L
45	Work Top (1)	$\frac{3}{4}$" x 25$\frac{5}{8}$" x 40$\frac{1}{2}$"
46	Work Top Frame Left End (1)	$\frac{3}{4}$" x 3" x 25$\frac{5}{8}$"
47	Work Top Frame Right End (1)	$\frac{3}{4}$" x 2" x 25$\frac{5}{8}$"
48	Work Top Frame Supports (2)	$\frac{3}{4}$" x 1$\frac{7}{8}$" x 25$\frac{5}{8}$"
49	Work Top Frame Sides (2)	$\frac{3}{4}$" x 4" x 48"
50	Towel Bar (1)	1$\frac{1}{4}$" Dia. x 26$\frac{3}{8}$""
51	Glue Blocks (8)	$\frac{3}{4}$" x 2" x 2"
52	Casters (2)	3$\frac{7}{8}$" Swivel
53	Foot Sides (2)	$\frac{3}{4}$" x 3$\frac{7}{8}$" x 24"
54	Foot Top (1)	$\frac{3}{4}$" x 1$\frac{7}{8}$" x 24"
55	Foot Ends (2)	$\frac{3}{4}$" x 1$\frac{7}{8}$" x 3$\frac{1}{8}$"

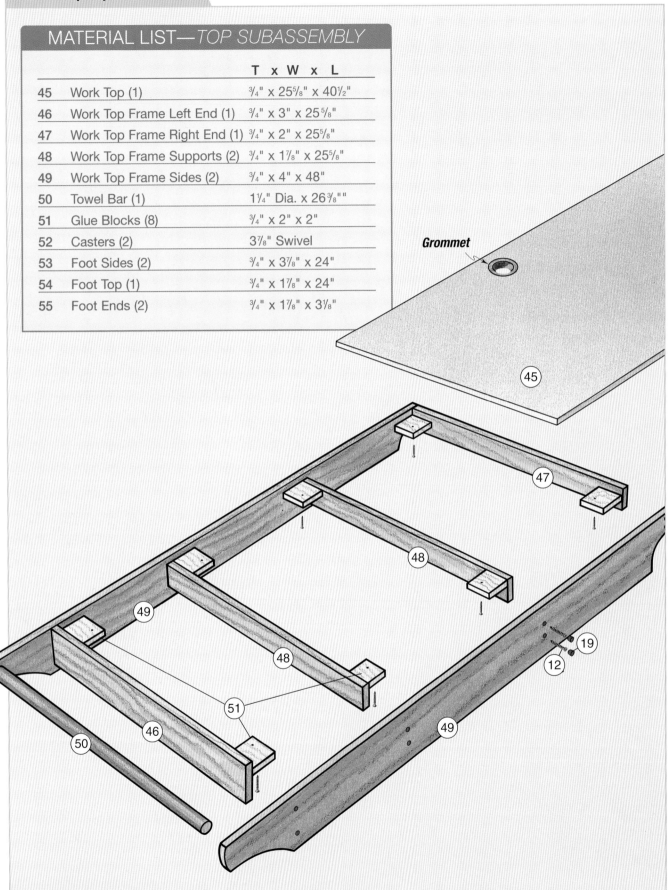

Grommet

power sharpening system and plan to use a magnifying lamp for better viewing (a good idea, by the way), bore an access hole through the work top for running the power cords neatly behind the station. Protect the cords from abrasion with a grommet inserted in the access hole (see the *illustration* on the facing page).

Now the fun begins. Start a search through your shop for all your containers of oil and mineral spirits, emery paper, stones and files. You'll probably be amazed at how much you've accumulated over the years. While you're at it, pick a couple of plane irons and chisels to give your new sharpening station a christening!

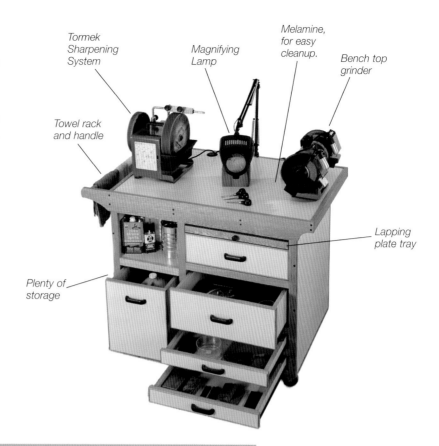

Tormek Sharpening System

Magnifying Lamp

Melamine, for easy cleanup.

Bench top grinder

Towel rack and handle

Lapping plate tray

Plenty of storage

THE TORMEK SHARPENING SYSTEM

One of the premier sharpening machines on the market, the Tormek sells for about $400. At that price it may not be for everyone, but its versatility demands a look. Replete with tons of gizmos to put an edge on everything from a curved gouge to a long planer knife, this British import is the real deal. Pair it with a traditional grinder and the only thing you won't be able to sharpen is your wits.

Two auxiliary sharpening aids team up to hone curved gouges, making a difficult task much easier.

Keep the knives of your benchtop planer or jointer razor sharp on the water-bathed honing wheel.

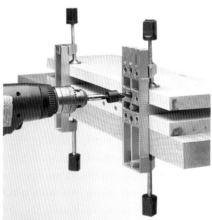

Use a Doweling Jig

Dowels are easier to install accurately for face frame and other joinery if you can drill their holes squarely. Fixtures like the Dowel Pro Jig shown here are a slick and easy way to use dowels like a pro. They provide drilling guides, and most also center the holes automatically on the thickness of your material.

Downdraft Workbench

Contributing editor Rick White admitted a little guilt when he designed and built this project just for his shop. But he'd been pining for a work center large enough to assemble big casework projects on and strong enough to withstand some serious pounding. He also needed more storage space ... and a downdraft table was still the missing link in his pursuit of a truly dust-free shop.

Meanwhile, Rick's trusty old workbench was making the discussion somewhat irrelevant, since it was already occupying most of the space in the center of his shop.

When the answer came to him, it was just too simple: Make a new work center that serves all these functions! A workbench that also incorporates a downdraft table. Sometimes when you can't get what you want, you have to settle for something even better! Rick's downdraft workbench features a power strip, full-extension pullout shelves and room for sanders, drill drivers and routers, in addition to an efficient, built-in downdraft unit. For durability and strength, it has a solid maple top, and for good measure he tossed in a vise and an interchangeable second top. As you can see in the finished project, Rick's downdraft workbench turned out great, and his guilt melted away quickly.

From the Bottom Up

Start this project with basic casework joinery on the carcass. The stiles and rails as well as the end and back panels (pieces 1 though 9) are made from solid hardwood lumber. Rick used hard maple to match the top. Find the dimensions for all these pieces in the Material List on page 23. The machining details and the subassemblies you'll be creating are shown in the Elevation Drawings, also on the following pages.

Make the front, back and end subassemblies separately. Where the stiles and rails meet, Rick joined them with dowels so the joints would really stand up to a beating. Glue up the solid panels (pieces 7 and 8) a bit oversized, then trim and sand them smooth after the glue cures. Form 1/4" tongues on their edges, as shown in the *Drawings*. Note that where the stiles and rails capture the end and back panels, you will need to rout stopped grooves (Rick used a hand-held router and a slot cutter for this task) to accept the tongues on the panels' edges. Glue and clamp up the four separate subassemblies, checking to be sure they are square as the glue cures.

While you wait for the glue to dry, grab your plywood sheetstock and slice up the dividers and the bottom (pieces 10 and 11).

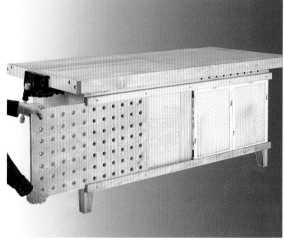

The worktop of this bench has two inserts that fit into a rabbeted opening over the downdraft unit. When not in use, either insert can easily be stored on the back face of the bench.

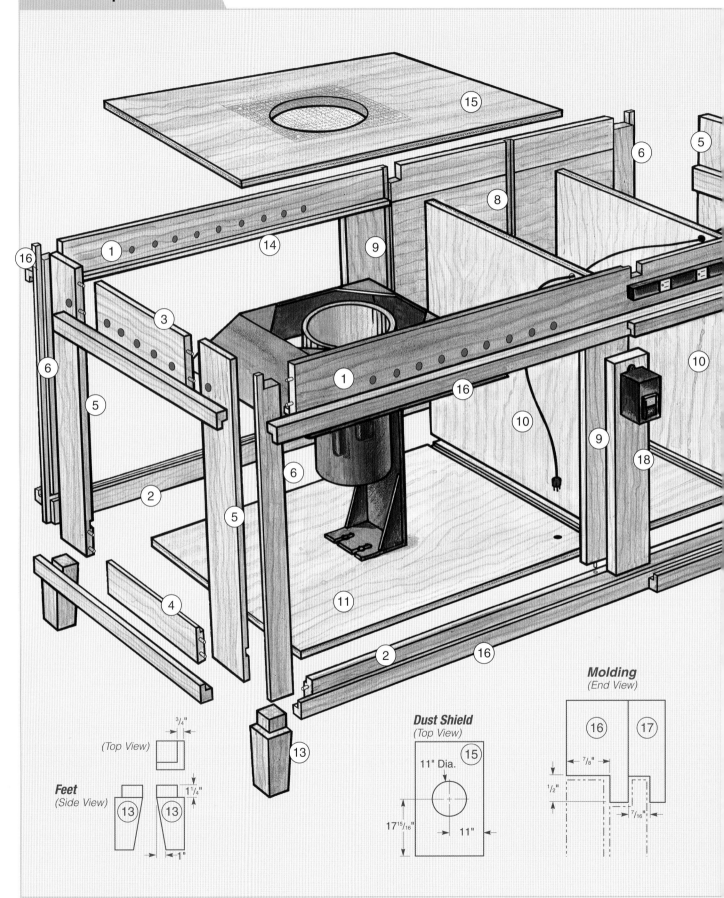

Feet
(Side View)

(Top View)

3/4"

1 1/4"

1"

Dust Shield
(Top View)

11" Dia.

11"

17 15/16"

Molding
(End View)

7/8"

1/2"

7/16"

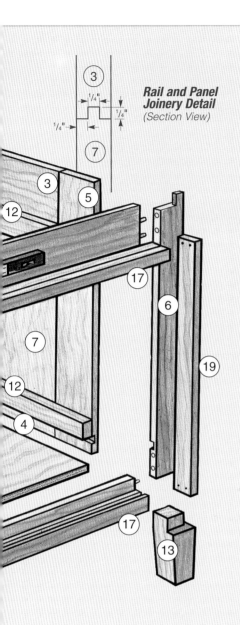

Rail and Panel Joinery Detail
(Section View)

1/4" 1/4" 1/4"

MATERIAL LIST—*CARCASS*

#	Part	T x W x L
1	Upper Long Rails (2)	³⁄₄" x 5⅝" x 66"
2	Lower Long Rails (2)	³⁄₄" x 2" x 66"
3	Upper Short Rails (2)	³⁄₄" x 5⅝" x 14½"
4	Lower Short Rails (2)	³⁄₄" x 2" x 14½"
5	End Stiles (4)	³⁄₄" x 3⅞" x 26¼"
6	Front & Back Stiles (4)	³⁄₄" x 2" x 26¼"
7	End Panel (1)	³⁄₄" x 19" x 15"
8	Back Panel (1)	³⁄₄" x 19" x 31"
9	Center Stiles (2)	³⁄₄" x 5" x 18½"
10	Dividers (2)	³⁄₄" x 22½" x 24½"
11	Bottom (1)	³⁄₄" x 22½" x 69"
12	Spacers (2)	1¼" x 2¼" x 22"
13	Feet (4)	2¾" x 2¾" x 6¾"
14	Cleats (2)	³⁄₄" x ³⁄₄" x 36"
15	Dust Shield (1)	³⁄₄" x 22" x 35⅞"
16	Large Molding (1)	1¼" x 2" x 328"
17	Small Molding (1)	³⁄₄" x 2" x 72"
18	Door Cap (1)	³⁄₄" x 2" x 23"
19	Door Stop (1)	1¼" x 3⅛" x 19"
20	Sliding Doors (2)	³⁄₄" x 16½" x 19⅞"

Door
(Front View)

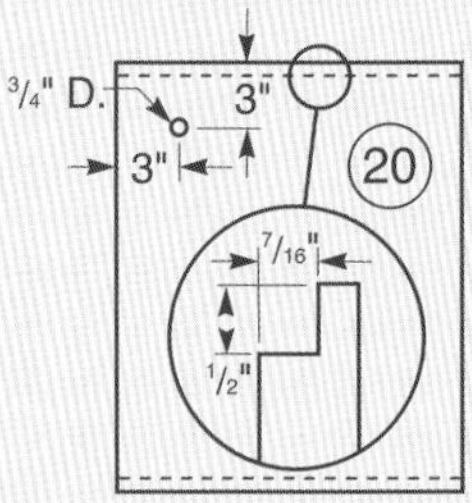

³⁄₄" D. 3"
3" (20)
7/16"
1/2"

NOTE: Rabbet top
and bottom edges
of one of the doors.

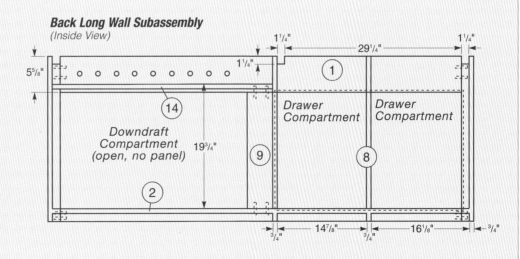

Back Long Wall Subassembly
(Inside View)

1¼" 29¼" 1¼"

5⅝" 1¼"

(14)

Downdraft
Compartment
(open, no panel)

19¾"

Drawer
Compartment

Drawer
Compartment

(9) (8)

(2)

³⁄₄" 14⅞" ³⁄₄" 16⅛" ³⁄₄"

Bottom *(Top View)*

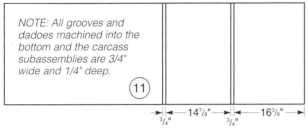

NOTE: All grooves and dadoes machined into the bottom and the carcass subassemblies are 3/4" wide and 1/4" deep.

⑪

←14⁷⁄₈"→ ←16³⁄₈"→
³⁄₄"   ³⁄₄"

End Wall Subassembly
Downdraft Compartment
(Inside View)

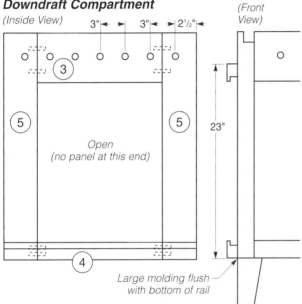

3" 3" 2¹⁄₂"

③

⑤   ⑤

Open
(no panel at this end)

23"

④

(Front View)

Large molding flush with bottom of rail

End Wall Subassembly
Drawer Compartment
(Inside View)

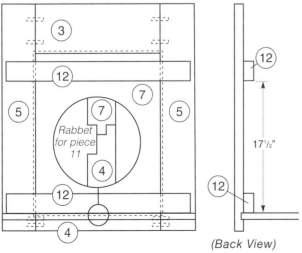

③

⑫

⑦

⑤   ⑦   ⑤

Rabbet for piece 11

④

⑫

④

⑫

⑫

17¹⁄₂"

(Back View)

MATERIAL LIST—*TOP SUBASSEMBLY*

		T x W x L
21	Laminated Top Pieces (9)	1¹⁄₄" x 3⁵⁄₈" x 79¹⁄₂"
22	Splines (8)	¹⁄₂" x 1" x 79¹⁄₂"
23	Side Rails (2)	1¹⁄₄" x 2⁷⁄₈" x 79¹⁄₂"
24	Cross Braces (3)	1¹⁄₄" x 1¹⁄₂" x 32³⁄₈"
25	Long Cleats (2)	1¹⁄₄" x 1¹⁄₂" x 79¹⁄₂"
26	End Caps (2)	1¹⁄₄" x 2⁷⁄₈" x 34⁷⁄₈"
27	Draft Vent (1)	³⁄₄" x 20" x 36"
28	Cover (1)	³⁄₄" x 20" x 36"
29	Vise Block (1)	1¹⁄₄" x 5¹⁄₂" x 15"
30	Vise (1)	*Steel screw type*

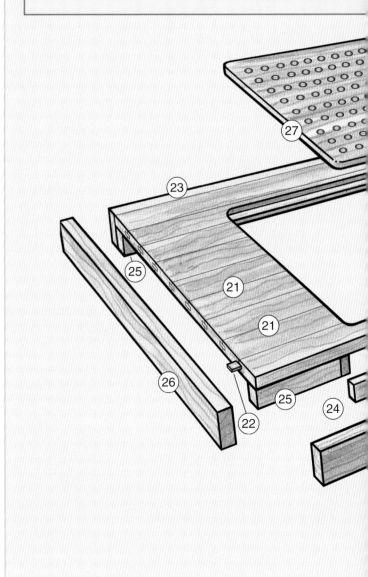

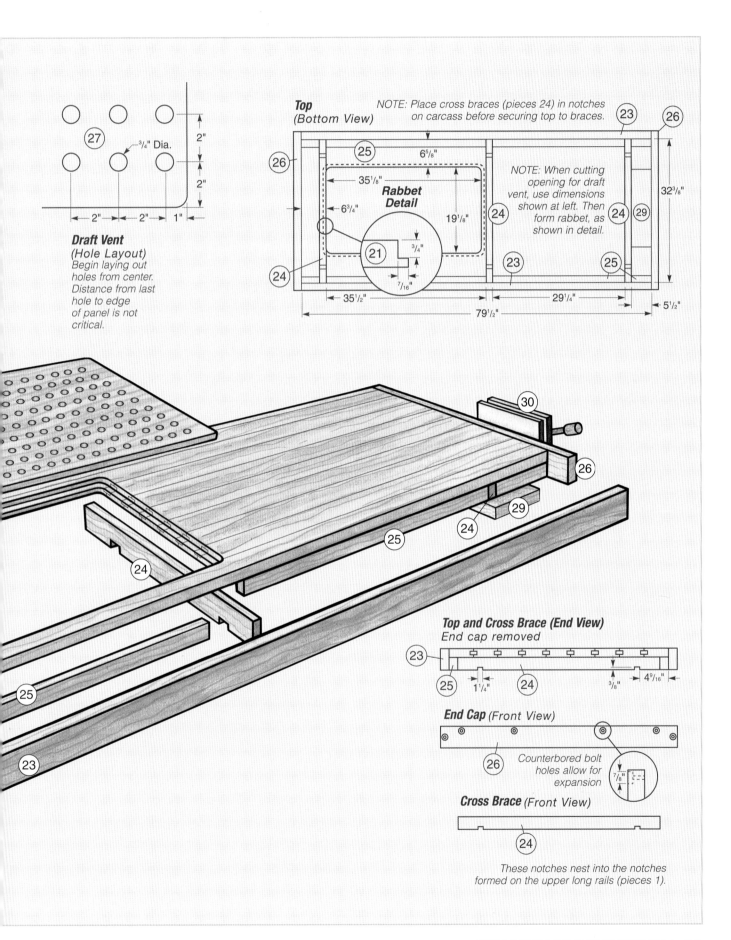

Draft Vent
(Hole Layout)
Begin laying out
holes from center.
Distance from last
hole to edge
of panel is not
critical.

27

³/₄" Dia.

2"

2"

2"   2"   1"

Top
(Bottom View)

NOTE: Place cross braces (pieces 24) in notches
on carcass before securing top to braces.

23   26

25   6⁵/₈"

26

35¹/₈"

**Rabbet
Detail**

6³/₄"

19¹/₈"

NOTE: When cutting
opening for draft
vent, use dimensions
shown at left. Then
form rabbet, as
shown in detail.

24

24   29

32³/₈"

21   ³/₄"

24

7/₁₆"

23   25

35¹/₂"   29¹/₄"   5¹/₂"

79¹/₂"

30

26

29

24

25

24

25

Top and Cross Brace (End View)
End cap removed

23

25   1¹/₄"   24   ³/₈"   4⁹/₁₆"

End Cap (Front View)

26   Counterbored bolt
holes allow for
expansion

7/₈"

Cross Brace (Front View)

24

These notches nest into the notches
formed on the upper long rails (pieces 1).

24

23

DOWNDRAFT WORKBENCH 25

Grooves, Holes and Rabbets

Now that the subassemblies have cured, you need to do a little more machining to each of them. With a hand-held router and straight edge, plow matching grooves and dadoes for the bottom and dadoes for the dividers (there are dadoes in the bottom, too). Don't worry when the grooves and dadoes nip into the panels' tongue and groove joints; it will work out fine. Using the same setup, form the rabbets at the edges of the front and back stiles (pieces 6).

Put the router aside and grab your jig saw to cut the six notches on the top edges of the two long rails. These will serve to capture the notched cross braces later on. The last bit of machining before you put together the subassemblies is to drill the safety vent holes in the upper rails. (Note: If all the holes on the draft vent happened to get covered, these holes will prevent the motor from overheating.) These safety holes are best bored on the drill press, so you'll need either a buddy to help you hold up the frames as you drill or use a couple of roller stands.

Now predrill the counterbored screw holes though the front and back stiles and test-fit the carcass together. (This is another process that a helper will make much easier.) Once everything fits together, assemble the carcass with glue, screws and clamps. While the carcass is clamped-up and the glue is curing, make the spacers, feet, cleats and dust shield (pieces 12, 13, 14 and 15). As shown in the *Elevations* on the previous pages, the feet have tapers on their inside faces and a rabbet on the opposing faces. When the carcass is out of its clamps, attach the feet, cleats and spacers with glue and screws. Plug all the exposed screw holes and sand them flush.

Monster Moldings

The filters, sliding doors and spare insert are all held in place with molding. It's not hard to make; you just need to make a bunch of it. First rip enough stock to make the large and small molding (pieces 16 and 17), then get your table saw set up with a dado blade and a featherboard. Plow the rabbet into the large molding stock as shown in the *Drawings*. Readjust the saw setup to make the small molding and create enough to make the two pieces required to hold the second sliding door. Now is also a good time to make the door cap, door stop and sliding doors (pieces 18 through 20). The door stop and cap are simply sticked up hardwood, but one of the doors has a couple of rabbeted edges and both have finger holes to be machined. Look to the *Elevation Drawings* for these details. Again, predrill counterbored screw holes and mount the molding and assorted parts

as shown in the *Exploded View* and *Elevation Drawings* — you are really making progress now. Plug the screw holes, sand them flush and get ready to do some laminating.

A Laminated Top

The glued-up maple top on this bench is a substantial bit of work. The basic top is made of nine pieces of maple with splines to help align the glue-up (pieces 21 and 22). Take care to surface this wood to very close tolerances — it will help you in the long run. Once you glue up the top and trim it to size, you will need to determine how you will flatten it. See the sidebar on page 28 for some options and techniques that will help with this process.

When the top is flat, glue the side rails (piece 23) in place. Scrape the squeeze-out off and install the cross braces (pieces 24). As mentioned earlier, the cross braces have notches cut into them that fit into the notches you formed earlier in the long rails (pieces 1). You'll need to rip the long cleats (pieces 25) from solid stock and then cut and fit them once the cross braces are in place. Gluing and clamping are sufficient to secure these cleats in place.

Next, form the end caps (piece 26) boring the two-step holes for the lag bolts that attach the end caps to the top. Make the through holes for the bolts oversized to accommodate seasonal wood movement.

SANDING
DOGS

When using the downdraft table, Rick finds these sanding dogs very useful. They fit into the vent holes and keep your stock from moving during sanding.

After a little experimentation, the author arrived at the perfect number of holes for the draft vent top. See the Draft Vent Hole Layout Detail on page 25.

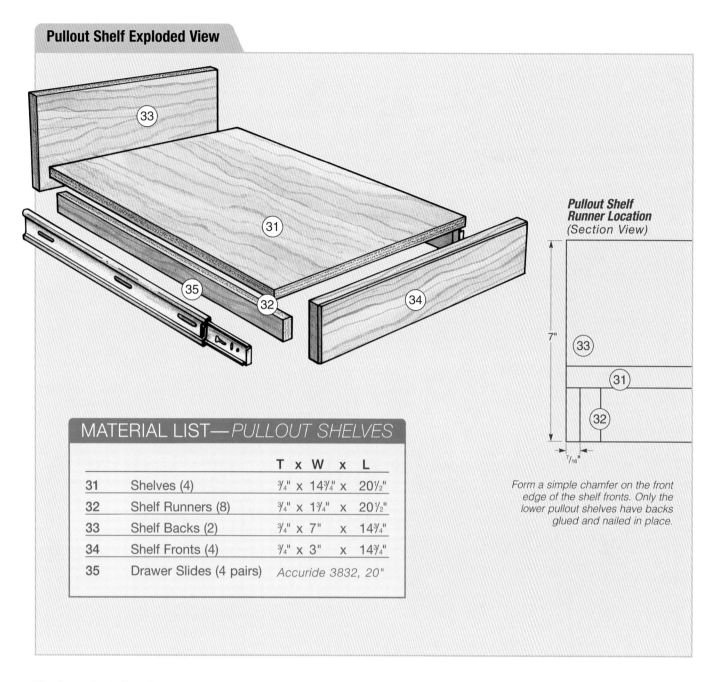

**Pullout Shelf
Runner Location**
(Section View)

7"

⁷/₁₆

*Form a simple chamfer on the front
edge of the shelf fronts. Only the
lower pullout shelves have backs
glued and nailed in place.*

MATERIAL LIST—*PULLOUT SHELVES*					
		T	x W	x	L
31	Shelves (4)	¾"	x 14¾"	x	20½"
32	Shelf Runners (8)	¾"	x 1¾"	x	20½"
33	Shelf Backs (2)	¾"	x 7"	x	14¾"
34	Shelf Fronts (4)	¾"	x 3"	x	14¾"
35	Drawer Slides (4 pairs)	*Accuride 3832, 20"*			

The Downdraft Opening

Cutting a huge gaping hole in a perfectly good top is an admittedly disturbing task, but you can't have a downdraft table without it. Use a straight bit in your hand-held router and make a template (see the Drawings for the proper opening size) to guide the router to the dimension of the inside of the opening. Use several passes to cut through the top. Then switch to a rabbeting bit to create a rabbet around the upper edge of the opening. The rabbet will hold the draft vent.

Make the draft vent and the cover (pieces 27 and 28) to fit your opening. Lay out the vent holes and use a sharp Forstner bit to bore them, as shown in the photo on page 26. Follow behind with your router and a roundover bit to soften the upper edges of the vent holes. Bore a single finger hole in the cover and round over the top and bottom edge of that hole. If you choose to put an end vise on the top, install the vise block and vise (pieces 29 and 30), as shown in the Drawings on page 25.

Pullouts and Shelves

Pullout shelves make it possible to store tools in this bench without also having to climb in to get them. The top shelves serve as a little extra tabletop to place your in-use tools on, and the bottom pullouts feature a high back to keep power tools from shifting and falling off the back.

Cut the shelves, runners, fronts and backs (pieces 31 through 34) to size and set up a "mini-assembly line" to build them. Before you continue, ease the sharp edges

FLATTENING A BENCHTOP

A well fettled plane is the best tool for removing the high areas of the workbench's top. Work diagonal to the grain for best results.

Another option is to use coarse-grit paper and your belt sander to remove the high spots. Work in the pattern shown below.

With a straightedge, establish and mark the low areas of the glued-up top with a pencil.

A dead-flat work surface is an essential element in any workbench. Flattening a glued-up top is not too hard if you take it one step at a time. You can cart your glued-up top to a cabinet shop and have it surfaced by a large stationary belt sander, but if you choose to do it yourself, here's how to go about it.

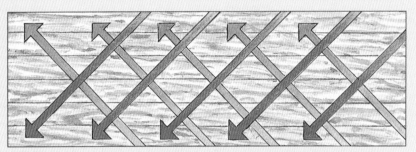

First mark the low areas in the glued up top. Next, with your plane or belt sander, remove the high areas as you work in an opposing diagonal pattern. Again, using your straightedge, mark the low areas once more and repeat the pattern. Repeat this process until you flatten the top.

and ends of the front pieces with a chamfer bit in the router. Use finish nails and glue to attach the runners and fronts to the shelves. Inset the runners 7/16" from the edge of the shelves to accommodate the drawer slides (pieces 35). On the two lower pullouts, glue and screw the backs in place. Mount the drawer slides in their proper places and you are ready to move on to the final details.

Now is as good a time as any to do a once-over sanding and surface preparation. Rick sealed his bench with several coats of a hard-drying oil finish. He wanted something that would seal the wood but also be easy to retouch whenever necessary. (Don't use linseed or mineral oils, which don't cure hard enough to repel dust.)

High-tech Hardware

The downdraft hardware and power strip are final touches that make this project sing (or at least hum). You can find these items as well as the finishing supplies and drawer slides by contacting Rockler at (800) 610-0883 or www.rockler.com.

Rick mounted the power strip over the pullout shelves and eventually mounted a second strip on the back side of the table as well. There's no limit to how much access to power you can have — especially at the workbench. For more convenience, wire the power strip through the ON/OFF switch of the downdraft unit so there will be a single power cord exiting the bench.

Add-Ons and Personal Preferences

Workbenches should be tailor-made to suit the main user. Bench height is one area where people differ. Most woodworkers prefer the bench top to sit at half their height. (If you are 6' tall, the top should be 36".) Perhaps you would like bench dogs in your workbench ... this top is designed so that is an option. You can drill additional holes or you can use the sanding dogs (shown on page 26) along with your vise to secure longer stock or panels while machining.

Even though this project was just for Rick, he got over the guilt really fast ... let us know how you feel when you're done with yours!

Quick Tip

Holder for a Drafting Lamp

Having supplemental task lighting at the workbench is essential, especially for spotting flaws during finishing and for doing other detail work. Here's a quick way to retrofit a drafting lamp onto any workbench with bench dog holes. Just take a piece of 2 x 4 and drill two holes several inches apart. One should fit the lamp base, while the other should be the same diameter as a bench dog. Glue a dowel into the second hole so you can mount your lamp into any hole on the benchtop. From there, the hinged arm allows you to focus light wherever you need it most.

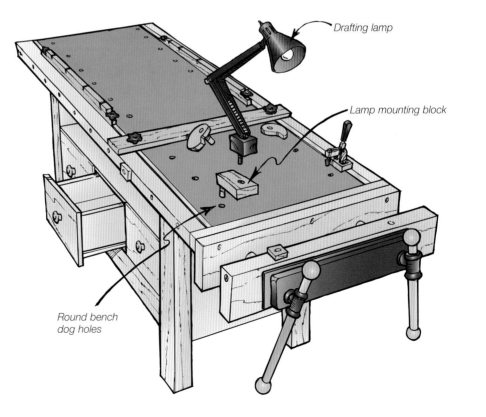

Drafting lamp

Lamp mounting block

Round bench dog holes

Lumber and Plywood Storage Options

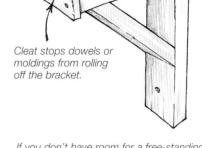

Lumber storage is an issue for any size workshop. What starts out long or wide ends up as much shorter offcuts that are sometimes too valuable to throw away. A good lumber rack needs to stow the big stuff so it's easy to load and unload while also storing shorter pieces so they're easy to sort and see. Here are two good plans for full-duty lumber racks and a couple options for simpler bracket systems. One of these styles is sure to suit your shop.

Cleat stops dowels or moldings from rolling off the bracket.

If you don't have room for a free-standing lumber rack, simple wall-mounted brackets are a good alternative.

The Mobile Rack

This mobile rack is designed to store all the essentials: Full sheets of plywood and composites, partial sheets, long lengths of lumber and short lengths. The rack is mounted on casters so it can be moved out of the way for cars.

The key to the design is a wide and stable base platform, upon which the rack is built. The platform is a 2x4 frame topped off with a 1/2"–thick oriented strand board (OSB) skin. Four large, 4" diameter heavy-duty casters are attached to the bottom of the frame: two fixed casters at one end and a pair of swivel caster at the other. The rack steers somewhat like a car.

A 2x4 is attached vertically to the platform about halfway across each end. In front of these posts, a couple of bins with angled tops provide storage for short lengths of lumber and partial sheets. Behind the posts is a space for full sheets of plywood and other sheet goods. On top of this rear compartment is a rack for long lengths of lumber, pipe and other awkward stock.

The Stationary Rack

The key to the second lumber storage system for a basement is standard 1" ID black gas pipe: As designed, there are three lengths of pipe that run from floor to ceiling, each positioned 42" away from its neighbor.

These are not continuous lengths: We installed T-shaped connectors at various intervals along the pipe (see the top right *Drawing*, next page), including one at floor level. Tie these three uprights together with 3/4" ID pipe, running it about 16" off the floor, and the same distance from the ceiling. Anchor the rack using circular metal pipe flanges, screwing them to cleats between the joists in your basement ceiling.

To convert this skeleton into a rack, screw a 21"-long piece of threaded pipe into each of the T's in each upright. Then, to provide a stable base for the rack, use short elbows to cap off the lowest piece of pipe, which creates feet for the unit. With the pipes all in place, you're ready to start building the rest of the system with AC plywood. Two 1/2" plywood boxes (9" x 30" x 40"

long) roll in under the rack, each mounted on a set of four 1½" diameter casters. These boxes hold hardwood and softwood shorts (pieces of stock under 40" long). Above

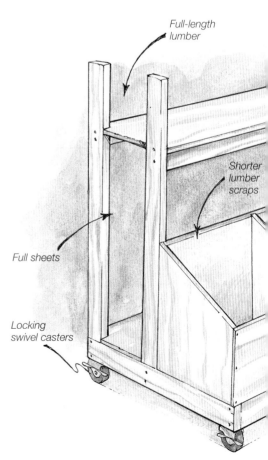

Full-length lumber

Shorter lumber scraps

Full sheets

Locking swivel casters

them, two pairs of pipe arms support 8'-long lengths of thick (over 4/4) lumber.

The next three sets of arms each support an 8'-long tray. These 8"-high by 24"-wide trays hold stock that measures from 3' to 7' long. The two spaces above these trays are reserved for stock that is over 8' long.

Three trays should be sufficient to manage all the medium length stock in a serious hobby shop. These are made of 1/2" AC plywood, glued and screwed together. Round over a radius on the top front corner of each end piece to avoid catching yourself on a sharp corner or splintering the plywood.

Insert dividers in the trays if you wish to further organize wood by species, thickness or other characteristics pertinent to your work.

Simpler solutions

If both of these storage racks are a bit ambitious for your needs, maybe a simpler rack will do. See the *Drawing* on the preceding page for a sturdy wall bracket design or the L-bracket system in the tint box, below right.

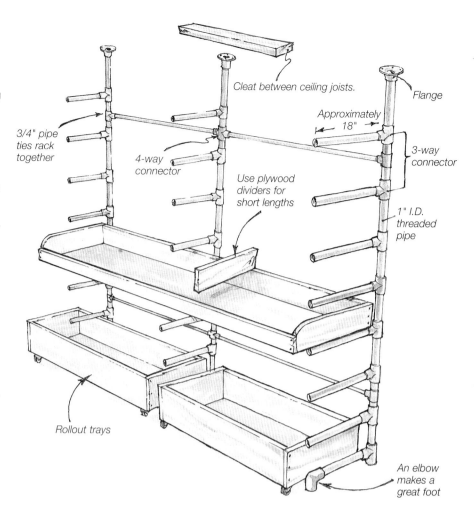

Cleat between ceiling joists.

Flange

3/4" pipe ties rack together

4-way connector

Approximately 18"

Use plywood dividers for short lengths

3-way connector

1" I.D. threaded pipe

Rollout trays

An elbow makes a great foot

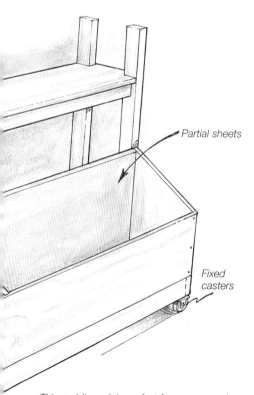

Partial sheets

Fixed casters

This mobile rack is perfect for garage workshops, especially when you're forced to park a car right in the middle of your shop.

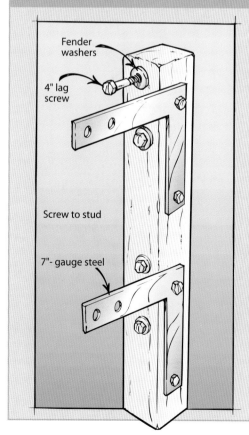

A WALL-MOUNTED LUMBER RACK

Fender washers

4" lag screw

Screw to stud

7"- gauge steel

Here's an option for a space-saving, low-tech lumber rack that you can build easily in an afternoon. Metal L-brackets serve as shelf brackets here. You can also use them as connection points for continuous wood shelving. Look for brackets that are at least 7-gauge steel for maximum strength. Mount these brackets directly to the wall studs with lag screws if your shop walls have exposed studs. For drywall-sheathed walls, screw the brackets onto lengths of 2" x 2" lumber and bolt these to the wall studs instead. Make sure the lag screws are driven at least two inches into the studs, and use fender washers to help distribute the weight.

A Mobile Clamping Cart for the Small Shop

Necessity is the mother of invention. In some shops, that's not a clever proverb, it's a design philosophy. Assembly supplies start to pile up so you design a storage fixture for them. This one has caught the eye of more than one visitor, so we thought we'd present it to you. It's a great solution to organizing clutter in a small shop.

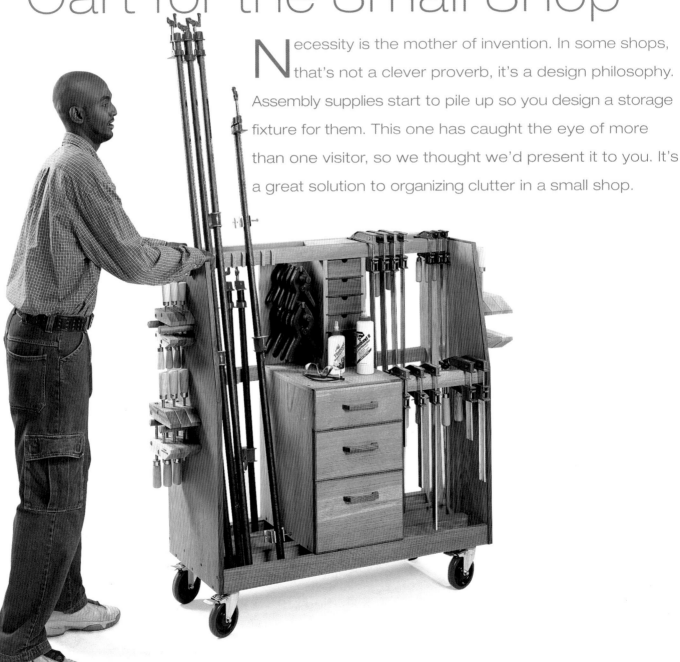

Roll your clamps right to your work station and the appropriate supplies – glue, screws and biscuits will be close at hand.

Slicing Up the Sheet Stock

Begin your journey toward more organized clamping and gluing sessions by cutting the cart's sides and bottom to size (pieces 1 and 2) on the table saw. Create the angle on the front corner of the sides (see the *Elevation Drawings* on the next page) with a hand-held circular saw guided by a straightedge. Rip solid stock to make pieces 3 though 6. While you're at the saw, rip the walnut banding (piece 7), too. Apply the banding to the sides and allow the glue to cure. Now, form the rabbet on the front rail with a dado head in your table saw and notch one of the long rails, as shown in the *Drawings*. Clamp and glue pairs of long and short rails together and, after the glue

Rip the large plywood pieces first. The sides and bottom form the shell of this rolling cart.

has cured, cut them to length. Attach the appropriate rails and cabinet support to the cart bottom with glue and screws. To assemble the sides and bottom, pre-drill counterbored screw holes and, with the help of a friend, bring the pieces together. NOTE: Secure just the middle long rail at this time. See the *Drawings* for details.

Making the Center Cabinet

A clamp cart should hold more than just clamps; you also need glue, biscuits, screws and other fasteners as well. The center drawers on this cart should tidy things up well. Begin making the center storage cabinet by cutting its plywood parts (pieces 8 through 11) to size and shape (form the notch to accommodate the back rail as well). Rip some oak banding (piece 12) and use it to cover the exposed edges of the plywood pieces. Pre-drill counterbored screw holes, assemble the cabinet (without the back) and slide it into place on the cart subassembly. Secure it to the rails with screws. Now go ahead and secure the back with glue and screws.

Cut the parts for the tray bank sides and top (pieces 13 and 14) and band their edges. Notch the upper corner for the rails. Put a 1/4" dado head in your table saw and plow a series of

3/8"-deep dadoes to accept the dust proof tray bottoms, as shown in the *Elevation Drawings*. Locate and cut the biscuit joints on the cabinet top and the tray bank sides. From 1/4" hardboard, cut the tray bank divider (piece 15). Now install the tray bank sides and divider with glue, screws and biscuits securing the joints.

With that subassembly in place you can install the remaining rails, both long and short. Next, cut all ten clamp dowels (pieces 16) to length (mount them to best accommodate the clamps you own), and the pipe dividers (pieces 17). Again, determine whether you have 3/4"- or 1/2"-diameter pipe clamps before you attach them. The drawer slides, casters and the hinge (pieces 18 through 20) will be mounted a bit later.

Building Drawers and Trays

The drawer faces (pieces 21, 22 and 23) are cut from 3/4" plywood and edged with the walnut banding. The drawer sides, fronts and backs (pieces 24 through 29) are made from 1/2" plywood with locking corner joints. (See the *Detail*, on page 35.) Plow the dadoes in the sides and fronts for the drawer bottoms (pieces 30) and you're ready to assemble the drawers.

The tray sides, fronts and backs (pieces 31 and 32) are assembled with the same corner joints as the drawers. Their bottoms (pieces 33), are glued and pin-nailed in

Cart Carcass Exploded View

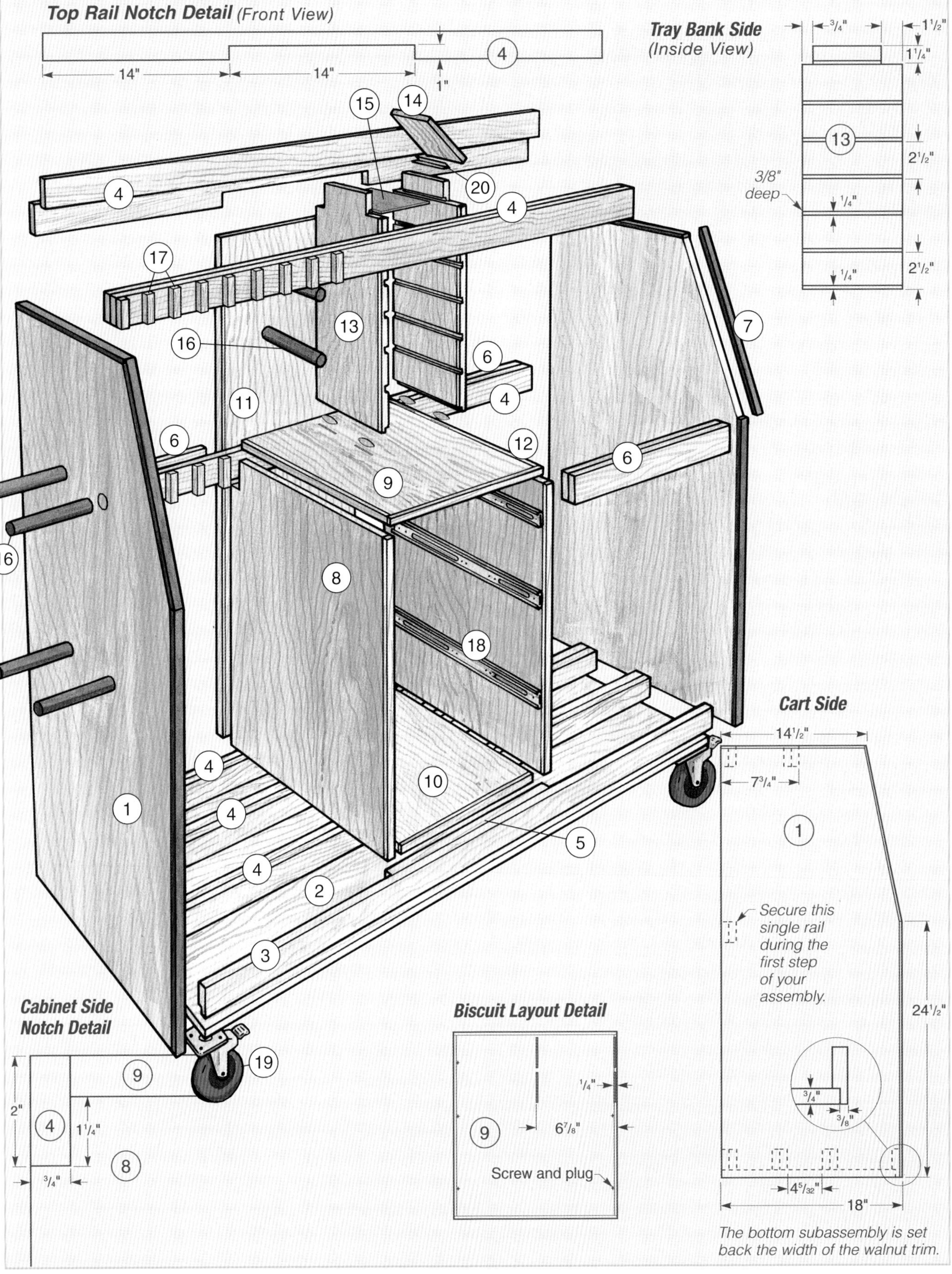

Top Rail Notch Detail (Front View)

4

14" 14" 1"

15 14

20

4 4

17

16 13

6

16 11 6 4

7

6 6

12

9

8

18

10

4 5

4

2

4

3

19

Tray Bank Side
(Inside View)

3/4" 1 1/2"

1 1/4"

13 2 1/2"

3/8"
deep 1/4"

1/4" 2 1/2"

Cart Side

14 1/2"

7 3/4"

1

Secure this
single rail
during the
first step
of your
assembly.

24 1/2"

3/4"

3/8"

4 5/32"

18"

The bottom subassembly is set
back the width of the walnut trim.

**Cabinet Side
Notch Detail**

9

2" 4 1 1/4"

3/4"

8

Biscuit Layout Detail

1/4"

9 6 7/8"

Screw and plug

MATERIAL LIST—*CART CARCASS*

		T x W x L
1	Sides (2)	¾" x 17¾" x 41½"
2	Bottom (1)	¾" x 17⅞" x 42"
3	Front Bottom Rail (1)	¾" x 2¾" x 42"
4	Long Rails (11)	¾" x 2" x 42"
5	Cabinet Support (1)	¾" x 2" x 14"
6	Short Rails (4)	¾" x 2" x 14"
7	Walnut Banding (1)	¼" x ¾" x 260"
8	Cabinet Sides (2)	¾" x 16" x 21"
9	Cabinet Top (1)	¾" x 13½" x 15¼"
10	Cabinet Bottom (1)	¾" x 12½" x 16"
11	Cabinet Back (1)	¾" x 13½" x 38"
12	Oak Banding (1)	¼" x ¾" x 115"
13	Tray Bank Sides (2)	¾" x 7" x 16½"
14	Tray Bank Top (1)	¾" x 4¾" x 7"
15	Tray Bank Divider (1)	¼" x 6¼" x 4¾"
16	Clamp Dowels (8)	1" Dia. x 8"
17	Pipe Dividers (30)	½" x ½" x 2"
18	Drawer Slides (3 sets)	16" *Full-extension*
19	Casters (4)	*Locking*
20	Piano Hinge (1)	*Brass*

Drawer & Trays Exploded View

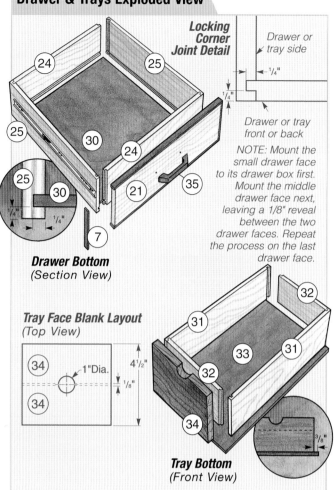

Locking Corner Joint Detail

Drawer or tray side

Drawer Bottom (Section View)

Tray Face Blank Layout (Top View)

1"Dia.

Tray Bottom (Front View)

Drawer or tray front or back

NOTE: Mount the small drawer face to its drawer box first. Mount the middle drawer face next, leaving a 1/8" reveal between the two drawer faces. Repeat the process on the last drawer face.

place. Note that on the overhanging edges of the bottoms, these fit into the dadoes you cut in the tray bank sides. The walnut tray faces (pieces 34) are made in pairs—first drill the finger hole and then slice the blank down the center (see *Tray Face Blank Layout Detail*, above right). Attach them with screws.

Now mount the drawer pulls (pieces 35), casters, and the hinge on the tray bank top, and you are nearly done. Cover all exposed screw holes with walnut plugs and topcoat with a penetrating finish.

You will likely want to modify the cart to suit your specific clamp collection. Keep in mind that you can fit a lot in those drawers ... that's where all our C-clamps and band clamps go.

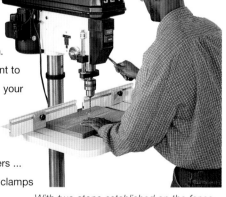

With two stops established on the fence, drill the holes to mount the drawer pulls.

MATERIAL LIST—*DRAWER & TRAYS*

		T x W x L
21	Small Face (1)	¾" x 4¼" x 13½"
22	Middle Face (1)	¾" x 6¼" x 13½"
23	Large Face (1)	¾" x 9¼" x 13½"
24	Small Front & Back (2)	½" x 2½" x 11"
25	Small Sides (2)	½" x 3¾" x 15½"
26	Middle Front & Back (2)	½" x 6" x 11"
27	Middle Sides (2)	½" x 6" x 15½"
28	Large Front & Back (2)	½" x 8" x 11"
29	Large Sides (2)	½" x 8" x 15½"
30	Bottoms (3)	¼" x 11" x 15"
31	Tray Sides (12)	½" x 1¾" x 6¼"
32	Tray Fronts & Backs (12)	½" x 1½" x 4⅞"
33	Tray Bottoms (6)	¼" x 6¼" x 7"
34	Tray Faces (6)	¾" x 2³⁄₁₆" x 5½"
35	Pulls (3)	*Wood*

Use a single liner or both at once to effectively grip and secure a wide variety of moldings or other shaped pieces. Even difficult end grain drilling is made easy with this vise fixture.

Woodworker's Magnetic Drill Press Vise

Every now and then it's necessary to clamp odd-shaped or small parts to a drill press table to drill them safely and accurately. If your only option is a metalworking vise, you've probably discovered that the jaws aren't really shaped correctly for woodworking. It's virtually impossible to clamp a wooden dowel or molding securely between them without doing damage to the wood. No one likes to sacrifice a carefully made part! If you cringe each time you tighten the screw, we've got a more gentle option here. Build this wood-jawed vise and put your other one out to pasture.

If you're still using a metalworking vise to hold (and crush!) delicate wood parts, this drill press vise fixture is a gentler solution for woodworking.

Every vise is built around a screw or spindle mechanism. If only one jaw moves, this is a single threaded spindle, and it's the common configuration for metalworking vises. In designing this project, we wanted a vise with both jaws controlled from a single handle, eventually meeting in the center of the fixture. Two moving wooden jaws would make the vise easier to operate as well as provide a more forgiving clamping surface.

Starting with the Jaws

We built this vise out of oak because it's easy to work with and plenty strong. To take maximum advantage of that strength, face-glue and screw eight pieces of stock together to create the laminated jaws (pieces 1). Predrill for the twelve screws (pieces 2: see *Elevation Drawings* on page 38 for locations) and counterbore the screw holes for walnut plugs (pieces 3). The screws add extra strength to the finished jaws and work as clamps during the glue-up process.

After the glue dries, use the *Face and End Views Drawing* and *Figure 1* on page 38 to locate and drill holes for the ring magnets (pieces 4) in the front face of each jaw. This is easier to do while the jaws are still rectangular. We used 3/4"-diameter magnets, but you should have yours in hand before drilling any holes to drill accurately. You want the magnets to drop into their shallow bores

with a snug friction fit. Use a Forstner bit on the drill press to bore these holes cleanly.

Now cut each jaw to shape on your band saw (see *Figure 2* and the *Jaw and Drive Block Subassembly Drawing*). Glue and plug the screw bores and, after the glue dries, trim the plugs flush with a sharp chisel. Then sand the jaws and set them aside.

Building Removable Liners

Not everything a woodworker needs to clamp is nice and square, and the removable jaw liners on this vise are designed to handle a diverse assortment of shapes. By inserting just one liner, you can clamp irregular stock such as triangular or decorative moldings that only have one flat surface. With both liners installed, drilling dowels and other round stock is a breeze to clamp firmly either vertically or horizontally.

After cutting the liners (pieces 5) to size, set your table saw blade to 45° and use a combination of the saw's miter gauge and rip fence to create the angled grooves in their faces. You'll find all the dimensions for setting up these angled cuts in the *drawings* on the next two pages.

Set the saw back to 90° to clean out the squared-off bottom of each groove, then head for the drill press to bore holes for the magnets that hold the liners to the vise jaws (but don't install the magnets yet).

Making the Frame

The jaws of this vise slide along a frame composed of two sides (pieces 6) and a couple of endcaps with removable wedges (pieces 7 and 8). The sides are rectangular stock with a rabbet cut on one edge (see the *Side Detail* on page 38). Cut these rabbets on your table saw, then adjust the height of the blade and use your miter gauge to nibble out the notches on the ends of each frame side. You could do this on your band saw, but it might be difficult to get an absolutely square cut.

See the *Frame Endcap With Wedge Drawing* to locate the 1/2"-diameter hole (for the threaded spindle) in each endcap, then drill these holes. To make assembling the vise easier, a wedge-shaped part of each endcap must lift off. With your drill press, predrill and countersink holes for the two screws (pieces 9) used to reattach the wedges, then follow the *drawings* and use your scroll saw to remove each wedge.

To complete the frame assembly, predrill and counterbore holes for the screws to hold the assembly together (pieces 10) and the plugs to cap them (pieces 11). Now bore ten holes in the frame sides for the magnets (see the *drawings* for hole locations). Magnets will help in set-ups, but don't rely on their holding strength alone; the vise should always be clamped securely to the

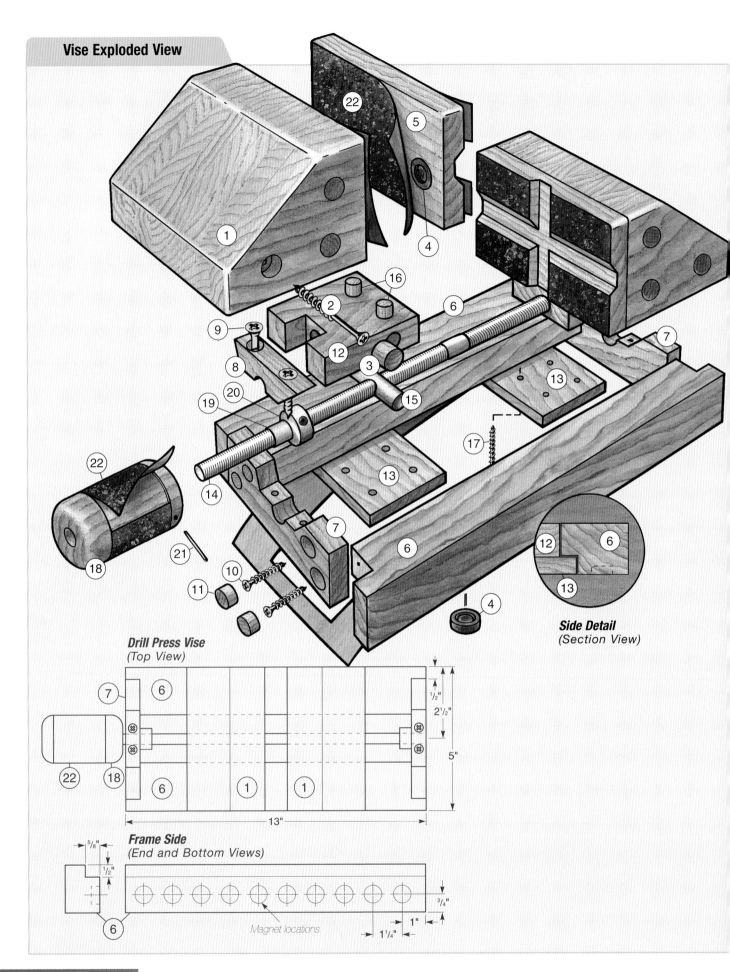

Drill Press Vise
(Top View)

2½"
½"
5"
13"

Side Detail
(Section View)

Frame Side
(End and Bottom Views)

⅝"
½"
¾"
1"
1¼"

Magnet locations

MATERIAL LIST

		T x W x L			T x W x L
1	Laminated Jaws (2)	3" x 6" x 3 3/8"	12	Drive Blocks (2)	7/8" x 2" x 2 3/8"
2	Jaw Screws (12)	2 1/2" x #10 *Square-X*	13	Lock Plates (2)	9/16" x 2 3/4" x 2 7/8"
3	Jaw Plugs (12)	5/8" Dia. x 3/8"	14	Double Threaded Spindle (1)	7/16" Dia. x 14 1/4"
4	Ring Magnets (32)	3/4" OD	15	Spindle Nuts (2)	5/8" Dia. x 1 3/4"
5	Liners (2)	3/4" x 3" x 6"	16	Drive Block Dowels (4)	1/2" Dia. x 1 1/2"
6	Frame Sides (2)	1 1/2" x 2" x 13"	17	Drive Block Screws (8)	1" x #6, *Square-X*
7	Frame Endcaps (2)	5/8" x 1 1/2" x 5"	18	Handle (1)	2" Dia. x 3 1/2"
8	Wedges (2)	5/8" x 1/2" x 2 3/8"	19	Brass Sleeves (4)	1/2" OD x 5/8"
9	Endcap Wedge Screws (4)	1 1/4" x #6, *Brass*	20	Spindle Collars (2)	1/2" ID
10	Frame Screws (8)	1 1/2" x #8, *Square-X*	21	Retaining Pin (1)	1/8" Dia. x 1 7/8"
11	Frame Screw Plugs (8)	5/8" Dia. x 1/4"	22	Non-skid Tape (1)	3" x 60"

Jaw and Drive Block Subassembly
(Face and End Views)

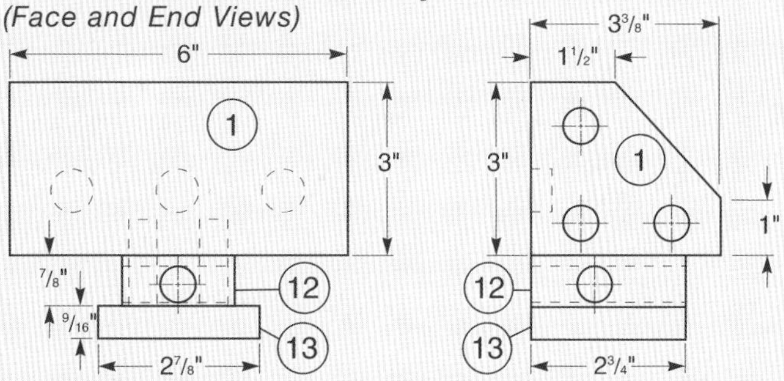

Drill Press Vise
(Side View)

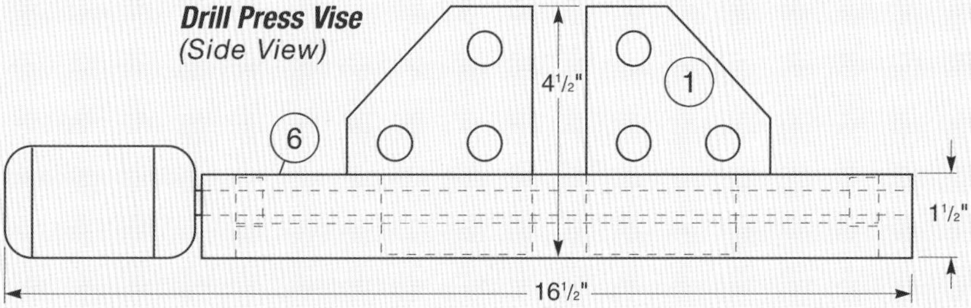

Frame Endcap with Wedge
(End View)

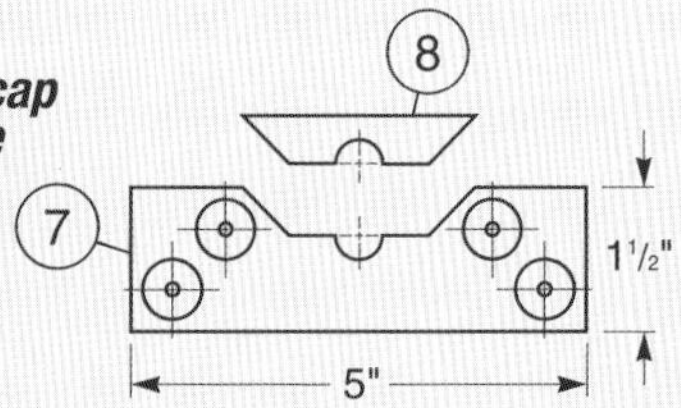

drill press table during use. Complete the frame by gluing and screwing it together, then install and sand the plugs.

Adding Drive Blocks and Lock Plates

An oak drive block (piece 12) is attached to the bottom of each jaw: these ride between the frame sides to keep the jaws in line. A simple rectangular lock plate (piece 13) is attached to the bottom of each drive block (one of the final assembly steps). These plates ride in the rabbets on the frame sides and prevent the jaws from lifting off the frame during clamping.

After cutting the drive blocks to size, use your miter gauge to nibble a rectangular notch in one end of each (see the *Exploded View Drawing* on the facing page). Then move to your drill press and (using your old steel vise one last time!) bore a 1/2"-diameter hole through the middle of each block; this allows the threaded spindle (piece 14) to pass through.

Switch to a 5/8"-diameter bit to bore a large hole across the grain in each drive block (see *drawing* for location). These holes are for the cylindrical spindle nuts (pieces

15) that thread onto the spindle and allow the blocks to move when the spindle is turned. Predrill for the dowels (pieces 16) and screws (pieces 17) to lock the blocks to the jaws. All of these locations can be found on the *drawings*.

Use dowel centers to lay out the dowel drilling locations in the bottom of each jaw and drill these holes. When everything lines up, glue the dowels in place and glue the blocks to the jaws, but leave the lock plates aside until final assembly.

Turning the Handle

The cylindrical handle (piece 18) on this vise is large enough to grasp and twist tightly, yet its shape allows for delicate adjustments equally well.

If you don't own a lathe, you should be able to locate 2" oak handrail stock at your local lumberyard. If you decide to turn the handle, use glued-up stock rather than a single piece of wood, to avoid splitting. Either way, bore the center out on your drill press (for the spindle) before rounding over the ends. Make this this boring 7/16" in diameter. Then round over the ends of the handle on your router table, using a bearing-guided 3/8"-radius roundover bit. If you're

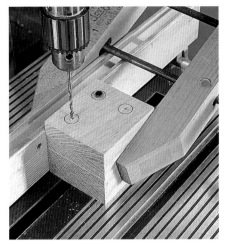

Figure 1: Make the laminated oak sliding jaws first. Stack the jaw parts and machine them while they are still rectangular in shape.

turning the handle on a lathe, do all your shaping and sanding while the handle is chucked in the machine.

Sand all the wooden parts and dry-fit them together, then apply your finish. Use a hard finish like varnish here; oil is not a good choice, as it tends to soak into clamped parts when they are under pressure.

Time for Final Assembly

Begin the assembly process by sliding the spindle nuts into their borings in the drive blocks, then threading the spindle through them. Twirl the drive blocks (and, of

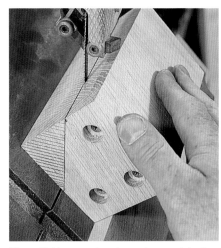

Figure 2: Use your band saw to complete the laminated jaw's shape. See the Elevation Drawings *for all the dimension details.*

course, the jaws) until each is an equal distance from the unthreaded area in the middle of the spindle. Cut a pair of brass sleeves (pieces 19) from a length of rigid brass 1/2" OD tube. Now, with the wedges removed, spread epoxy on the top half of each of the frame's endcap holes (the halves drilled into the removable wedges) and press the brass sleeves in place.

After the epoxy sets, slip a couple more brass sleeves onto the spindle, then slide the spindle collars (pieces 20) over these. Pass the spindle ends through the brass sleeves in the frame endcaps, then

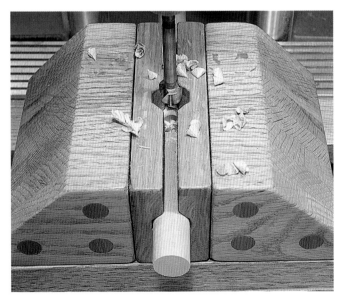

With magnets to hold this drill press vise in place and a variety of clamping options available, drilling dowels and circular-shaped objects is a breeze. We used oak to ensure strength and durability.

Drilling odd-shaped stock is easy with this drill press fixture. The double threaded spindle allows for single-handed adjustability, and the overall stability adds a level of safety to drilling operations.

The operating hardware for this drill press vise is a double threaded spindle (allowing both jaws to be driven by a single handle) teamed up with spindle nuts and collars.

line up the spindle/drive block assembly on the frame and screw the wedges (piece 13) in place. Secure the lock plates with screws driven into their predrilled holes (don't epoxy them in — you may need to remove them in the future), then center the jaws along the frame and secure them there by tightening the Allen bolts in the spindle collars.

Slide the handle onto the long end of the spindle, and drill a 1/8"-diameter hole through it at the location shown on the *Elevation Drawings* so it pierces the handle and the spindle, then remove the handle. Apply epoxy in the handle cavity and remount the handle on the spindle, capping its end with a plug. While the epoxy is still

liquid, secure the retaining pin (piece 21) in the handle with more epoxy dabbed in the 1/8" hole you just drilled.

Continue using epoxy to secure all the magnets in place, keeping in mind the ones in the jaws and liners should be installed so they attract rather than repel (a matter of flipping them the correct side). To finish up, apply non-skid tape (piece 22) to the jaw and liner faces, the frame bottom and the handle as shown on the *Exploded View Drawing*. All that's left to do is to find some strangely shaped parts to lock into your new drill press vise, because you're ready to make some shavings!

Quick Tip

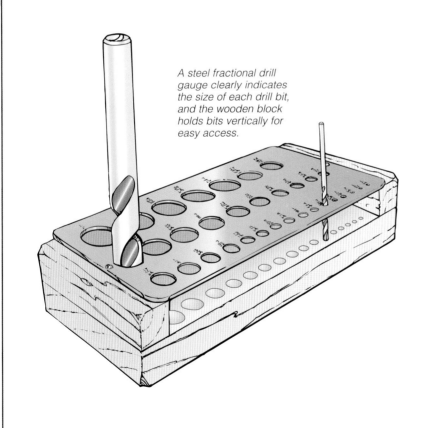

A steel fractional drill gauge clearly indicates the size of each drill bit, and the wooden block holds bits vertically for easy access.

Drill Bit Holder

If you only have a few twist drill bits, finding the one you need usually isn't a problem — but it's a bigger hassle if you own a full fractional set. Here's a clever way to keep them all organized next to your drill press: Buy a fractional gauge from a metalworking mail-order catalog. This is a 3" x 6" metal plate with holes ranging from 1/16" to 1/2", in 1/64" increments. Screw the plate to two wood blocks glued to a wooden base. Use your drill press to drill down into the base through each of the fractional gauge holes with the correct diameter bit. Make a 1/2"- or 3/8"-deep hole for each bit. This way, the holes in the base will hold the bits securely and straight up. Then load the holder with bits. Now your bits are visibly numbered and neatly organized. Store them with the cutting end down for added safety.

Shop-built Disc Sander

A dedicated disc sander is a useful addition to any shop, but it's another tool expense that often falls down the list of "must haves" until it never gets purchased. What you may not know is that an ordinary bench grinder is easy to convert into a disc sander by simply replacing a grinding wheel with a plywood disk and a spacer (see page 46). Once you've made that switch, your new "sander" will need a sturdy platform and sanding table — the genesis for this project. If you're the resourceful sort or feed your woodworking hobby from a lean budget, this Shop-built Disc Sander should have instant curb appeal!

If you decide to build this project, use a grinder that revolves at 1,725 RPM to avoid burning your wood. The slow-speed variety used for sharpening turning tools is ideal.

Making the Base Cabinet

Get started on the cabinet by cutting the bottom, shelf, top, sides, front and back (pieces 1 through 7) from a sheet of oak veneered plywood. And while you're at the table saw, make the storage bin shelves (pieces 8) from 1/4" plywood.

While most of the milling on this project takes place on the edges of the stock, there is a little routing required. Chuck a 3/4"

straight bit in your router and clamp a straightedge in place to plow the dado in the cabinet back for the cabinet shelf. Its location is shown in the Elevation Drawings on page 45. Switch to a 1/4" bit and mill the dadoes for the storage bin shelves on the inside faces of the upper sides.

All the panels are trimmed to some degree with 1/4"-thick solid walnut (piece 9), and some of this trim must be attached before you start milling grooves. See the technique shown on the next page to attach trim to the back edge of the cabinet top, the front edge of the shelf and both the front and back edges of the cabinet bottom.

When the glue is dry, mount a 3/8" dado head in your table saw and mill the appropriate dadoes, grooves and rabbets, as shown in the *drawings*. The grooves will be captured by the hardwood edging. As you assemble the cabinet, the method behind this construction technique will become clear.

Assembling the Base

Glue and clamp walnut trim (ripped to 1/4" thickness) along the remaining plywood edges of the cabinet pieces, as shown in the Exploded View on page 45. Note that the trim stops short of the rabbets on the front, back and shelf. Dry-fit and temporarily clamp the front, back, bottom and shelf together. Double-check the size and fit of the lower side and upper sides. The sides are installed with biscuits, so you can mark their locations and cut their slots now. Glue up and clamp the cabinet, dropping the lower side (and its biscuits) in place as you do.

Next, install the upper sides and the top with glue, clamps and biscuits, capturing the storage bin shelves. Check that everything is square as you tighten the clamps.

Converting the Grinder

Here's how to convert your grinder to a sander: We decided to retrofit ours with a 12" disc to match the standard size stick-on discs available through catalogs and home

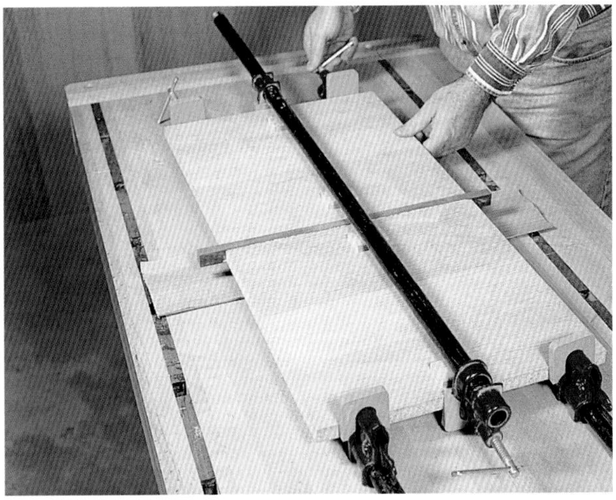

Start by gluing and clamping a strip of solid hardwood between two pieces of plywood. With this approach, the clamping pressure is even and strong across the entire joint.

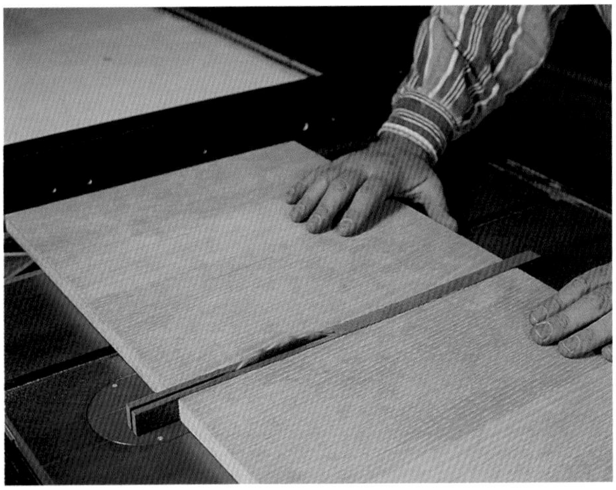

Rip the assembled pieces down the middle, leaving two securely attached strips of hardwood in place. The strip is machined to be a bit thicker than the plywood.

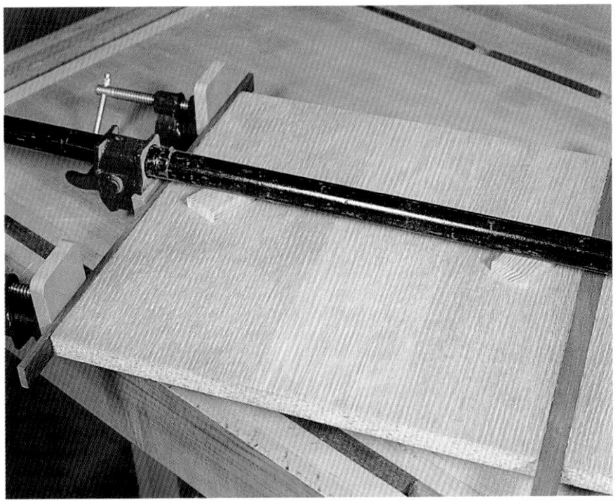

Now simply spin the plywood panels around and repeat the process. Whenever your trim is likely to get abuse, this method of glue-up provides a slightly stronger bond.

Carcass Exploded View

MATERIAL LIST—*CARCASS*

		T x W x L
1	Cabinet Bottom (1)	3/4" x 16" x 15 1/2"
2	Cabinet Front (1)	3/4" x 16" x 16 1/2"
3	Cabinet Shelf (1)	3/4" x 16" x 15 3/8
4	Cabinet Lower Side (1)	3/4" x 16 1/8" x 14 1/2"
5	Cabinet Upper Sides (2)	3/4" x 12 1/4" x 12 1/2"
6	Cabinet Top (1)	3/4" x 16" x 12 3/4"
7	Cabinet Back (1)	3/4" x 16" x 29 3/4"
8	Storage Bin Shelves (2)	1/4" x 15 3/4" x 11 7/8"
9	Walnut Trim (1)	1/4" x 3/4" x 400"
10	Disc (1)	3/4" x 12"
11	Disc Laminate (1)	1/32" x 13" x 13"
12	Disc Spacer (1)	*Cut to fit*
13	Grinder Sub-base (1)	*Cut to fit*
14	Table (1)	1 1/2" x 12" x 18"
15	Walnut Table Edging (1)	1/2" x 1 1/2" x 43"
16	Table Laminate (1)	1/32" x 13" x 19"
17	Miter Gauge Channel (1)	*Aluminum, trim to length*
18	Table Mounting Blocks (2)	1 1/2" x 5" x 12"
19	Block Bolts & Nuts (4 Sets)	5/16" x 4"
20	Table Hinges (1 Pair)	1 1/2" Brass
21	Table Support (1)	*Brass lid support*
22	Cabinet Casters (2)	3" *Dia.*
23	Cabinet Feet (2)	1 1/2" x 3" x 3 1/2"
24	Cabinet Handle (1)	1 1/4" *Dia.* x 14 1/2"
25	Cabinet Handle Brackets (2)	1 1/2" x 3" x 3 1/2"

The handle brackets and cabinet feet are shaped exactly the same. The brackets for the feet have no borings for a handle.

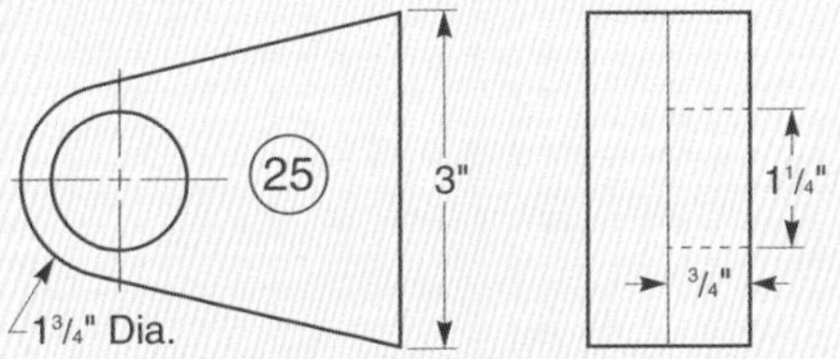

Handle Brackets
(Inside and End Views)

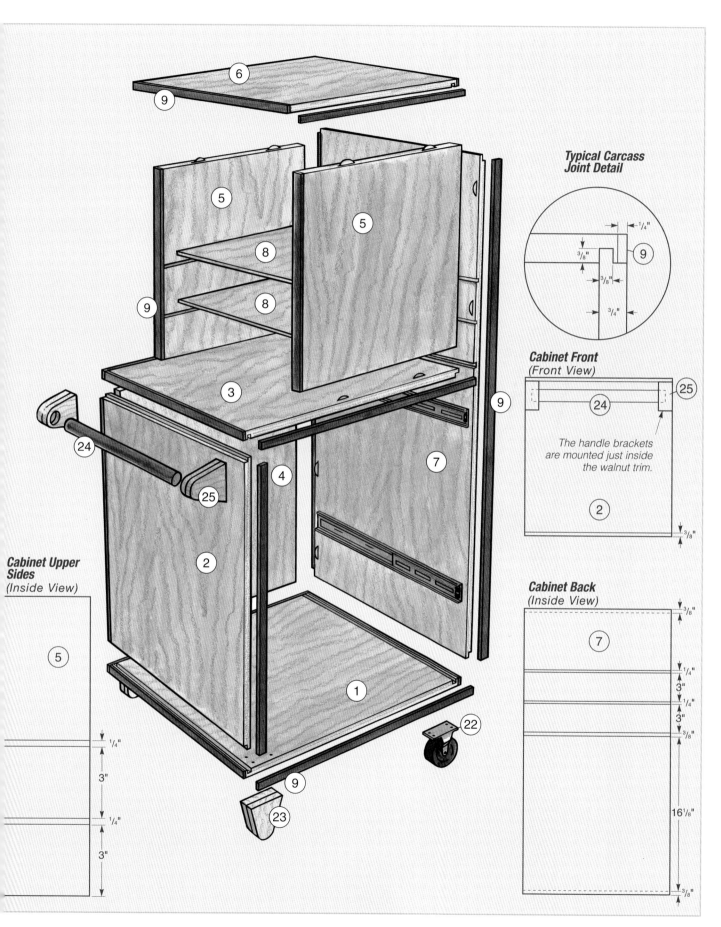

Typical Carcass Joint Detail

Cabinet Front
(Front View)

The handle brackets are mounted just inside the walnut trim.

Cabinet Back
(Inside View)

Cabinet Upper Sides
(Inside View)

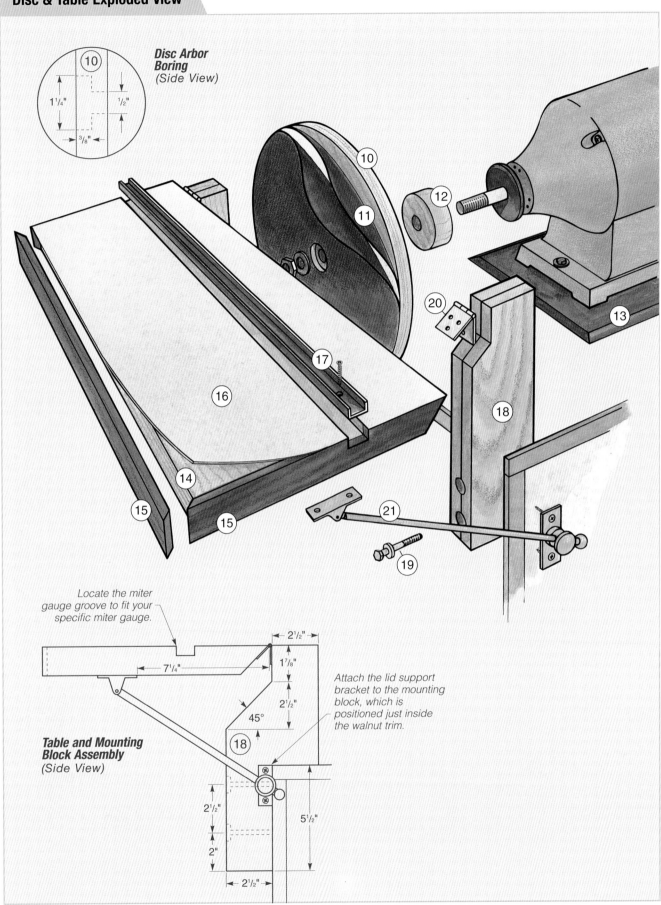

Disc Arbor Boring (Side View)

1¼"   ½"
3/8"

10

11

10

12

13

20

17

16

18

14

15

15

21

19

Locate the miter gauge groove to fit your specific miter gauge.

2½"

7¼"

1⅞"

2½"

45°

Attach the lid support bracket to the mounting block, which is positioned just inside the walnut trim.

Table and Mounting Block Assembly (Side View)

18

2½"

5½"

2"

2½"

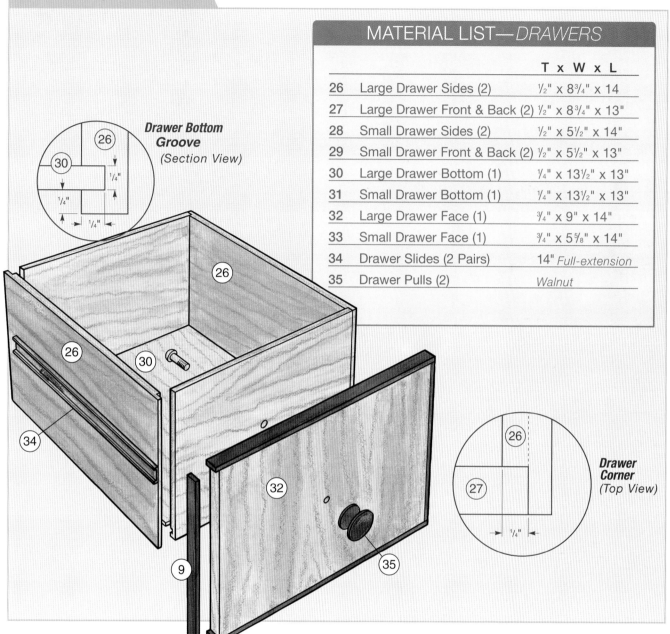

MATERIAL LIST—*DRAWERS*

		T x W x L
26	Large Drawer Sides (2)	1/2" x 8 3/4" x 14
27	Large Drawer Front & Back (2)	1/2" x 8 3/4" x 13"
28	Small Drawer Sides (2)	1/2" x 5 1/2" x 14"
29	Small Drawer Front & Back (2)	1/2" x 5 1/2" x 13"
30	Large Drawer Bottom (1)	1/4" x 13 1/2" x 13"
31	Small Drawer Bottom (1)	1/4" x 13 1/2" x 13"
32	Large Drawer Face (1)	3/4" x 9" x 14"
33	Small Drawer Face (1)	3/4" x 5 5/8" x 14"
34	Drawer Slides (2 Pairs)	14" *Full-extension*
35	Drawer Pulls (2)	*Walnut*

Drawer Bottom Groove
(Section View)

Drawer Corner
(Top View)

improvement centers. Use plywood for making the disc (piece 10). MDF and particleboard are not structurally stable enough for this application. Start with a plywood blank, and drill a step-down center hole to match the diameter of your grinder's arbor as well as the nut and washer, then cut the disc to size on the band saw. Stay just outside your layout lines and finish to the center of the pencil line with a belt sander.

Apply plastic laminate (piece 11) to the sandpaper side of the disc, using a good-quality contact adhesive, then trim it to size

with a bearing-guided flush-trim bit in a router. Break the sharp edges of the disc with sandpaper, and don't forget to remove the laminate over the center hole.

The cylindrical hardwood spacer (piece 12) provides support for the disc, but it also takes up space on the arbor so the threads are set in from the sanding disc face. Bandsaw the spacer after boring the arbor hole on the drill press (to ensure that it is exactly 90° to the disc face). Slide the spacer and disc onto the arbor and lock them in place with the nut and a washer. Then stick on an

80-grit disc and mount the grinder on the cabinet. Depending on the model, you may have to install a sub-base (piece 13) under your grinder to achieve 1/4" of clearance between the bottom of the disc and the top of the cabinet. Alter the thickness of this piece as required by your machine.

Building an Adjustable Table

The tabletop (piece 14) is comprised of three thicknesses of 1/2" plywood, face-glued together. The hinged edge is chamfered on the table saw at 45°, and the other

Storage is always useful in the shop, and the two drawers in this cabinet will hold plenty of supplies.

By adding a miter gauge slot, this shop-built disc sander can help create compound angles.

This heavy-duty lid support allows for accurate and infinite angle adjustments. Drop the table down for storage.

three edges are then laminated with 1/2"-thick walnut table edging (piece 15), mitered at the corners. After sanding, apply plastic laminate (piece 16) to the top surface, then use a straight bit in your router table to plow the groove for the aluminum miter gauge channel (piece 17). Locate this groove so the edge of your miter gauge (use the one from your table saw) is about 1/4" away from the disc when it's set at 60°, then screw the channel in place.

Glue up two thicknesses of 1x stock to form blanks for the two mounting blocks (pieces 18), and band-saw them to the shape shown in the *drawings*. Sand the blocks smooth, then secure each to the cabinet with a pair of predrilled, counterbored bolts (pieces 19), washers and nuts. Attach the table to the mounts with a pair of brass hinges (pieces 20), making sure the screws are not so long that they penetrate the tabletop.

You can adjust and set the angle of the table with a heavy-duty brass lid support (piece 21). This is surface-mounted by means of predrilled screws at the locations shown on the *drawings*.

Mobilizing the Cabinet

To make the disc sanding center mobile, add two locking casters (pieces 22), a pair of feet (pieces 23) and a handle (piece 24). The feet and the handle brackets (pieces 25) are identical, except that the brackets feature a shallow bore to accommodate the walnut handle (see the *drawings*). All four parts are secured with predrilled screws driven home from inside the drawer cavity. The casters are simply screwed to the bottom of the cabinet.

Building the Drawers

Choose high-quality, 1/2" plywood for the drawer sides, fronts and backs (pieces 26 through 29). Baltic birch is an excellent choice. After cutting these parts to size, install a 1/2" dado head in the table saw and plow two rabbets on the inside face of each drawer side (see the *drawings*). Switch to a 1/4" dado head to mill a groove in each drawer side, front and back for the drawer bottoms (pieces 30 and 31). Assemble the drawers with glue and clamps.

Both drawers fit in the same opening, so it's a good idea to install them before sizing the drawer faces (pieces 32 and 33). Use full-extension slides (pieces 34), following the manufacturer's instructions. Mount the slides after placing the drawers in the opening.

Cut the drawer faces from 3/4" plywood, with the grain running vertically. Wrap the edges with walnut trim. Test-fit the drawer faces using double-faced tape (allow 1/8" between the two drawers). Permanently mount the drawer faces with glue and screws, then drill a hole dead-center in each and install the hardwood pulls (pieces 35).

After sanding the entire project down to 180 grit, spray or brush on three coats of satin finish. Now you have an extremely useful addition to your woodworking tool arsenal. Better yet, half the grinder still remains for touching up those chisels or the mower blade!

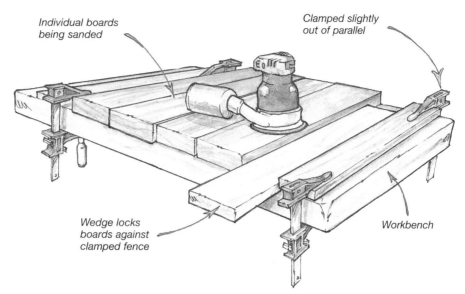

Individual boards being sanded

Clamped slightly out of parallel

Wedge locks boards against clamped fence

Workbench

Sanding Jig for Multiple Boards

When you need to sand several boards of the same size, clamp two fences to your bench, leaving one at a very slight angle to the other. Then load up the boards you need to sand and wedge them in place between the fences with a piece of scrap. It makes for quick and easy board changes, which is great on big jobs. Just make sure the fences and wedge are thinner than the boards being sanded so they don't get in the way along the edges of the outermost boards you're sanding.

Keep It Grounded

As dust flies through your collector hoses, it builds up static electricity on the walls of the hose. This can also occur if you use rigid plastic pipe for dust collection ductwork. To prevent sparks (and even explosions), ground metal hoses by attaching a piece of plastic-covered copper wire to the hose and a cold water pipe (or similar ground). Run bare wire through plastic hoses and ground one end of this in the same fashion.

One Person's Trash...

Anyone who owns farm animals or small pets like gerbils and hamsters would be delighted to get your sawdust for bedding. Just be sure you let them know what species

you've been milling, and have them call their vet to make sure the particular wood type won't harm the animals. For example, horses have been known to get colic when exposed to some species like walnut.

Making Perfectly Round Wheels

If you need a pair of wheels (or maybe even four), scribe circles on your stock and cut the wheels out on the band saw, staying just outside the lines. Drill a 1/4" hole at the center of each wheel, then slide the wheels onto a 1/4" threaded rod and tighten with nuts. Chuck the rod into your portable drill, clamp a wooden guide block onto the table of your disc sander and, with the drill in reverse, sand the wheels to their final size.

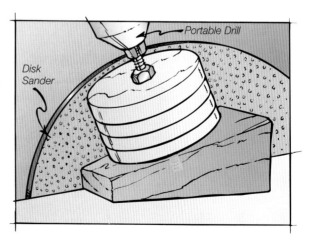

Portable Drill

Disk Sander

The alignment blocks don't just store the disks, they make it easy to center them on your orbital sander: just press down. The dust extraction holes line up every time.

Sandpaper Caddy

If finding a specific grit sandpaper in your sandpaper drawer is a frustrating chore, here's an easy way to bring some order to the chaos. A reader submitted this handy caddy design, which is basically an embellishment of a simple alignment block for installing orbital sanding disks on a sander (see photo, above). By making several of these alignment blocks (pieces 1) for each of the grits you use, all you need is a case to store them in. Suddenly that drawer is much less cluttered!

The concept here is simplicity itself: dowels on a board line up the holes on a sanding disk with your sander's pad. To install a disk, slip the orbital sander over the guide pins (pieces 2) of the appropriate block and press down. Lift off the sander and you're ready to sand. The critical dimension on these blocks is the location of the guide pins. Follow the *Elevation Drawing* at right and use one of your sanding disks to verify the layout marks. Make a cardboard template and use it as a guide for locating the pins.

The holes in the faceplate of the sander and the sanding disks are 3/8". Using 5/16" dowels for the pins allows for some slight misalignment but still provides a good match between the holes in the paper and the dust extraction openings in the pad. Make

enough storage blocks for the various grits you use. Five should cover it, for 60, 80, 100, 150 and 220 grits.

Once you've made the alignment blocks, build the storage cabinet shown in the *Exploded View*. It simply consists of an open-faced rectangular box with a series of runners that hold the different alignment blocks.

Rather than fabricating the sides (pieces 3) individually, cut a board 13" wide by 10 7/8" high. Use 1/4" hardboard for the sides. Glue the five runners (pieces 4 and 5) in place at their proper locations (see *Elevation Drawing*). After the glue dries, cut the assembly in half vertically and trim each half

to width to make two identical case sides. Cut the top, bottom and back of the cabinet (pieces 6 and 7) to size, and glue them to the cabinet sides, starting with the top and bottom. Make the back from hardboard. Pin the joints with brads or finish nails if you wish to hold them in place while the glue dries. To identify the grit of the paper stored on each block, attach a label to each. They're quick to make on a computer.

This handy sanding caddy holds five grit's worth of sanding disks. Use the blocks to mount disks on your sander and to make each grit easy to find.

MATERIAL LIST

		T x W x L
1	Alignment Blocks (5)	¾" x 5⅞" x 5⅞"
2	Guide Pins (20)	⁵⁄₁₆" Dia. x 1¼"
3	Sides (2)	¼" x 5⅞" x 10⅞"
4	Middle Runners (8)	⅜" x ⅜" x 5⅞"
5	Bottom Runners (2)	⅜" x ⅝" x 5⅞"
6	Top/bottom (2)	¾" x 5⅞" x 5⅞"
7	Back (1)	¼" x 6⅜" x 10⅞"

Alignment Block
(Top View)

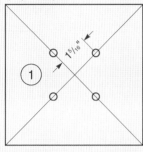

1⁵⁄₁₆"

Note: The easiest way to locate the pin holes is to draw the layout lines shown at left, then lay a disk in place and rotate it until four of the holes intersect the lines. Or measure out from the center as shown.

Storage Cabinet Side
(Section View)

2½"

4¼"

6"

7¾"

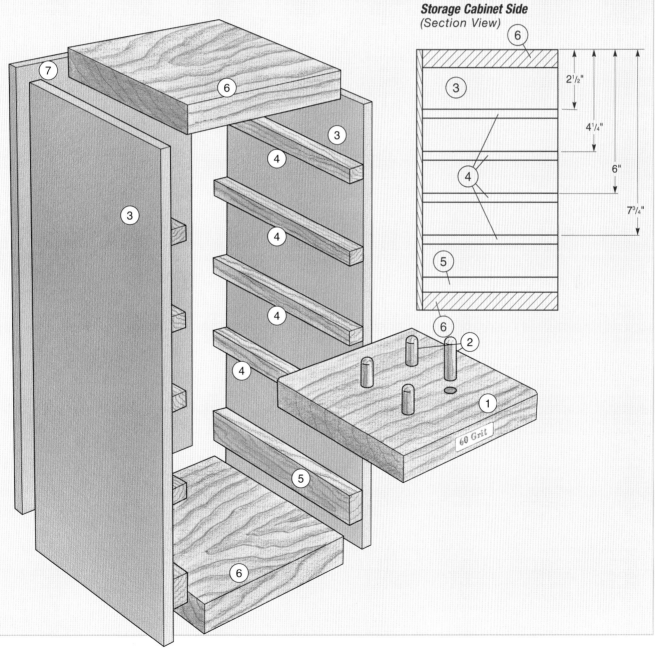

60 Grit

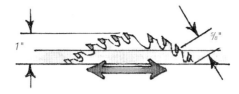

Figure 1: A blade set too low causes the teeth to cut more horizontally than vertically, which increases the chances of kickback.

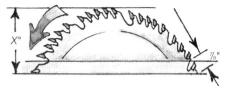

Figure 2: When a blade is set high, the teeth are traveling downward as they enter the workpiece, forcing it safely onto the table.

Avoiding Kickback and Binding

Occasionally readers ask us: "What's the most dangerous tool in the shop?" Among our staff, the consensus is, it's the one you're most afraid of. The second most dangerous tool is the one that you're sure won't hurt you. If you respect the power of woodworking tools, your caution will be rewarded with safe, precise work. With that in mind, let's take a look at four problem areas encountered during basic table saw operations.

Kickback During Ripping

Kickback simply means that the workpiece is kicked, or driven back toward the operator. When most woodworkers hear the term, they think of a ripping operation coming to a sudden and dramatic stop. There are two interrelated causes for this: an underpowered saw, and incorrect blade height.

Forensic scientists have long known that a bullet causes its greatest damage as its velocity decreases (small entry/large exit). The same is true with kickback, which occurs when a saw blade is slowing down. If the saw has enough power to keep driving, it won't kick back. Not only does the sheer power of the saw come into play here, but the physical weight does too: if the motor, saw arbor and blade are heavy enough, their momentum should keep the blade spinning during a sharp impact.

The second cause of this type of kick-

back (and many other problems too) is a blade that's set too low. Your high school shop teacher may have told you to set the blade as low as possible - just above the top of the wood (see *Figure 1*). But that blade position means the teeth are cutting more horizontally than vertically.

When the teeth do catch, they're traveling at the top of the blade's rotation. If the blade is set high (as shown in Figure 2), the teeth are traveling downward, forcing the workpiece onto the table, instead of back

NEVER, NEVER

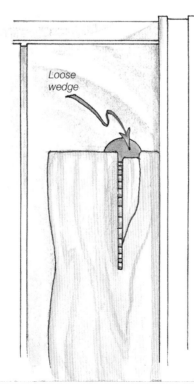

Loose wedge

No matter how rough things get, or how probable a kickback will be, don't ever let go of the wood! Even if you think you're Speedy Gonzales, you're simply not fast enough to get out of the way of a 50 mile-per-hour projectile. More often than not, by holding fast you actually will prevent the kickback. The trick is to train your reflexes not to panic and jump away so that you can hold on even tighter and even drive the piece forward if you can. Let go, and there's no telling where the wood will end up.

On long rips, stand at the end of the board to the left and walk it through. This is not only safest, but it also produces a smoother cut.

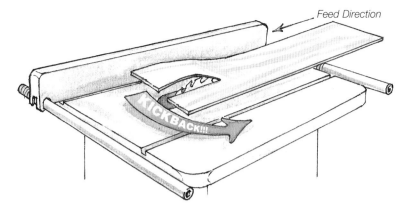

Figure 3: With over-the-top kickback, the wood is lifted off the table and dropped back on top of the blade, which then throws it toward the operator at about 50 mph.

toward the operator. A low blade also causes motor drag because there are more teeth in contact with the wood. Each tooth, instead of cutting through a little more than $\frac{3}{4}$" of stock, is cutting through more than twice that amount of material. With a $\frac{3}{4}$" board and $\frac{1}{4}$" of blade protrusion on a 10" blade, the teeth must cut through a full $1\frac{5}{8}$" of material. This heats up the teeth and the wood, increases drag on the motor, and reduces the feed rate. Not only does heat cause metal fatigue, but it may cause some species of wood to expel oils that gum up the blade, further reducing its life. Since the blade is already slowing down and the motor is operating closer to its stall rate than necessary, kickbacks are far more likely.

Over-the-Top Kickback

One reader once reported that the first shop he worked in had a 2'x3' piece of plywood mounted on the wall with the boss's name written on it. This piece had a distinctive semi-circular gouge out of one face. The boss wouldn't tell what caused it, only that it "had to stay on the wall until someone else makes one like it". Had he explained how it happened, the culprit was actually over-the-top kickback.

Over-the-top kickback is the most dangerous type because the wood is thrown toward the operator at close to blade speed (about 52 mph!). The workpiece catches the rear teeth of the blade (*Figure 3*), and the teeth lift the wood off the table. As the saw teeth travel up and forward, they drive the wood toward the operator. Speed increases and the blade cuts less while digging in more. That decreasing difference in speed between the blade and wood means the teeth no longer cut but dig in like baseball cleats and kick back.

Ripping Lumber and Sheet Products

We've seen woodworkers rip a long board by standing close to the saw and pulling the workpiece through in short choppy spurts. To them we say the best method for ripping a long board is to stand at the back left side of the board and walk it into the saw. This will result in a smooth, continuous rip. Keeping your left hand fairly far forward during this operation helps push the edge of the board safely toward the fence.

On sheet products, it can help to deliberately hold the sheet very slightly crooked with only the front corner touching the fence (full sheets or long rips). Slowly ease the sheet forward until you hear the blade make its first contact. Then immediately straighten the sheet tight to the fence. This ensures that the rip starts with the front of the sheet tight to the fence. As the sheet is straightened, the blade holds the front in place and you can exert pressure with your left hand to keep the workpiece against the fence.

Crosscut Binding

Often you'll need to cut a piece of wood that's wider than it is long. Regardless of grain direction, this is a cross-cut. The safety issue here is binding, which occurs when the workpiece twists away from the fence. This is one of those operations where things can go wrong very quickly. Don't attempt it if you're not comfortable with your saw. The safest way to tackle this cut is to use a sliding cutoff jig. One final thought: it's a good idea to keep the saw table waxed and the rip fence properly aligned with the blade.

NEVER...LET GO OF THE WORKPIECE!

YIKES!

Switch

A reader told us he once was ripping some oak for face frames and either didn't notice the end check (a split at the end of the board), or didn't think much of it. But this check was unusual: it ran diagonally at about 20°, perhaps 6" into the wood. When the blade hit the end of the check, it cut off a wedge-shaped piece that got jammed into its own slot. This increased pressure on the side of the blade. At the moment, he was eight feet behind the saw's OFF switch, so his only choice was to hold tight until the thermal overload tripped. He had to ask himself if it was more important to have the saw motor burn out or end up with a three-pound chunk of oak sticking out of his ear. Had he let go, the small wedge would surely have been free to fly.

Keep in mind that, although some circumstances may leave you no choice but to bail out, the majority of sawing problems are best handled by holding onto that wood, no matter what.

Deluxe Drum Sander

If you want to build a better mousetrap, the best starting point is a list of the limitations of your old one. As far as drum sanding on a drill press goes, most sanding jigs lack dust control, and the drums tend to clog too soon. This jig addresses both problems: It has a built-in dust collection port, and the drum can be raised or lowered through the tabletop, so you can work with a new, unclogged part of the sleeve as often as needed.

There's another advantage to this jig: The cube in the center can be revolved to present different sized holes for various drum diameters, so it supports the workpiece right up to the drum. That makes it easier to sand thin or delicate stock that might otherwise break off or get trapped.

The inner cube measures 4" on all sides, and we built it from ½" Finnish birch plywood. Measure your six most frequently used drums and drill appropriately sized holes in the cube. Then construct the main box (also ½" stock) so that the 4" cube is absolutely flush with its top.

The vacuum port in the jig is standard 1¼" ID plastic plumbing pipe, but you'll have to adjust that to fit your own shop's dust collector hose.

Two dozen ¾" diameter rare-earth magnets hold the jig to the drill press table, eliminating the need for clamps. Drill ⅜"-deep holes in the bottom for these magnets and secure them with silicone adhesive. Finally, cover the bottom with non-slip rubber (the type used on steps or ramps), and you're ready to start sanding.

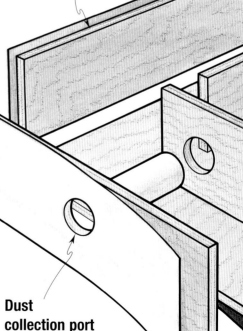

1/2" Plywood

Dust collection port

Non-slip rubber

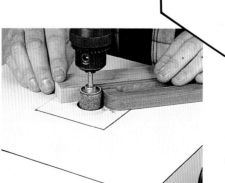

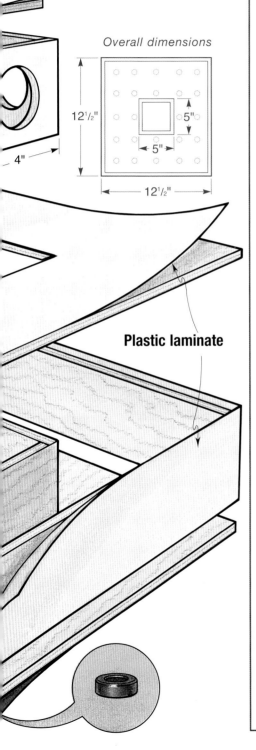

Overall dimensions

12½"

5"

5"

12½"

4"

Plastic laminate

Budget Beaters

When you need to sand tight corners, try wrapping self-adhesive sandpaper around your jigsaw blade to create an instant detail sander.

Jigsander

One way to power-sand those intricate cuts that no sander can reach is to wrap a piece of self-adhesive sandpaper around the blade. You'll have to open the cooling blocks on your jigsaw for this trick to work, and use a stiff blade. There's no need to wrap the blade with excess paper; just two wraps should do it.

Budget Bushings

When a number of perpendicular holes have to be drilled, drill bit guide bushings sure come in very handy. If you're ever caught without one, try grabbing an appropriate sized T-nut instead. Install one in a piece of scrap and drill it out for the correct size drill bit. This trick won't hold up in daily use, but it sure works well for 10 to 20 holes.

Pizza Pedestals

Save the plastic spacers that come with your home-delivered pizza. After you collect a few, they make handy supports for elevating small projects when spraying or brushing on a finish. Sure beats excess finish sticking a project to the newpaper it's sitting on!

Options for Drawing a Smooth Curve

An old band saw blade works wonderfully for drawing smooth curves. Drive nails at key spots along the waste side of the curve, then bend the blade against the nails to draw the final curve.

Another option for scribing smooth curves is to use a piece of stiff electrical wire. Ten- to six-gauge wire will provide enough stiffness for the wire to hold its shape but still be flexible enough to bend easily to shape.

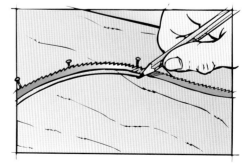

Home Projects

A dozen furniture and accent projects that will beautify
your home and sharpen your woodworking skills.

Greene & Greene Serving Table

Moving from the verdant east to a dry, southern California landscape had a formative effect on the Greene brothers. Charles and Henry moved to Pasadena in 1893 and shortly thereafter created their own distinct architectural style.

Espousing a similar philosophy to the celebrated Frank Lloyd Wright, the Greenes believed an architect's duty lay beyond floor plans: They designed the furniture, lighting and accents in many homes they built. Charles, who had been affected by a Japanese furniture exhibit at the World's Columbian Exposition in 1893, was primarily responsible for creating those classic interiors. This reproduction serving table features many of the facets that set Charles' designs apart. Bold horizontal lines, wide aprons and a cantilevered top suggest strength, functionality and honest craftsmanship. A broad expanse of Honduras mahogany is deftly balanced by small, ebonized accents. Square plugs hide the screw heads, and splines hold the tabletop's breadboard endcaps in place.

Buying Materials

It's always a good idea to buy stock for a project several weeks in advance of when you plan to start building. That's what we did for the mahogany used on this table. Doing so allows the wood to acclimate to the temperature and humidity of your shop. This is especially true of the board used to make the top (piece 1) of this server: Because of the large cantilever on either end, the tabletop must be a stable, properly cured piece of stock. Another important note before you start: If you will be using the water-based aniline dye we recommend for this project (see page 62), it is important to use a brown polyurethane glue. This will prevent dark lines from appearing, because the water-based glue will absorb the dye at a different rate than the mahogany.

After cutting the top to size (see the Material List on page 61), use a bearing-guided straight bit in your portable router to create the tenon on each end. (Refer to the Exploded View Drawing on page 60 and the project's Elevation Drawings shown on pages 64 and 65 for machining and assembly details.) It's a good idea to cut these tenons before jointing the long edges of the top, as any blowout will be cleaned up by the jointer. If the piece is too large to handle comfortably on your jointer, another option is to clamp a long straightedge to the workpiece and joint the edges with a straight bit chucked in your router.

Milling the Tabletop

The procedure for creating the breadboard endcaps (pieces 2) is described in detail in the sidebar on page 63. These caps serve two functions: they dress up the ends of the tabletop, and they also help prevent this wide piece from warping widthwise.

Refer to the sidebar on "Making the Ebonized Plugs and Splines," page 64, before chopping the square mortises in the endcaps for the ebonized plugs (pieces 3) that hide the screws (pieces 4). A good technique here is to drill out most of the mortise waste with a Forstner bit, then use a sharp knife to score the squared-up ends before trimming to their final dimensions with a sharp chisel. This will reduce tearout and create sharp, crisp corners on the mortises. Use the same technique to create the spline mortises on both the top and the endcaps. Note that these are matching mortises that accept a single piece between them. Use the Elevation Drawings to lay these out.

Screw (don't glue) the breadboard endcaps to the top through the equally spaced

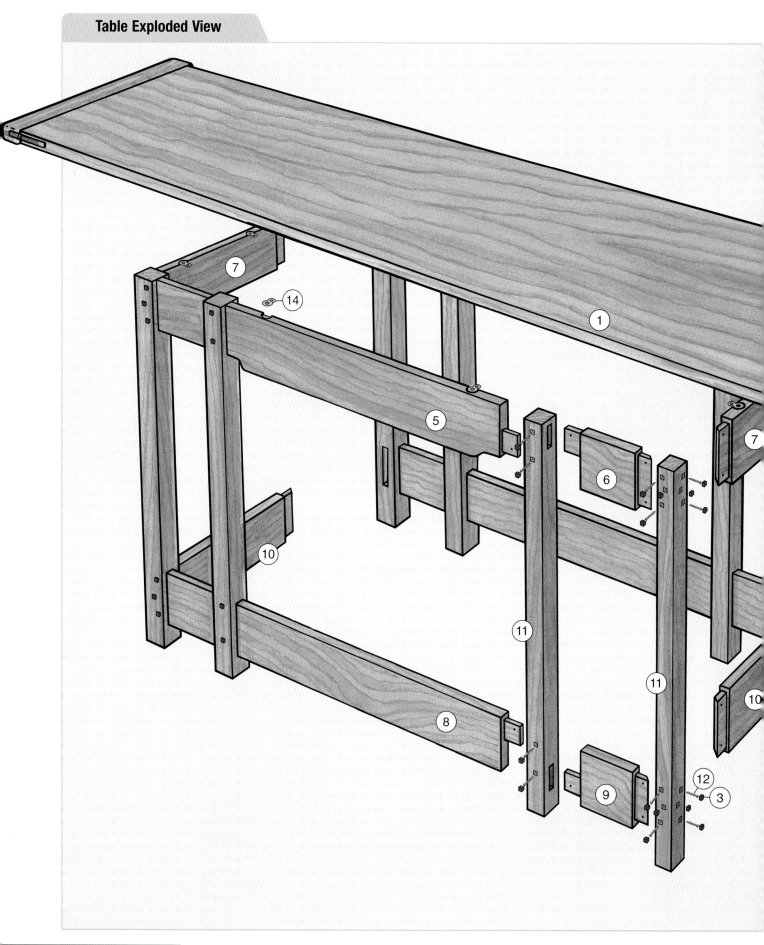

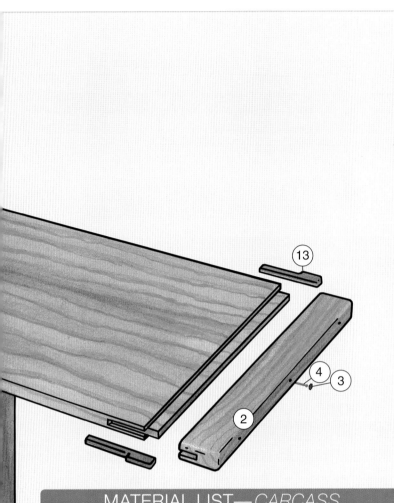

mortises and pre-drilled screw holes. These holes are drilled slightly oversized through the endcaps so the screw shanks have extra play all around. Space created by the enlarged holes allows the top to expand or contract across its grain and will help prevent cracking. Cover the holes with the ebonized plugs, secured with just a drop of glue. Gently break the long edges of the top with sandpaper, then sand the entire top and set it aside while you build the leg assembly.

Making the Tenoned Aprons

Harmony and simplicity were guiding principles of the Arts & Crafts movement, so it's a good idea to keep both concepts in mind when selecting stock for the top and bottom aprons (pieces 5 through 10). Above all, the wood should be consistent in color. If its grain patterns also match, so much the better.

Cut all sixteen of the apron parts to size, according to the Material List on this page, then lay out the asymmetrical and mitered tenons on the ends of the aprons. Use the Elevation Drawings on pages 64 and 65 to create the proper offset for the aprons joining the central legs. You can cut all these tenons on the table saw using a dado head and the saw's miter gauge, as shown on the next page. Note that some of the tenons are notched and some are mitered. Cut the notches on the band saw and the miters on the full-width tenons with your table saw. After the tenons are cut, use the Full-size Patterns on the *inside front cover* to lay out, then band saw the stepped profile on the bottom edge of both the top center aprons. Clean up the saw marks with a drum sander mounted in your drill press.

Mortising the Legs

If you own a mortising machine or an attachment for your drill press, chopping mortises in the legs (pieces 11) should be a quick and easy task, as all of them are the same width (see the *Elevation Drawings* on pages 64 and 65 for details). Even doing it the old-fashioned way (see the *sidebar* on the next page) is a relatively simple task. Carefully lay out the mortises for each individual leg. (The four inner legs are similar and the

MATERIAL LIST—*CARCASS*

		T x W x L
1	Top (1)	1" x 15 7/16" x 73"
2	Breadboard Endcaps (2)	1 1/4" x 1 7/8" x 15 3/4"
3	Ebonized Plugs (70)	3/8" x 3/8" x 9/16"
4	Endcap Screws (6)	#8 x 1 3/4"
5	Top Center Aprons (2)	3/4" x 5" x 24 5/8"
6	Top Side Aprons (4)	3/4" x 4 1/2" x 4 3/4"
7	Top End Aprons (2)	3/4" x 4 1/2" x 9 1/16"
8	Bottom Center Aprons (2)	3/4" x 4 1/2" x 24 5/8"
9	Bottom Side Aprons (4)	3/4" x 4 1/2" x 4 3/4"
10	Bottom End Aprons (2)	3/4" x 4 1/2" x 9 11/16"
11	Legs (8)	1 13/16" x 1 13/16" x 26 7/8"
12	Screws (48)	#6 x 1"
13	Ebonized Splines (4)	3/8" x 1 1/2" x 4"
14	Tabletop Fasteners (10)	*Metal*

MAKING THE MORTISE AND TENON JOINTS

Before cutting the shaped profile on the top center aprons, reveal the tenons on their ends using a dado head in your table saw.

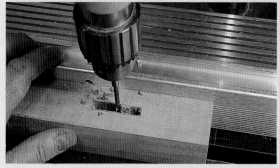

A Forstner bit chucked in your drill press will remove most of the mortise waste, and the bit's design leaves a nice, flat-bottomed cavity.

After laying out the matching mortises in the legs, score them with a sharp utility knife to avoid tearout as you drill.

Clean up with a sharp chisel, cutting across the grain on the top and bottom first, then with the grain along the sides.

four corner legs match each other in the same fashion.) The apron tenons are asymmetrical and the mortises must match them exactly. Clamp a fence to your drill press and, as the Forstner bit removes most of the waste, slide each leg across the table against the fence. Clean up each pocket with a sharp chisel, then stay at the drill press to make all the small, square mortises in the legs for the plugs (these are similar to the plug mortises you already cut in the breadboard endcaps). When you're done, switch bits again and drill pilot holes for all the screws. Chisel the plug mortises square.

Using the *Exploded View* drawing on page 60 as a guide, dry-fit the aprons to the legs. Make any necessary adjustments, then use the screw holes in the legs as guides to extend pilot holes into the apron tenons. Disassemble the legset and give all the pieces their final 120-grit sanding before raising the grain with a water-dampened sponge. When this dries, sand with 220-grit paper before applying a stain or other colorant to bring out the richness of the wood. Before you go on, mask off the areas where the aprons and the legs meet. This will keep those areas free of dye as you proceed with the finishing process.

Applying an Aniline Dye Finish

In keeping with the habits of the Greene brothers, we applied a water-based aniline dye to all the legset and tabletop mahogany parts. If you haven't used aniline dyes before, here are some tips to help you get top-notch results: Use a drop of dish soap in water-based dye to break the surface adhesion, and apply the product with a foam brush. Wipe it off immediately with paper towels, then let it dry. It is important to dye the wood before you assemble the piece. It is virtually impossible to achieve uniformity of color if you try to dye the assembled server.

From this stage on, you should wear utility gloves (latex medical versions or standard household rubber gloves will both work fine) whenever you handle any of the dyed parts: otherwise you may leave oil residue on the dye or dissolve the dye with ambient moisture from your hands. Both will show up as smudges on the finished piece. A little caution here will save you heartache later.

After the dye dries, remove the masking tape and use a utility knife to create small, V-shaped channels in the hidden surfaces, wherever glue might squeeze out of a joint. These little glue traps (see *Figure 1*, next page) will save you frustration — they're an excellent alternative to refinishing all the parts that might be affected by squeeze-out, since wiping off the wet glue will also smudge the dyed surfaces.

You can now reassemble the legset using glue sparingly. Make sure everything is square and plumb as you tighten the clamps, then set this subassembly aside to dry. After the glue has cured, remove the clamps and drive home the screws (pieces 12) to complete the joint.

Final Thoughts

After all the plugs (pieces 3) and splines (pieces 13) are made, there are a couple of items that need your attention before these accents can be installed. First on the list is attaching the tabletop to the legset. Refer to the *Exploded View* or *Elevation Drawings* to locate and drill simple round mortises with a Forstner bit in the top of the legset for the tabletop fasteners (pieces 14), then screw the fasteners to the legset. Lay the top face-down on a soft surface (towels laid across cardboard works well), and drill pilot holes in its underside (be careful!) for the fastener screws. Then, screw the legset and top together.

Apply three coats of a satin or semi-gloss finish to all surfaces to achieve the soft yet durable finish the Greenes preferred. One of the best options out there is a gel varnish such as Bartley's — it's tough, easy to apply and has great visual depth. As mentioned earlier, a brown polyurethane glue is a good choice for securing the plugs and splines in their mortises. However, only glue the splines to the tabletop and not to the end-caps. This will allow your top to expand and contract with the seasons during a lifetime of useful service.

Charles and Henry Greene became known for their fine architecture and furni-ture design, developing a style of their own from a world of influences. Now you can serve your food from atop a stylish piece of true Americana that you've built yourself.

Figure 1: Slice tiny v-channels around the perimeter of the joint areas with a sharp chisel or utility knife to help prevent glue squeeze out from smudging the dye.

MAKING BREADBOARD ENDS

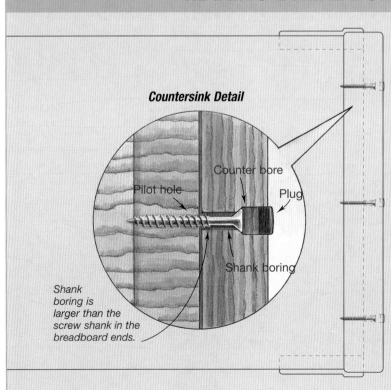

Countersink Detail

Counter bore

Pilot hole

Plug

Shank boring

Shank boring is larger than the screw shank in the breadboard ends.

Whether it's a glued-up lamination or a single wide board, wood likes to wiggle with the weather. Old-time cabinetmakers tried to eliminate this movement in breadboards by capping the ends with strips of solid hardwood. This treatment worked, but had its problems. You'll hear tales of folks awakened in the middle of the night by the loud report of maple and oak parting company under the tremendous pressures of moisture-related wood movement.

To prevent such a calamity from happening on this project, the tongue and groove joints on the breadboard ends allow the cross-grain joints to slip past one another as needed. The exclusion of glue here also helps. We used screws driven into counterbores with oversized shank holes to secure the ends. The space provided by these extra-large holes allows for the expansion and contraction of the top. Square up the counterbores to accept the ebony plugs that cap the screw heads and also add decorative detail.

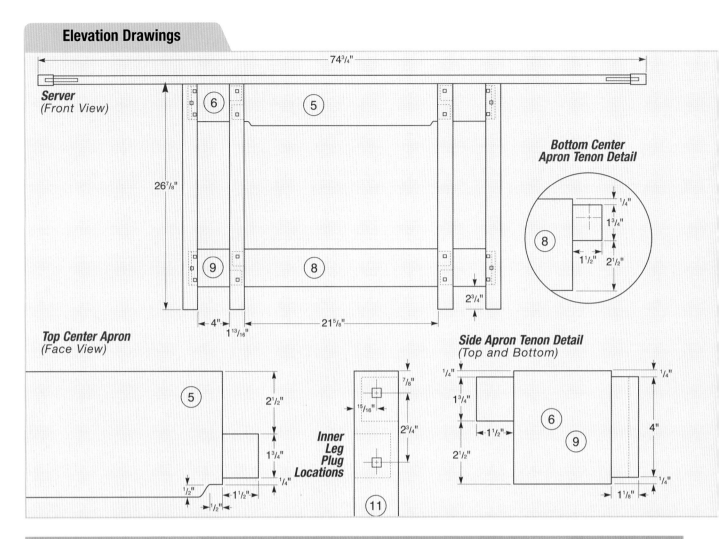

Server
(Front View)

74³/₄"

26⁷/₈"

6   5

9   8

4"   21⁵/₈"

1¹³/₁₆"

2³/₄"

**Bottom Center
Apron Tenon Detail**

8

¹/₄"

1³/₄"

1¹/₂"   2¹/₂"

Top Center Apron
(Face View)

5

2¹/₂"

1³/₄"

¹/₄"

¹/₂"   1¹/₂"

¹/₂"

**Inner
Leg
Plug
Locations**

7/₈"

15/₁₆"

2³/₄"

11

Side Apron Tenon Detail
(Top and Bottom)

¹/₄"

1³/₄"

1¹/₂"

2¹/₂"

6

9

¹/₄"

4"

¹/₄"

1¹/₈"

MAKING THE EBONIZED PLUGS AND SPLINES

Polish the Ebon-X plugs and splines to their final luster with a polishing wheel mounted in a bench top grinder.

Early in the new century, Charles Greene had the luxury of being able to specify ebony for the plug and spline accents in his most accomplished furniture pieces. While ebony is no longer as widely available or as inexpensive as it once was, there are some viable modern alternatives. Exotic Birch™ in its Charcole Ruby shade is a sound choice, as is the idea of ebonizing your own stock. Perhaps the most appealing option is Ebon-X™, an ebony substitute made by impregnating domestic hardwoods with non-toxic chemicals. Making plugs (pieces 3) with this material is relatively simple. Rip a length of material to 3/8" x 3/8", then create a gentle crown to both of its ends with a sander. Buff the ends of the stick on a grinder equipped with a polishing wheel to create an ultra smooth finish. Cut off 3/16"-long plugs using your band saw, then repeat the entire plug making process.

Cut the splines (pieces 13) to the shape found on the *inside back cover*. Again, use a sander to help create the gently rounded profiles on the splines. Move to the buffing wheel and repeat the buffing technique you used on the plugs. Polish the Ebon-X smooth as silk, bringing it to a high, rich luster.

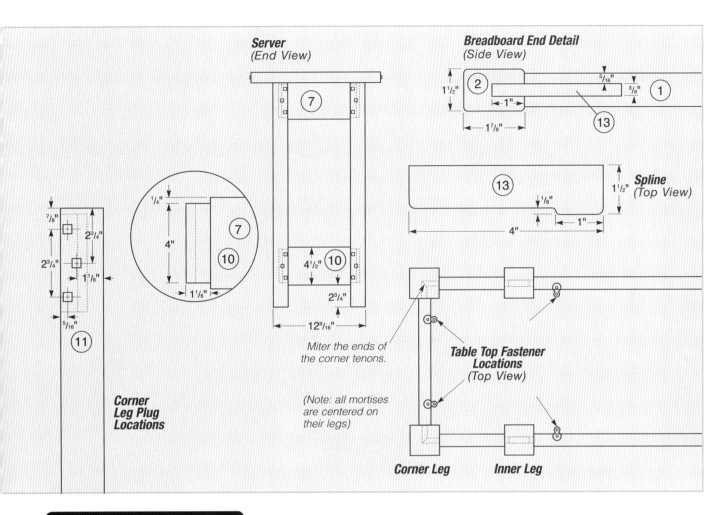

Server
(End View)

⑦

Breadboard End Detail
(Side View)

②　1½"　←1"→　←1⅞"→　⑬　5/16"　3/8"　①

Spline
(Top View)

⑬　1½"　⅛"　←1"→　4"

⑦
⑩

¼"　4"　1⅛"

**Corner
Leg Plug
Locations**

⑪

⅞"　2¾"　2¾"　1⅜"　5/16"

4½"　⑩
2¾"
←12⅞"→

Miter the ends of
the corner tenons.

(Note: all mortises
are centered on
their legs)

**Table Top Fastener
Locations**
(Top View)

Corner Leg　　**Inner Leg**

Quick Tips

Go with the Grain

If you're getting a little tearout or feathering on boards as you run them across the jointer, flip the board end for end to reverse the direction of the feed. Tearout usually means you're planing against the grain. By switching the front of the board to the back, the blades will shear with the grain direction and produce a much cleaner cut. If the knives are nicked, just loosen one and move it left or right, as far as it will go. Leave the others as they are and you'll get clean, sharp cuts.

Snipe Remedies

Snipe is that annoying little concave area that a jointer or thickness planer can leave on the last couple of inches of a board. It is caused by an outfeed table that is set lower than the knives or on workpieces that are just too short. Dealing with it involves adjusting the outfeed table, planing longer boards, or buying one of a new breed of planers that are marketed as being "snipe-free." Or you can cut your stock 6" or 8" too long, then trim off the snipe on the miter saw. It's not thrifty, but it works.

The Greene & Greene Coffee Table

Among contributing editor Mike McGlynn's favorite Arts & Crafts pieces are those either built by or based on designs by architects Charles and Henry Greene of Pasadena, California. For example, the original version of this reproduction is a coffee table from Greene & Greene's Pratt House, although that one was considerably larger. Its design was also more elaborate, and the construction details were quite involved.

While planning this reproduction for a client, budget and time constraints dictated that Mike scale back both the size and degree of difficulty if his bid was to be competitive. To accomplish this, he introduced some modern techniques and materials like biscuit joinery, MDF-core sheetstock and catalyzed lacquer, to name a few. But this would be consistent with the Greenes' approach. As furniture builders, they made extensive use of state-of-the-art technology.

Selecting the Wood

This table is built of Honduras mahogany to be as authentic as possible, but teak or walnut would also be acceptable; the Greenes made furniture out of all three species. You'll need 8/4 stock for the feet (pieces 1) and 6/4 for the legs (pieces 2), stretchers (pieces 3) and the tabletop frame elements (pieces 4, 5 and 6).

If you're wondering why Mike didn't use 5/4 material for the stretchers, since they're only 1" thick, there are two reasons: First, the grain and color of the legs, stretchers and tabletop edge should all match. Second,

Figure 1: When cutting parts for the tabletop frames, use a bevel gauge to transfer the angles from your pattern to the workpieces.

Figure 2: Mortises for the traditional Greene & Greene ebony plugs can be cut with a mortising machine or drilled and chiseled square.

if you wanted to use 5/4 for the stretchers, you'd have to buy a full plank at most lumberyards. This is fine if you have other projects in mind. Or, just use one 6/4 board.

When choosing your lumber, look for a board that's at least half the width of each leg, as these will be glued up. Try for a board that has a ribbon stripe grain to it — this will make the glue joint in the legs less visible and also will help make the tabletop edges flow together better.

Before You Start Cutting

Let the mahogany sit in your shop for a couple of days so it adjusts to the new range of humidity and temperature. Then, when you do cut the pieces out, leave them oversize 1/4" in width and 1" in length. Give

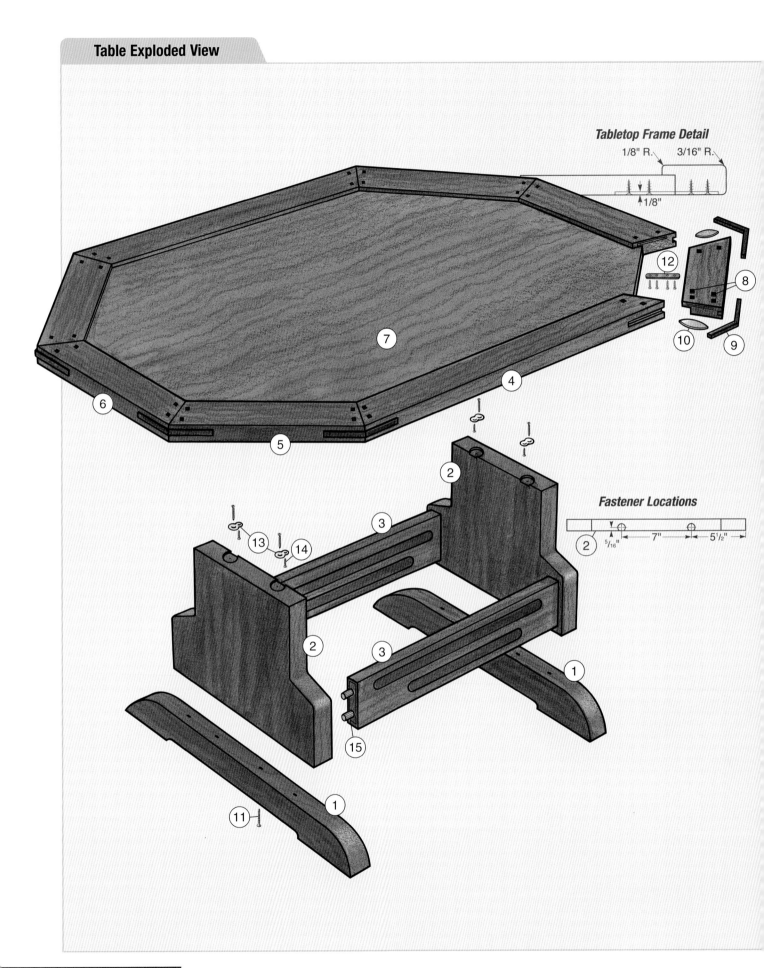

Tabletop Frame Detail

1/8" R. 3/16" R.

1/8"

Fastener Locations

7" 5¹/₂"

⁵/₁₆"

MATERIAL LIST

		T x W x L
1	Feet (2)	1¾" x 2¼" x 26"
2	Legs (2)	1⅛" x 18" x 12⅜"
3	Stretchers (2)	1" x 4" x 16¾"
4	Tabletop Frames, Long (2)	1⅛" x 2½" x 23⁷⁄₁₆"
5	Tabletop Frames, Short (2)	1⅛" x 2½" x 10¹⁵⁄₁₆"
6	Tabletop Frames, Medium (4)	1⅛" x 2½" x 14½"
7	Tabletop Panel (1)	¾" x 27" x 36"
8	Decorative Plugs (32)	⅜" x ⅜" x ³⁄₁₆"
9	Decorative Splines (8)	⅜" x 1½" x 5 ½"
10	Biscuits (8)	#0 (1¾" x ⅝")
11	Leg/Foot Joint Screws(8)	#8 x 3"
12	Retaining Brackets (10)	⅛" x ⅝" x 4"
13	Tabletop Fasteners (4)	⅛" x ¾" x ¹⁵⁄₁₆"
14	Fastener & Bracket Screws (48)	#6 x ⅝"
15	Stretcher Dowels (8)	⅜" Dia. x 1½"

Stretcher Elevation
Side View

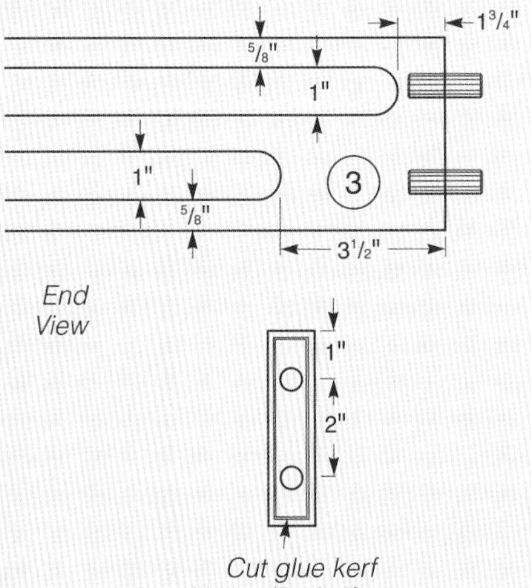

End
View

Cut glue kerf
with a utility knife.

some thought to how the grain is going to align on the seams in the legs. You will want to arrange your stock so that this seam ends up being as invisible as possible.

After rough sizing, continue the milling process by face-jointing (a hand plane will work if your jointer bed is too narrow) and planing the leg boards to thickness, then joint the edges you want at the seam. Place three biscuit joints along the glue line, to aid with alignment and lend a little strength. If you're going to use the recommended water based aniline dye (see page 71), use a waterproof glue such as Titebond II or Gorilla Glue, so the dye won't leave a dark line. Then glue up the legs and clamp them for a nice tight joint. As the glue is drying, cut and joint the stretchers to length and width. You can also cut and joint the feet to width, leaving them about 1" too long.

Preparing Plugs and Splines

The tabletop panel (piece 7) is surrounded by a solid hardwood frame that requires a number of angled cuts. The best way to make these cuts is to tape a tabletop pattern (see *inside front cover*) onto a sheet of scrap ply, and then dry-fit the pieces by laying them directly on top of this drawing. The drawing is also useful for picking off angles with your sliding bevel gauge, so you can transfer them accurately to the workpieces (see *Figure 1*). Cut the frame elements to the lengths listed in the *Material List* on this page, then use the bevel gauge to set your table saw's miter gauge and miter the ends of all eight pieces.

Following in the Greene & Greene style, ebony plugs (pieces 8) decorate each joint. If you're not comfortable using ebony, use Ebon-X™, a product made by Michigan-based Supertech. With the frame elements dry-fitted together, you can lay out and cut mortises for these plugs. Use the Scaled Pattern on the *inside front cover* to mark their locations. Cut them with a mortising machine, or make them the old-fashioned

Figure 3: Locate the spline mortises exactly halfway up the frame, then cut them on your router table and square the ends with a chisel.

way on a drill press, and chisel them square as shown in *Figure 2*.

At each joint in the frame, insert ebony splines (pieces 9). Lay out stopped mortises for these splines (see *inside front cover*) so they are exactly in the center of the frame members (top to bottom); that way it won't matter which face you have against your router table fence when you cut a slot (see *Figure 3*, above). Use a 3/8" bit in your router table, and clamp a stop block to the fence. Chisel the end out square.

Milling the Tabletop Frame

Although each joint is held together by a spline, these are primarily decorative. For additional strength and gluing surface, add a #0 biscuit (piece 10). As you can see in the *drawings*, the placement of these biscuit joints is precise, so it's a good idea to have some scrap pieces to experiment on first. After cutting the biscuit joints (see *Figure 4*), set up your router table with the appropriate size roundover bits (see *Tabletop Frame Detail* on page 68) and round over the two outside edges and the top inside edge of each frame element. Note that the inside edge is a smaller radius. If you wait until after assembly to perform this step, the bit won't reach the inside joints.

The last step before sanding and assembly is to cut a rabbet on the inside bottom edge of each piece, to accept the tabletop. Cut this rabbet with two passes on your table saw. The key here is that the

height of the rabbet should be exactly the same as the thickness of the top. Make sure you have the tabletop on hand — made of either sheet stock (an MDF core with factory applied veneers on top and bottom) or a glued up and sanded solid-wood panel.

Framing the Tabletop

Working your way down through the grits to 120, sand the top, inside and bottom faces of the tabletop frame pieces as well as the inside roundover. The outside face and the outside roundover can be sanded after the frame is assembled.

As you sand, it's important to avoid rounding the mitered ends of the frame elements. The best way to do this is to back up the paper with a sanding block. As each part is sanded, dry-fit it again to make sure it's perfect. Make corrections now — not when the glue is wet.

When everything fits, get all of your gluing necessities together. These should include 3M clear packing tape (it is far better than many other brands), waterproof glue, glue brushes, the biscuits and a wet rag. Apply the glue to the biscuit slots and miters, then install the biscuits and stretch tape across the joints. The tape has a "memory" and as it tries to return to its former unstretched shape, it pulls the joint together. When applying tape on the top face, it's a good idea to put small sticks on either side of the joint to keep the tape out

Figure 4: An ebony spline at each frame joint provides alignment and a gluing surface, but the joint's real strength comes from a biscuit.

of the glue: This greatly simplifies clean up. After you've glued up the frame, lay it on a flat surface and weight or clamp it down while drying, so it doesn't dry with a twist.

Figure 5: Drill the ends of the slots with a 1" Forstner bit and rout the rest of the waste in several passes, raising your straight bit by 1/8" on each pass.

Milling the Stretchers

As the frame is drying, you can start work on the base. Doweling the legs and stretchers is the first step here. Your layout on this step must be done accurately, so take your time and carefully follow the measurements in the *Stretcher Elevation Detail* on page 69 and on the *inside front cover*.

After you've laid out the locations of the dowel holes, drill them with a combination of a drill press (for the legs) and a doweling jig (for the stretchers). Take a sharp awl and create a starting point for the drill bit at each dowel location, then use a brad point or Forstner bit to prevent wandering off center.

Following the measurements on page 69, locate the two decorative slots in each stretcher. Drill the end of each slot with a 1" Forstner bit chucked in your drill press, then connect the holes with progressively deeper passes made on a router table with a 1/2" straight bit, as shown in *Figure 5,* above. Follow up with a 1/8" roundover bit, and soften all the edges of the openings.

Using this same roundover bit in the router table, mill the top and bottom edges of the stretchers, being careful not to round over any part of the ends, or the joinery here won't look as clean as it should.

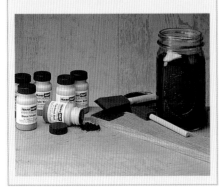
Assembling the Base

Refer to the measurements on the *drawings* again, this time to lay out the relief cuts on the feet and the pattern of the legs. Make these cuts on the band saw, then use a roundover bit to soften the outside edges of the legs and the tops of the feet.

Clamp the feet and legs together in their correct alignment, and drill pilot holes through the feet into the legs. These holes are for the #8 x 3" screws (pieces 11) that will hold them together: The holes should be large enough in the feet to allow the screw shaft to slide through freely and just large enough in the legs to allow the threads to grip solidly. Countersink the screw heads and, before assembling the leg set, finish these parts according to the instructions in "Finishing Tips" *sidebar* at left.

After finishing, glue up the leg assembly using enough glue to do the job, but not so much that it squeezes out and ruins the stain (Mike recommends cutting a glue relief groove on the end of the stretchers, as shown on page 69). Now clamp the assembly together, using pads to protect the finish. When it's dry, the feet can be glued and screwed in place.

Completing the Tabletop

Mike made the tabletop out of 3/4" MDF for stability with factory-adhered ribbon stripe mahogany veneer on both faces because of the veneer's consistent grain pattern. Lay the completed tabletop frame on your sheetstock or glued-up panel, orienting it parallel to the grain, then use a pencil to trace the edge of the rabbet onto the tabletop. Be careful to hold or clamp the frame firmly so the pencil tip doesn't slip. Cut to the line with a band saw, then test-fit the piece to see if it slips freely into the rabbet. If not, trim it with a block plane.

Set the tabletop aside for now while you clean up the frame. Remove any small beads of glue with a sharp chisel and sand the outside face and outside roundover.

Figure 6: To make the decorative plugs for this project, a 3/8" x 3/8" stick of ebony (or an ebony substitute) is sanded, buffed and cut to length.

Soften each corner slightly, then slip the frame over the tabletop and use a sharp chisel to cut mortises (see *inside front cover* for locations) in both the frame and the panel for the eight retaining brackets (pieces 12). Go through the same dye finishing process used earlier on the leg set, then screw the brackets in place, thereby securing the tabletop to its frame.

Use a Forstner bit to create mortises in the tops of the legs for the tabletop fasteners (pieces 13) as shown in the *Fastener Locations* drawing on page 68. Then turn the tabletop upside down on a padded surface and center the base on the top. Secure the base to the top with the correct length screws (pieces 14) — this is a bad time to use a screw that's too long! After assembly, refer again to the *sidebar* on finishing for some tips on topcoating your aniline dye.

Make the decorative plugs from a 3/8" x 3/8" stick of ebony. Sand and buff the ends of the stick on a grinder equipped with a polishing wheel (see *Figure 6*), then cut off 3/16"-long pieces. Try to give the plugs a softened, slightly domed appearance. Give the splines the same softened, polished surface on the buffer. Your final construction step is to put a small drop of Gorilla Glue in each mortise or slot and gently tap the plugs and splines home, using a rag to absorb the hammer's impact.

Bowfront Bureau

Bending wood can be a challenge, but don't let the graceful curves of this bureau put you off. By using a combination of easy-to-build bending jigs and bendable plywood, you'll ease right through the tricky parts.

This bowfront bureau is designed to compliment the reader bed project on page 84. As you can see, we stayed with the arch theme in the bureau's design. A single template lets you lay out the long, lazy arches for the top of the mirror, the leading edge of the tabletop, and the bowed drawer fronts. We stayed with the bed's color scheme too: white ash accented by dark walnut trim.

Building a Bending Form

This project begins with the top of the mirror frame, because the curve established here is used to create all the other curves in the dresser. The arched top is made up of several thin laminations that are face-glued together and clamped to a bowed form to dry. The first step in the form's construction is to lay it out with pencil lines on 3/4" plywood. Drive an 8d finish nail into the plywood at each end of the curve, 65½" apart, as shown in the *photo* on the next page. Connect the nails with a pencil line and draw a second, intersecting line halfway along it, at 90°.

Drive a third nail exactly 2¹⁵⁄₁₆" up this line. Bend a strip of thin hardwood (or plywood) so it touches all three nails — you might need help here — and draw a curved line along the bottom edge. Extend the line a few inches past each nail.

Clamp a second piece of 3/4" plywood below the first, then jigsaw both pieces at the same time, staying just outside your layout line. Leave the clamps in place and belt-sand precisely to the line. Keep the sander moving, so you don't create any flat spots.

Predrill for screws, then glue and screw several 3" spacers between the two sheets of plywood, as shown in the *illustration* at the top of the next page. Use a square to make sure the bowed edges line up perfectly as you drive the screws home.

Laminating the Arch

The mirror arch is made up of five 3/8"-thick boards. Four of these (pieces 1) are ash, while the top one (piece 2) is walnut.

It's a good idea to spread a single layer of wax paper along the form before you start gluing. This will prevent the laminated arch from sticking to the form. You should also make sure you have enough clamps on hand before you start gluing. You'll need about 20: one placed every six or eight inches on both top and bottom.

Leave the laminations about 3" longer and 1/4" wider than their finished size, then spread the glue with a brush or roller to get even and complete coverage. Work quickly or the glue will begin to set. Make sure the laminations' edges all line up as closely as possible, then start applying clamps from the center out. If you see a small gap, move the clamps closer together.

Let the glued assembly dry for at least 24 hours before removing any clamps. While it's drying, you can make the mirror posts.

Making the Mirror Posts

Like the arch, the large posts (pieces 3) that frame the mirror are also laminated. This makes them more stable than a single large piece of stock that might twist or split over the years. It's also easier to find 3/4" clear stock than 2¼"-thick boards.

Leave the laminations about 1/8" wider and an inch longer than their final sizes (see the *Material List* on page 75), then laminate

A SIMPLE BENDING JIG

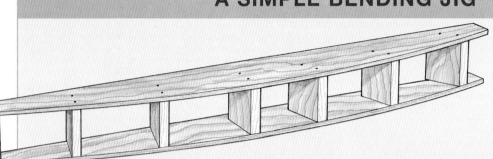

The jig to create the gently curved mirror arch is made from plywood and spacers.

As you laminate the arch, the jig will be subjected to a lot of stress, so be sure to use plenty of glue and screws when you make it.

To begin making the bending jig, strike the gentle curve of the mirror arch onto a piece of plywood. This curve must be fair and true.

After using a band saw or hand-held jigsaw to rough-cut the curve, carefully sand right to the line with your belt sander.

three boards together to make each post. After the glue dries, remove your clamps and dress one laminated face of each post on the jointer. Then place the jointed face against the table saw fence and rip each post to a hair over its final dimension. Make one final pass per post on the jointer, to clean up the ripped face, then square off the bottom of each post on the miter saw.

Transfer the radius of the arch to the top of each post, and band-saw it to shape. Keep in mind that you'll need a right and a left post. Then sand the cuts smooth.

Milling the Arch

Before assembling the arch on its posts, clean up its edges, trim it to length and chamfer the bottom edge. After removing the clamps, begin by running the arch across the jointer to clean one side, then rip

it 1/16" oversize on the table saw before jointing the other side. Trim it to length so the bottom edge is 67⅜" long.

The chamfering is done with a 45° bearing-guided router bit. To reduce tearout, chamfer the ends first, then the front — along the bottom edge only. Then switch to a

While the arched mirror top may seem to present a machining challenge, simply take the curved piece in stride without fear.

rabbeting bit to plow the stopped rabbet along the bottom edge of the back. Stay with this bit to rabbet the inside back edge of each post, remembering that they're mirror images, not identical shapes.

Make sure the back edges are flush as you connect the arch to the posts with 3" flathead wood screws, driven into counterbored pilot holes.

The final arch lamination, the walnut cap (piece 2), can be applied now. Glue and clamp it in place. After the glue dries, remove the clamps and trim the edges flush with the ash. A bearing-guided flush-trimming bit works well on the sides, but use a belt sander on the ends to prevent tearout.

Use the bending form to lay out the curves on the arched walnut trim piece (piece 4) that backs up the mirror frame. Miter the ends of this piece while it's still rectangular, then cut it to size and shape on the band saw. Cut the straight trim for the sides and bottom (pieces 5 and 6) to size and miter the remaining corners to fit. Test-fit the pieces into the rabbets you just made in the post and arch subassembly.

Making the Mirror Frame

The arched mirror will be surrounded by an ash frame. This frame is glued in front of the walnut trim that you just made. Making the frame is very similar to the process used to make the walnut trim. Begin by striking the curve for the arched top of the frame (piece 7), then miter its ends before band-sawing it to shape. Cut the remaining parts (the sides and bottom, pieces 8 and 9) to size, miter their corners and add biscuit mortises for even more stability. Form the rabbets on the back edges

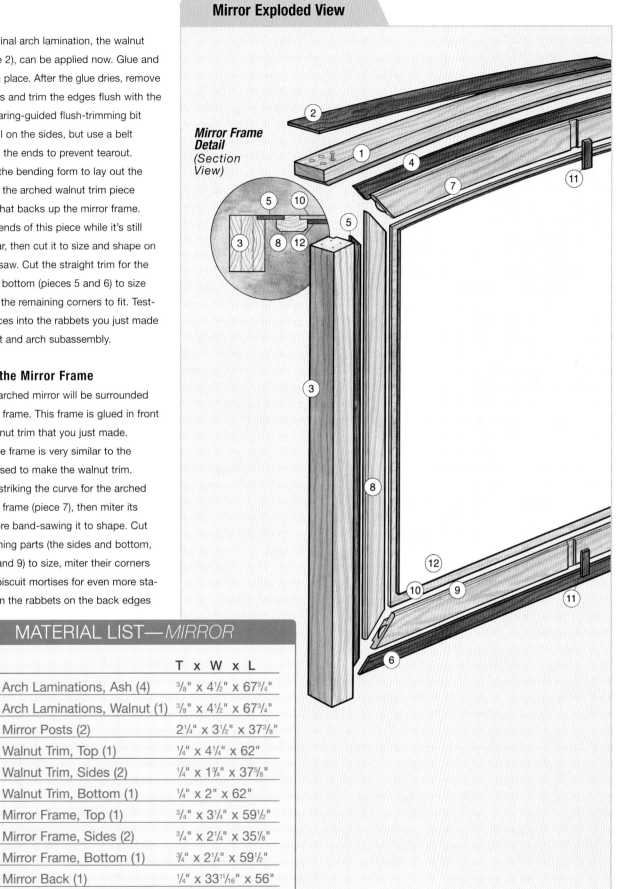

Mirror Exploded View

Mirror Frame Detail
(Section View)

MATERIAL LIST—*MIRROR*

		T x W x L
1	Arch Laminations, Ash (4)	³⁄₈" x 4¹⁄₂" x 67³⁄₄"
2	Arch Laminations, Walnut (1)	³⁄₈" x 4¹⁄₂" x 67³⁄₄"
3	Mirror Posts (2)	2¹⁄₄" x 3¹⁄₂" x 37³⁄₈"
4	Walnut Trim, Top (1)	¹⁄₄" x 4¹⁄₄" x 62"
5	Walnut Trim, Sides (2)	¹⁄₄" x 1³⁄₄" x 37⁵⁄₈"
6	Walnut Trim, Bottom (1)	¹⁄₄" x 2" x 62"
7	Mirror Frame, Top (1)	³⁄₄" x 3¹⁄₄" x 59¹⁄₂"
8	Mirror Frame, Sides (2)	³⁄₄" x 2¹⁄₄" x 35¹⁄₈"
9	Mirror Frame, Bottom (1)	³⁄₄" x 2¹⁄₄" x 59¹⁄₂"
10	Mirror Back (1)	¹⁄₄" x 33¹¹⁄₁₆" x 56"
11	Walnut Frame Inserts (4)	¹⁄₄" x ³⁄₄" x 2¹⁄₄"
12	Mirror (1)	¹⁄₄" *(cut to fit)*

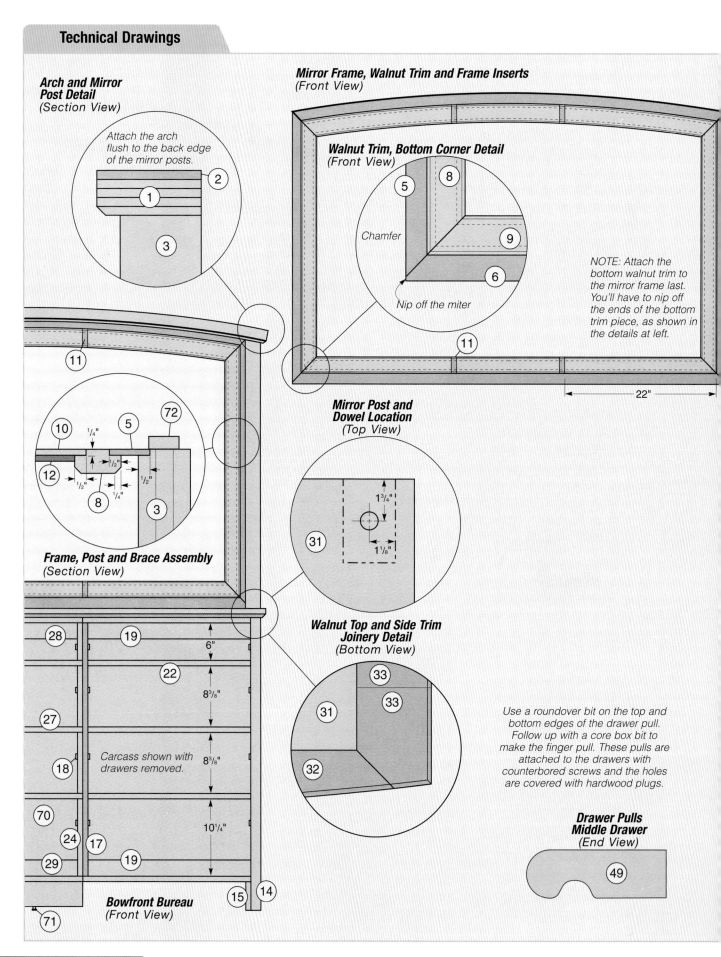

Arch and Mirror Post Detail
(Section View)

Attach the arch flush to the back edge of the mirror posts.

Mirror Frame, Walnut Trim and Frame Inserts
(Front View)

Walnut Trim, Bottom Corner Detail
(Front View)

Chamfer

Nip off the miter

NOTE: Attach the bottom walnut trim to the mirror frame last. You'll have to nip off the ends of the bottom trim piece, as shown in the details at left.

22"

Frame, Post and Brace Assembly
(Section View)

1/4"
1/2"
1/2"
1/4"
1/2"

Mirror Post and Dowel Location
(Top View)

1 3/4"
1 1/8"

Walnut Top and Side Trim Joinery Detail
(Bottom View)

Use a roundover bit on the top and bottom edges of the drawer pull. Follow up with a core box bit to make the finger pull. These pulls are attached to the drawers with counterbored screws and the holes are covered with hardwood plugs.

Drawer Pulls Middle Drawer
(End View)

6"
8 3/8"
8 3/8"
Carcass shown with drawers removed.
10 1/4"

Bowfront Bureau
(Front View)

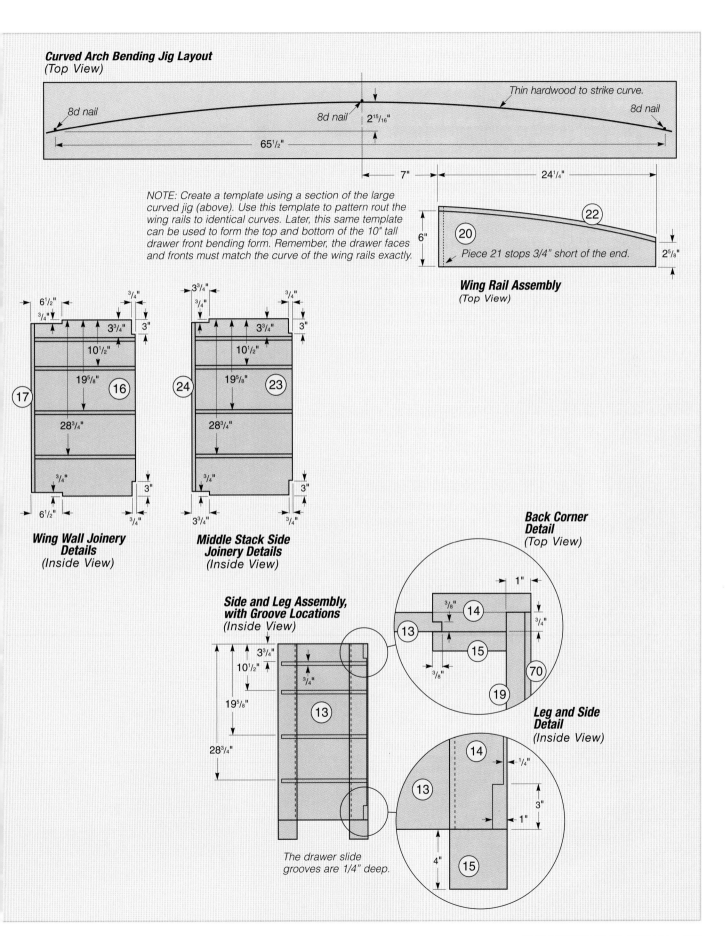

Curved Arch Bending Jig Layout
(Top View)

8d nail

8d nail   2¹⁵/₁₆"

Thin hardwood to strike curve.

8d nail

65¹/₂"

7"

24¹/₄"

NOTE: Create a template using a section of the large curved jig (above). Use this template to pattern rout the wing rails to identical curves. Later, this same template can be used to form the top and bottom of the 10" tall drawer front bending form. Remember, the drawer faces and fronts must match the curve of the wing rails exactly.

22

20

6"

Piece 21 stops 3/4" short of the end.

2⁵/₈"

Wing Rail Assembly
(Top View)

6¹/₂"   3/4"
3/4"
3³/₄"   3"
10¹/₂"
17   19⁵/₈"   16
28³/₄"
3/4"   3"
6¹/₂"   3/4"

Wing Wall Joinery Details
(Inside View)

3³/₄"   3/4"
3³/₄"
3³/₄"   3"
10¹/₂"
24   19⁵/₈"   23
28³/₄"
3/4"   3"
3³/₄"   3/4"

Middle Stack Side Joinery Details
(Inside View)

Back Corner Detail
(Top View)

1"
3/8"   14
13   3/4"
15
3/8"   70
19

Side and Leg Assembly, with Groove Locations
(Inside View)

3³/₄"
10¹/₂"
3/4"
19⁵/₈"   13
28³/₄"

The drawer slide grooves are 1/4" deep.

Leg and Side Detail
(Inside View)

14
13   1/4"
3"
4"   1"
15

of the frame (see the *Mirror Frame Detail* on this page) to accept the trim and mirror back (piece 10). Now is also the time to chamfer the forward edges of the frame. Sand all four parts, dry-fit them to the mirror assembly to check their fit, then assemble with glue and biscuits. Before you go any further, clamp a straightedge in place to guide your router while you mill four dadoes for the walnut inlays (pieces 11) in the frame. Glue the inserts in place and sand them flush after the glue dries.

Install the back with glue and clamps. When this subassembly is dry, glue and clamp the mirror frame in place, centering it on the walnut trim. At this point, you're ready to order your mirror glass (piece 12), so the glazier can be working on it while you get busy building the dresser carcass.

Building Three Drawer Stacks

There are 12 drawers in the bureau — three stacks with four drawers each —

and the logical way to build such a large piece is to break it into these three separate subassemblies. As the two wing units are mirror images of each other, you can build both at the same time.

Begin by cutting the bureau sides (pieces 13) to size. These are 3/4" ash veneered plywood, as their outer faces will be visible. Plow the rabbet in each long edge and set the sides aside. Next, cut the legs and leg blocks (pieces 14 and 15) from solid-ash lumber. With your portable router, mill grooves to receive the bureau sides and create a rabbet down the rear legs' back edge to receive the bureau's back later. Glue and clamp them together, but be sure to make a right and left panel here.

Cut the wing walls (pieces 16) to size next, notching all four corners as shown on the *Technical Drawings*. These walls will be hidden, so a less-expensive grade of plywood will do nicely. Trim the front edge of each wall with solid-walnut stock (piece 17). Chuck a 3/4 straight bit into your router and plow stopped dadoes into the inside faces of the walls and sides to hold the drawer

The arc of the curved rails on the wing sections must be identical. To achieve this, cut the rails to within 1/16" of their shape and remove the last bit of stock with a jig and template-routing bit.

Carcass Exploded View

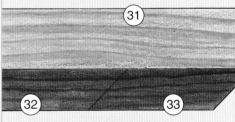

Front View

Chamfered Shadow Lines

An elegant shadow line along the front of the bureau is emphasized by adding walnut accents. To create the same look along the sides, glue up short lengths of walnut and apply them with the end grain exposed. This way, the accent wood can move in concert with the top during seasonal humidity changes.

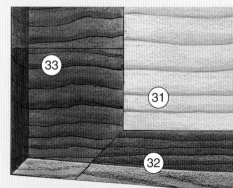

Bottom View

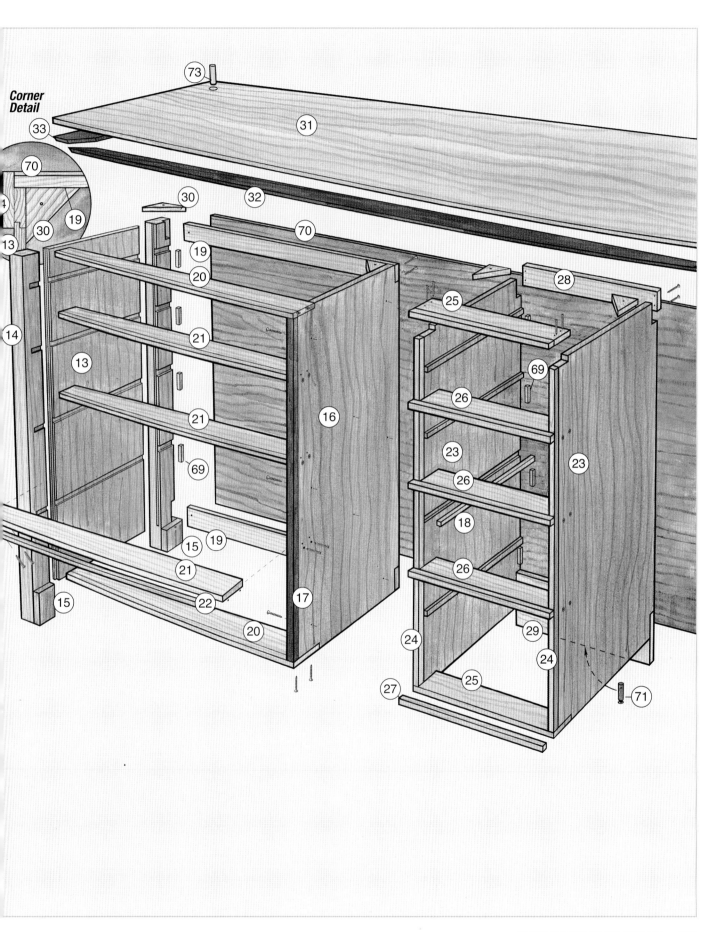

Corner Detail

slides (pieces 18). This is a good time to form the small rabbets on the back legs to accept the back stringers (pieces 19). Glue and clamp the drawer slides into all four panels next. Cut these from hardwood.

Making the Curved Rails

Each of the wings features drawer fronts that pick up the curve of the mirror. You can use that bending form as a template to lay out the curves on the wing rails and intermediate wing rails (pieces 20 and 21). We used a jig and a pattern-routing bit (see the photo) to be sure the front edges of each of these curved rails were identical. Apply solid-ash trim (piece 22) to the front of each rail, using glue and clamps to secure it. This is a very gentle curve, so the ash will have no problem bending around it, but leave the clamps on overnight just to give the glue ample time to reach full strength.

The curved rails are secured to the bureau sides with pocket hole joints on the ends that butt into the front legs. Glue these joints as well. Assemble the wings upside down on a flat work surface and make sure each subassembly is square and plumb as you work. A few clamps will help keep everything in position while the glue dries.

Constructing the Third Drawer Stack

The middle of the three drawer stacks is more economical to build. Its sides (pieces 23) are totally hidden, so there's no need to use ash-veneered plywood here. Cut the sides to size, then lay out the notches at all four corners of each. Cut these with a jigsaw, keeping in mind that you need a left and right panel that are mirror images of each other. Plow the dadoes for the drawer slide stock with a router and straight bit a or dado blade on the table saw (piece

The finger pulls on the curved drawer handles are plowed on the router table with a core box bit. Use a rounded "point fence" to get an extra measure of control as you move the curved piece across the router table from right to left.

18), then cut the ash trim for the front edges (piece 24) to size. Next, glue and clamp the trim and drawer slides in place.

As in the outer stacks, the top and bottom rails here (pieces 25) are a tad longer than the intermediate ones (pieces 26). They're not curved, however, so you can cut all five rails to size on the table saw. Apply solid-ash trim (piece 27) to the front edge of each. Cut the rear upper and lower stringers (pieces 28 and 29) to size. Note that the lower stringer is much wider than the upper. This allows you to place an adjustable leg into its edge. While this center support may not be necessary, better safe than sorry. Glue and screw the middle stack together, as you did with the wings. Screw locations are not critical as

TRICKS FOR BUILDING CURVED DRAWERS

Featuring curved fronts and sides of differing lengths, these drawers are not your typical cabinet fare.

After creating the drawer sides, use an angled dado head (see Technical Drawings) to form the dadoes for the fronts. Remember that you have to make right and left versions.

Fit the bottom to the curved fronts by tracing their curve and trimming to match. The curved fronts are glued up on pre-made jigs. You'll find Details in the Elevation Drawings to help here.

After a quick belt-sanding to extend the gentle curve of the drawer front through the corner joints, turn to the table saw to form the notches that are designed to accept the curved drawer pulls.

they will all be hidden. After the glue dries, sand all three drawer stacks down through the grits to 220. Now assemble the carcass. Glue and screw the wings to the middle stack, lining them up properly from front to back. Again, this is best done upside down on a flat surface. After assembly, glue and screw the corner blocks (pieces 30) in place. They should be predrilled to attach the top.

Making the Bureau Top

This is the least complicated subassembly in the entire project, and yet it may well be the most critical. Such a large expanse of ash is bound to attract admiring — and critical — glances. Begin making the top (piece 31) by selecting your best ash boards. Any width from 3" to 6" is acceptable. After jointing them, alternate their growth rings as you edge-glue the boards to make a panel. Sand it flat with a belt sander, or take it to a cabinet shop and have it sanded on a panel sander for best results. Then trim the top to size, but keep it as a rectangle for now. Next, glue and clamp the walnut accents (pieces 32 and 33) in place, mitering the corners. Note the unusual orientation of piece 33 on each end. This keeps expansion and contraction issues to a minimum. Cut and fit the back spacer (piece 34) and glue it in place. After the glue has cured, use the original bending form as a template to lay out the curve on the front edge of the dresser top. Band-saw close to the curved edge, and clean it up with your belt sander.

Switch to a chamfering bit to create the relief along the bottom edge of the top; the walnut lends an elegant effect to the dresser top when it's trimmed back in this manner. Work across the grain first, and then along it to minimize chipping and tearout.

Constructing the Drawers and Pulls

Eight of these drawers have curved fronts, while the four drawers in the middle stack are pretty standard fare. Let's begin with the center ones. All of these grooves, rabbets and dadoes can be milled on the table saw with a dado head set to the correct width. See the *Technical Drawings* for complete part dimensions.

All four middle drawers are constructed in the same manner; only their heights differ. Cut the sides (pieces 35 through 37) to size, then plow a groove on the outside of each for the drawer slide. Follow up with a groove along the inside for the drawer bottom, and mill two dadoes across the inside for the drawer back and front.

The backs (pieces 38, 39 and 40) require a 1/4" groove for the drawer bottoms. Plow this same groove in the drawer fronts (pieces 41, 42 and 43), then rabbet the ends of each drawer front. Cut the drawer bottoms (pieces 44) to size, then assemble the drawers with

glue and clamps. Don't glue the bottoms in their grooves; they should be free to move a little, to accommodate changes in humidity. After the glue dries, remove your clamps and slide each drawer into its opening to make sure it's a good fit before you make and mount the drawer faces (pieces 45, 46 and 47). The grain on the faces runs vertically, so crosscut a single piece of ash plywood to yield all four faces. This will give you continuous grain from top to bottom. Glue or iron on ash veneer edge tape (piece 48) to the vertical edges of each drawer face to cover the plywood edges. Trim the tape flush with a sharp utility knife, and turn to the drawer pulls next.

All four drawer pulls (pieces 49) can be cut from a single length of molding. Rip 60" of 1/2" solid ash to a width of 1¾", then use a bullnose bit to round over the front edges. Next, chuck a 5/16"-radius core box bit in your router and plow the finger groove in the bottom of the molding. Sand to 220 grit and crosscut the molding to make the four pulls. Install them with glue and counterbored screws. Plug the borings with ash plugs (pieces 50) made on your drill press with a plug cutter.

	MATERIAL LIST—*CARCASS*	T x W x L
13	Bureau Sides (2)	¾" x 12⅜" x 36¾"
14	Legs (4)	1½" x 4" x 40¾"
15	Legs Blocks (4)	¾" x 4" x 4"
16	Wing Walls (2)	¾" x 21½" x 36¾"
17	Wing Wall Trim (2) (Walnut)	¾" x ¾" x 35¼"
18	Drawer Slides (24)	½" x ¾" x 21½"
19	Back Stringers (4)	¾" x 3" x 25"
20	Wing Rails (4)	¾" x 6" x 24¼"
21	Intermediate Wing Rails (6)	¾" x 6" x 23½"
22	Rail Trim (1)	½" x ¾" x 250"
23	Middle Stack Sides (2)	¾" x 20¾" x 36¾"
24	Middle Stack Side Trim (2)	¾" x ¾" x 35¼"
25	Middle Stack Rails (2)	¾" x 3" x 14"
26	Middle Stack Intermediate Rails (3)	¾" x 3" x 12½"
27	Ash Rail Trim (1)	¾" x ¾" x 75"
28	Middle Upper Stringer (1)	¾" x 3" x 14"
29	Middle Lower Stringer (1)	¾" x 6½" x 14"
30	Corner Blocks (6)	¾" x 4" x 4"
31	Bureau Top (1)	¾" x 25" x 70"
32	Walnut Front Bureau Top Trim (1)	½" x 5" x 70"
33	Walnut Side Bureau Top Trim (2)	½" x 22" x 5"
34	Trim Spacer (1)	½" x 2" x 60"

Middle Drawer Exploded View

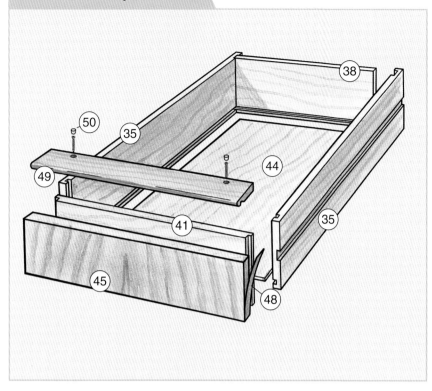

Wing Drawer Exploded View

The notches on the side pieces (for the pulls) are not cut until the drawer boxes are assembled.

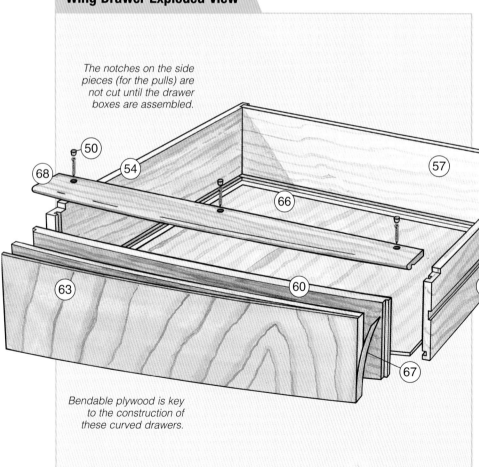

Bendable plywood is key to the construction of these curved drawers.

Forming Bowfront Drawers with Bendable Plywood

The bowed drawers are constructed in exactly the same manner as the middle drawers, except that the fronts and faces are bowed. Note that eight of the sides (pieces 51, 52 and 53) are shorter than the other eight (pieces 54, 55 and 56). You should also keep in mind that you're making two stacks of drawers that are mirror images of each other, so mark pieces as you go.

Cut all eight drawer backs (pieces 57, 58 and 59) to size. Then use your original bending form to lay out the curve for the drawer fronts and faces (pieces 60 through 65). You'll need to build a new bending form for the drawers, as they're taller than the original arch. Make this form large enough to handle the bottom drawer (10¾" high) and it can be used for all eight.

Make up each drawer front with three laminations of 1/4" bending ply, glued and clamped in place. It's a good idea to work with slightly oversized stock here, and trim it to final dimensions after the glue dries. See the steps in the *sidebar* on page 80 and on the *Technical Drawings* to accommodate the curved drawer construction.

Mill the dadoes for the backs and the grooves for the drawer bottoms (pieces 66) with the dado head reset to 90°, then cut the bottoms to size and shape on the table saw and band saw. Assemble the drawers, making sure they're square. Test-fit each in its cavity after the glue dries.

Use two laminations of bending ply and one of ash veneered plywood to make the curved drawer faces. Trim the edges with ash veneer edge tape (piece 67), and you're ready to make the pulls (pieces 68). These are created in exactly the same fashion as the ones you made earlier for the middle drawers, except that they are curved. Band-saw them to shape, bullnose the front edges, plow the finger groove with a core box bit and secure the pulls to the drawers with glue and plugged screws.

#		T x W x L
35	Top Middle Drawer Sides (2)	$^3/_4$" x 5$^3/_8$" x 21$^1/_4$"
36	Intermediate Middle Drawer Sides (4)	$^3/_4$" x 8" x 21$^1/_4$"
37	Bottom Middle Drawer Sides (2)	$^3/_4$" x 9$^5/_8$" x 21$^1/_4$"
38	Top Middle Drawer Back (1)	$^3/_4$" x 5$^3/_8$" x 11$^5/_8$"
39	Intermediate Middle Drawer Backs (2)	$^3/_4$" x 8" x 11$^5/_8$"
40	Bottom Middle Drawer Back (1)	$^3/_4$" x 9$^5/_8$" x 11$^5/_8$"
41	Top Middle Drawer Front (1)	$^3/_4$" x 5$^3/_8$" x 1$^5/_8$"
42	Intermediate Middle Drawer Fronts (2)	$^3/_4$" x 8" x 11$^5/_8$"
43	Bottom Middle Drawer Front (1)	$^3/_4$" x 9$^5/_8$" x 11$^5/_8$"
44	Middle Drawer Bottoms (4)	$^3/_4$" x 11$^5/_8$" x 20$^1/_2$"
45	Top Middle Drawer Face (1)	$^3/_4$" x 13$^{15}/_{16}$" x 5$^1/_4$"
46	Intermediate Middle Drawer Faces (2)	$^3/_4$" x 13$^{15}/_{16}$" x 8"
47	Bottom Middle Drawer Face (1)	$^3/_4$" x 13$^{15}/_{16}$" x 9$^5/_8$"
48	Middle Drawer Face Tape (1)	$^1/_{16}$" x $^3/_4$" x 70"
49	Middle Drawer Pull Molding (1)	$^1/_2$" x 1$^1/_2$" x 75"
50	Screw Plugs (48)	$^3/_8$" Dia.
51	Top Wing Drawers, Short Sides (2)	$^3/_4$" x 5$^1/_4$" x 18$^1/_4$"
52	Intermediate Wing Drawers, Short Sides (4)	$^3/_4$" x 8" x 18$^1/_4$"
53	Bottom Wing Drawers, Short Sides (2)	$^3/_4$" x 9$^5/_8$" x 18$^1/_4$"
54	Top Wing Drawers, Long Sides (2)	$^3/_4$" x 5$^1/_4$" x 21"
55	Intermediate Wing Drawers, Long Sides (4)	$^3/_4$" x 8" x 21"
56	Bottom Wing Drawers, Long Sides (2)	$^3/_4$" x 9$^5/_8$" x 21"
57	Top Wing Drawers, Backs (2)	$^3/_4$" x 5$^1/_4$" x 22$^5/_8$"
58	Intermediate Wing Drawers, Backs (4)	$^3/_4$" x 8" x 22$^5/_8$"
59	Bottom Wing Drawers, Backs (2)	$^3/_4$" x 9$^5/_8$" x 22$^5/_8$"
60	Top Wing Drawers, Fronts (2)	$^3/_4$" x 5$^1/_4$" x 22$^3/_4$"
61	Intermediate Wing Drawers, Fronts (4)	$^3/_4$" x 8" x 22$^3/_4$"
62	Bottom Wing Drawers, Fronts (2)	$^3/_4$" x 9$^5/_8$" x 22$^3/_4$"
63	Top Wing Drawer, Faces (2)	$^3/_4$" x 23$^5/_8$" x 5$^1/_2$"
64	Intermediate Wing Drawer Faces (4)	$^3/_4$" x 23$^5/_8$" x 8"
65	Bottom Wing Drawer Faces (2)	$^3/_4$" x 23$^5/_8$" x 9$^5/_8$"
66	Wing Drawer Bottoms (8)	$^1/_4$" x 22$^5/_8$" x 20$^1/_4$"
67	Wing Drawer Face Tape (1)	$^1/_{16}$" x $^3/_4$" x 140"
68	Wing Drawer Pulls, Molding (1)	$^1/_2$" x 2$^1/_2$" x 195"

Odds & Ends

69	Drawer Stops (24)	$^1/_2$" x $^1/_2$" x 2$^1/_2$"
70	Bureau Back (1)	$^1/_4$" x 36$^3/_4$" x 64"
71	Adjustable Support (1)	$^3/_4$" Dia.
72	Mirror Braces (2)	$^1/_2$" x 1$^1/_4$" x 60"
73	Dowels (2)	$^3/_4$" Dia. x 5"

Making the Drawer Stops and Bureau Back

This is one piece of furniture where lining up the drawers is easy. You'll want each drawer front to line up perfectly with the face frame of the dresser, and all you have to do to achieve this is to pop them into their openings, line them up, and then go around back and put a pencil mark on the slide at the back of each drawer. Then you can glue and screw stops (pieces 69) in place to limit each drawer's travel.

With the stops in place, cut the bureau back (piece 70) to size, then secure it in place with brads every 6" or so around the edge and up along the back edges of the middle stack sides. Now install the adjustable middle support (piece 71).

Slide the drawers into their various cavities and use double-sided tape to line up the drawer faces in their openings. When you're satisfied with their fit, mark the locations with a pencil, remove the tape and secure the faces to the drawer boxes with countersunk screws driven through the inside of the drawer fronts.

Some Final Thoughts

Sand the entire dresser, including the mirror frame, to 220 grit, then apply several coats of oil finish according to the manufacturer's instructions. After the finish dries, move the dresser to its new home before you mount the mirror. This can be done with two braces (pieces 72), coupled with 3/4" dowels (pieces 73). The braces are screwed into the mirror and the base and the dowels locate and secure the mirror posts on the top (see the *Mirror Post and Dowel Location Detail* on page 76 for locating the dowel holes carefully. Use glazier's mastic to secure the mirror to the mirror back.

Now all that's left is to justify to your wife why you need the majority of the drawers instead of her. It's probably a battle you'll lose before it even begins.

Build a Bed Designed for Readers

This queen-sized bed features a perfectly inclined backrest, three large storage compartments and three drawers for your bedside collectibles. The crowning touch: Open the middle drawer and drop the support down to make a rock-solid resting place for that steaming mug of tea.

There's an old adage that says, "The longer your years, the shorter your days." Whether you consider yourself over the hill or not, life just seems to get busier as the years pass. If the only quiet time you have to catch up on reading is late at night when the kids are asleep, you'll love this project.

Most beds are designed for lying down, not sitting up and reading. Plus, few styles offer convenient storage for all the catalogs, books and magazines you may need to get through. Even bedside tables offer limited storage space for reading material.

This multiple-use queen-sized bed addresses a number of these problems. It features comfortable back support for reading and lots of storage. One key feature is the flip-down doors that are supported by the pull-out drawers. The backs of the doors then become small, but sturdy tables to hold books, popcorn bowls or maybe even a remote control if you surf the channels instead of read yourself to sleep.

Simple Headboard Cabinet Design

The headboard is essentially just a plywood cabinet with nine separate compartments. This subassembly is secured between two legs and topped off with a gently curved pediment made of walnut and ash.

Begin building the cabinet by cutting the sides, dividers, top, bottom and shelves (pieces 1 through 6) to size. You'll want to check the *Exploded Views* and *Elevation Drawings* throughout this article for the construction details. As this is hardwood veneered plywood, make the straight cuts with a fine-toothed plywood blade on the table saw to minimize splintering the veneer. Keep the best-looking side of each panel facing up as you cut: the tearout will occur when the blade exits the workpiece. Grab your router and straight bit to plow three 3/16"-deep dadoes across each side and

four across each divider (two on each side), as shown in the *photo* below. As the *drawings* show, these are all through cuts. Once they're made, adjust the bit depth to 1/4" to create stopped rabbets along the back edge of each side and the top, to accommodate the back. With the routing completed, lay out the angled front edges of the sides and dividers. Trim the angled cuts close to your line with a jigsaw, then clamp on a straightedge and clean up the edges with a 3/4" straight bit chucked in your portable router, as shown in the *photos* on the next page.

Dry-fit the cabinet together, then mill enough cap stock (piece 7) to trim the front edges of all the cabinet parts. This is just square stock, ripped and planed to size.

Assemble the cabinet with glue and clamps, making sure that it's flat and square.

The dadoes for the headboard's straightforward joinery are plowed while the sides and dividers are still rectangular. The angled front edges are laid out and cut next.

Get close to the layout lines for the side with a hand-held jigsaw. Then finish the cut with a router and a straightedge jig, (left), to smooth the saw marks.

Use a straightedge jig and a router with a straight bit to trim the angled front edges smooth and straight.

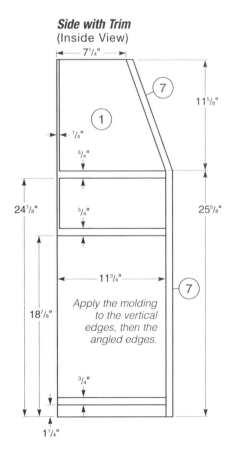

Side with Trim
(Inside View)

7¹/₄"

7

11⁵/₈"

1

¹/₄"

³/₄"

24⁷/₈"

³/₄"

25⁵/₈"

11³/₄"

7

18⁷/₈"

Apply the molding to the vertical edges, then the angled edges.

³/₄"

1¹/₄"

When the glue is dry, miter the cap stock to fit and apply it to the cabinet with glue and finish nails. Be sure to install the vertical strips first. Predrill pilot holes in the hardwood for the nails, and set the nail heads below the surface. The last trim to apply is the upper shelf trim (piece 8), which helps frame the drawer openings. Cover the holes with matching filler and sand it smooth after it dries. The plywood back (piece 9) and the lower panels (pieces 10 and 11) close up the headboard. Attach panel cleats (piece 12), setting them 7/8" in from the front of the headboard, and secure the panels with glue and screws. Fit the back into its rabbet and attach with brads.

Laminated Legs

The two headboard legs are created by laminating pieces of ash lumber to a 1/2"-thick walnut core. Face-glue and clamp one long ash lamination (piece 13) to each of the walnut laminations (pieces 14). After the glue dries, clamp the two short ash laminations (pieces 15 and 16) to the other side of the leg and clamp them in place.

When dry, run each assembled leg across the jointer. Later, you'll need to form gentle curves onto the top of each leg to mate them to the arched pediments.

Glue the leg laminations together, holding the parts with plenty of clamps until the glue sets. Check the joint initially to remedy any glue creeping.

Graceful Arched Pediment

The curved top of the headboard and the footboard (the pediments) are built up with a series of five 3/8"-thick ash laminations (pieces 17) that are glued together in a plywood form. A sixth walnut lamination (pieces 18) will be installed after the pediments are secured to the legs.

A bending form forces each lamination into an arched shape and holds them all tightly together while the glue dries. After you rip and crosscut all 12 laminations to size, refer to the *sidebar* (at right) and the *Elevation Drawings* for directions on building your form. Then apply a liberal amount of adhesive between five of the ash laminations and clamp them in place securely.

When the adhesive is dry, scrape off the excess and pass one edge of the pediment across the jointer. Set your table saw fence so it's 6⁵⁄₁₆" from a sharp ripping blade and rip the pediment to width. (You may need a helper for this task — the pediment is a handful.) Then pass the ripped edge across the jointer, reducing the part to its final 6¼" width. Crosscut it to 68½" long (measuring along the curve), then chamfer the bottom edge with a 45° bearing-guided chamfering bit. Run the bearing along the bottom face of the pediment so the router can ride the jointed sides (rather than having to follow the curve). Using several passes, shape the ends first, then the sides; this will eliminate any tearout from cutting across the grain on the ends. Before moving on, repeat this process to create the footboard pediment— it's identical to the headboard pediment.

Now clamp the legs temporarily in place on the headboard. Center one of the pediments on the two legs and trace its curve onto the face of the legs. Remove the legs and step to the band saw to cut the ends of each leg to the curved layout lines. Sand the curves smooth and exactly to the lines on a stationary disk sander. When the curves on the pediment and leg are a perfect match, glue and clamp the legs in place on the headboard.

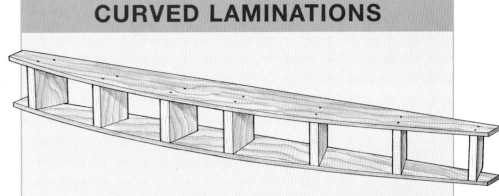

CURVED LAMINATIONS

The arched pediments on the foot of the bed are created by gluing hardwood laminations together while clamped to a curved form. Make the form from plywood shaped and mounted to dimension lumber with glue and screws. It is important that the form's curve be fair and true. To form the curve on your jig, mark the endpoints and centerpoint and flex a thin strip of hardboard to lay out the shape. Use a belt sander to smooth out the long gentle arc. The form also needs to provide good purchase for the many clamps it takes to apply even pressure to this pediment build-up. If you're limited to using shorter clamps, make some clamp cutouts, as shown in the *Elevation Drawing* on the next page.

The type of adhesive to use is a significant consideration for this task. White or yellow woodworking glues may work, but their elasticity could allow the curve to creep and change shape, even after the glue cures. Epoxy is a better choice for this operation — specifically a mixture with a long open time. The open time not only provides enough time to place the laminations around the form and clamp them properly, but it also allows the resin to infiltrate the wood fibers, thus creating a stronger bond. If epoxy isn't a reasonable option for you, polyurethane glue is another good choice for dry-bent laminations.

Use epoxy or polyurethane glues for dry-bent laminations like this one. Yellow or white glues are not recommended.

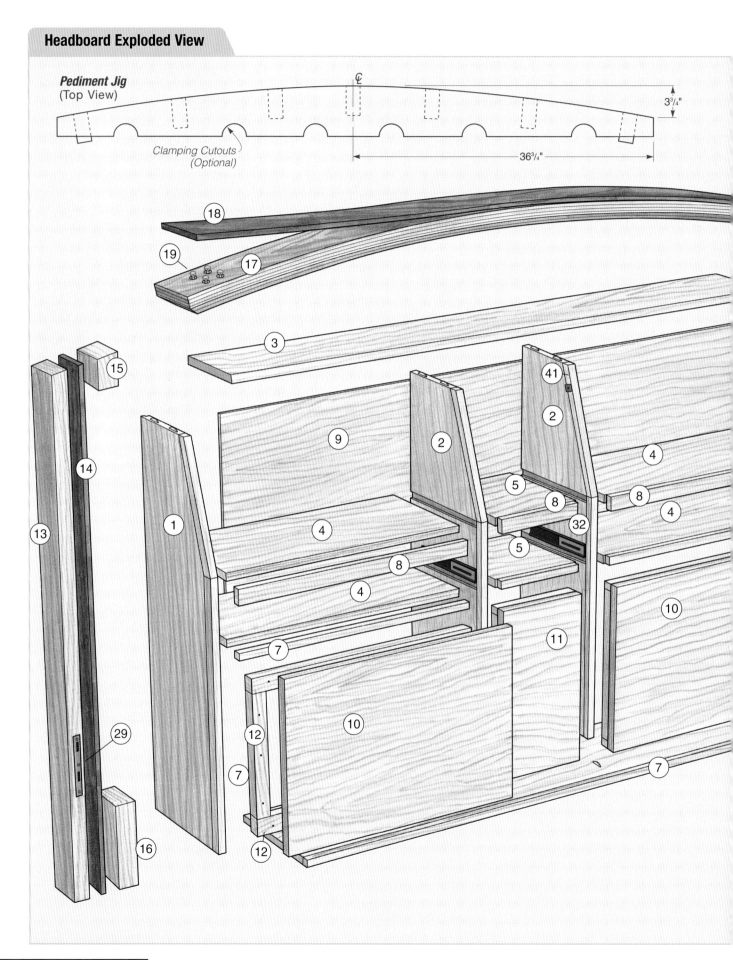

Pediment Jig
(Top View)

Clamping Cutouts
(Optional)

3³/₄"

36³/₄"

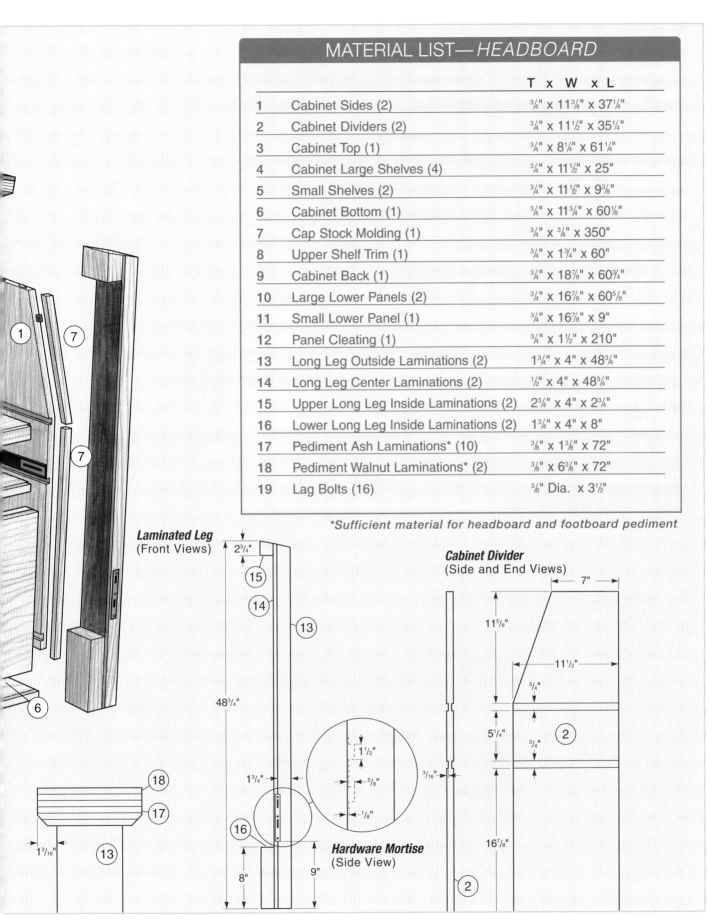

MATERIAL LIST—*HEADBOARD*

		T x W x L
1	Cabinet Sides (2)	$\frac{3}{4}$" x $11\frac{3}{4}$" x $37\frac{1}{4}$"
2	Cabinet Dividers (2)	$\frac{3}{4}$" x $11\frac{1}{2}$" x $35\frac{1}{4}$"
3	Cabinet Top (1)	$\frac{3}{4}$" x $8\frac{1}{4}$" x $61\frac{1}{4}$"
4	Cabinet Large Shelves (4)	$\frac{3}{4}$" x $11\frac{1}{2}$" x 25"
5	Small Shelves (2)	$\frac{3}{4}$" x $11\frac{1}{2}$" x $9\frac{3}{8}$"
6	Cabinet Bottom (1)	$\frac{3}{4}$" x $11\frac{3}{4}$" x $60\frac{1}{8}$"
7	Cap Stock Molding (1)	$\frac{3}{4}$" x $\frac{3}{4}$" x 350"
8	Upper Shelf Trim (1)	$\frac{3}{4}$" x $1\frac{3}{4}$" x 60"
9	Cabinet Back (1)	$\frac{3}{4}$" x $18\frac{7}{8}$" x $60\frac{3}{4}$"
10	Large Lower Panels (2)	$\frac{3}{4}$" x $16\frac{7}{8}$" x $60\frac{5}{8}$"
11	Small Lower Panel (1)	$\frac{3}{4}$" x $16\frac{7}{8}$" x 9"
12	Panel Cleating (1)	$\frac{3}{4}$" x $1\frac{1}{2}$" x 210"
13	Long Leg Outside Laminations (2)	$1\frac{3}{4}$" x 4" x $48\frac{3}{4}$"
14	Long Leg Center Laminations (2)	$\frac{1}{2}$" x 4" x $48\frac{3}{4}$"
15	Upper Long Leg Inside Laminations (2)	$2\frac{3}{4}$" x 4" x $2\frac{3}{4}$"
16	Lower Long Leg Inside Laminations (2)	$1\frac{3}{4}$" x 4" x 8"
17	Pediment Ash Laminations* (10)	$\frac{3}{8}$" x $1\frac{3}{8}$" x 72"
18	Pediment Walnut Laminations* (2)	$\frac{3}{8}$" x $6\frac{3}{8}$" x 72"
19	Lag Bolts (16)	$\frac{3}{8}$" Dia. x $3\frac{1}{2}$"

Sufficient material for headboard and footboard pediment

Laminated Leg
(Front Views)

Cabinet Divider
(Side and End Views)

Hardware Mortise
(Side View)

Grab one arched pediment and position it on the headboard subassembly. Mark the leg locations on its underside and bore pilot holes through the piece. Then attach the pediment to the legs, after predrilling for the 3½"-long lag bolts (pieces 19). The reason you're using such large bolts is that people are bound to use the arched pediments as handles to lift the bed, so these joints will be subject to some serious stress. Countersink for the bolt heads, making sure they are below the surface before you proceed to the next step.

Wrap up by gluing and clamping the final (walnut) lamination in place. After the glue dries, use a bearing-guided laminate trimming bit to pare the edges flush with the ash. Sand the edges, and you're ready to move on to the footboard.

Solid-Ash and Walnut Footboard

The only difference between the headboard and footboard (aside from height) is that the latter sports a couple of hardwood panels instead of a cabinet. Construction begins with the legs. Face-glue and clamp two ash laminations (pieces 20) around a walnut one (piece 21), and dress it on the jointer after the glue dries. Do this for each leg and then crosscut them to length. On the router table, plow stopped mortises into the inside faces of the legs and square up the ends of each mortise with a chisel.

Edge-glue hardwood stock to make the footboard panels (pieces 22 and 23), paying attention to the grain pattern. Size the panels to create the upper and lower sections and then plow a 1/2" groove along the joining edges. Cut the curved shape on the upper edge as shown in the *Elevation Drawings*. Mill the 1/2" x 1/2" tenons onto the panels ends with a dado blade in the table saw. Mill the decorative walnut strip (piece 24) that fits between the upper and lower panels to size. Sand both panels (and the walnut strip) to 180 grit, then glue and clamp the panel subassembly between the legs to complete the footboard.

Attach the footboard pediment (which you made earlier) in exactly the same fashion as the headboard version. Apply the final walnut lamination, clean up any glue squeeze-out and sand the edges smooth.

Side Rails and Moldings

There isn't much to the side rail assemblies: they're just a couple of lengths of molding (pieces 25) attached to boards (pieces 26). Rip the moldings to size, then lay out the five dadoes in each, at the locations shown in the *Elevation Drawings*. Make the dado cuts with the aid of your miter gauge. Glue the walnut accent strip (pieces 27) to the top edge of each rail.

After sanding the rails, screw and glue the moldings to them. Form five lengths of stock to serve as the rail slats (pieces 28). These fit into the dadoes in the side rail moldings and will support your box spring once the bed is assembled. Now you're ready to attach the rails to the headboard and footboard. This is done with bedframe hardware designed specifically for this application (pieces 29). It's strong, totally invisible and allows for disassembly when you need to move the bed elsewhere.

Heavy-duty lag bolts ensure that the arched pediments will not come loose from the bed's legs. Make sure you sink the heads below the level of the arch.

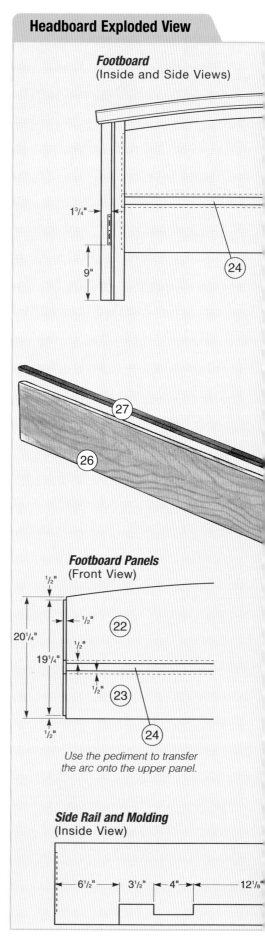

Footboard
(Inside and Side Views)

1³/₄"

9"

24

27

26

Footboard Panels
(Front View)

1/2"

20¹/₄"

19¹/₄"

1/2"

22

1/2"

23

1/2"

24

Use the pediment to transfer the arc onto the upper panel.

Side Rail and Molding
(Inside View)

6¹/₂"   3¹/₂"   4"   12¹/₈"

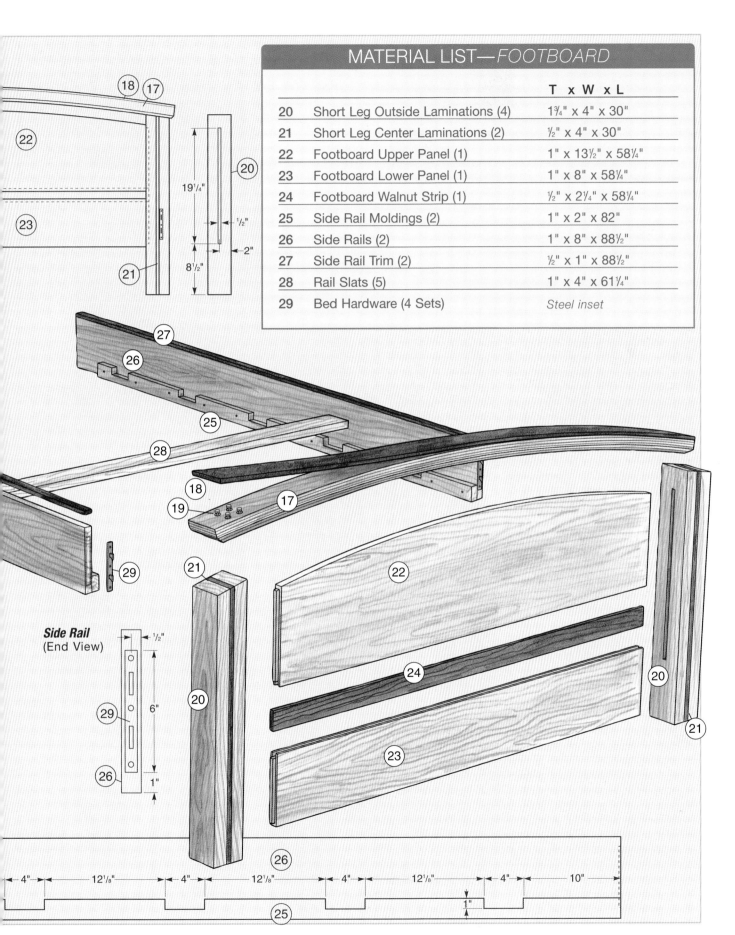

		T x W x L
20	Short Leg Outside Laminations (4)	1¾" x 4" x 30"
21	Short Leg Center Laminations (2)	½" x 4" x 30"
22	Footboard Upper Panel (1)	1" x 13½" x 58¼"
23	Footboard Lower Panel (1)	1" x 8" x 58¼"
24	Footboard Walnut Strip (1)	½" x 2¼" x 58¼"
25	Side Rail Moldings (2)	1" x 2" x 82"
26	Side Rails (2)	1" x 8" x 88½"
27	Side Rail Trim (2)	½" x 1" x 88½"
28	Rail Slats (5)	1" x 4" x 61¼"
29	Bed Hardware (4 Sets)	*Steel inset*

Side Rail
(End View)

½"

6"

1"

19¼"

½"

2"

8½"

4"   12⅛"   4"   12⅛"   4"   12⅛"   4"   10"

1"

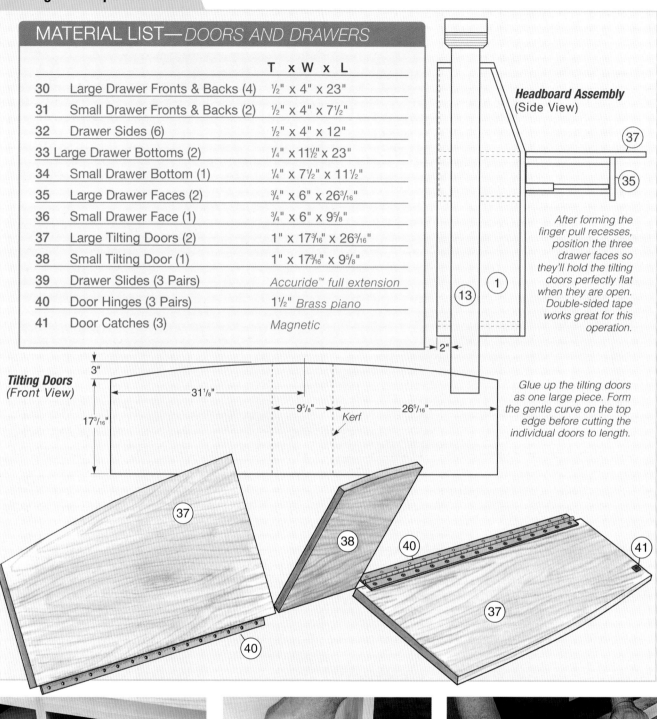

MATERIAL LIST—*DOORS AND DRAWERS*

		T x W x L
30	Large Drawer Fronts & Backs (4)	½" x 4" x 23"
31	Small Drawer Fronts & Backs (2)	½" x 4" x 7½"
32	Drawer Sides (6)	½" x 4" x 12"
33	Large Drawer Bottoms (2)	¼" x 11½" x 23"
34	Small Drawer Bottom (1)	¼" x 7½" x 11½"
35	Large Drawer Faces (2)	¾" x 6" x 26³⁄₁₆"
36	Small Drawer Face (1)	¾" x 6" x 9⅝"
37	Large Tilting Doors (2)	1" x 17³⁄₁₆" x 26³⁄₁₆"
38	Small Tilting Door (1)	1" x 17³⁄₁₆" x 9⅝"
39	Drawer Slides (3 Pairs)	*Accuride™ full extension*
40	Door Hinges (3 Pairs)	*1½" Brass piano*
41	Door Catches (3)	*Magnetic*

Headboard Assembly
(Side View)

After forming the finger pull recesses, position the three drawer faces so they'll hold the tilting doors perfectly flat when they are open. Double-sided tape works great for this operation.

Tilting Doors
(Front View)

3"

31⅛"

9⅝"

26⁵⁄₁₆"

Kerf

17³⁄₁₆"

2"

Glue up the tilting doors as one large piece. Form the gentle curve on the top edge before cutting the individual doors to length.

Putting It All Together. *Heavy-duty drawer slides are an important feature, as the drawers (when open) do double duty as door supports.*

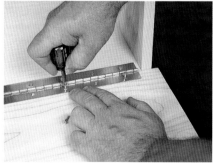

Sewing machine hinges were tested, but they weren't up to the job. Piano hinges offer the strength and support these doors need.

Installing knock-down bed rail hardware in mortises keeps it invisible when assembled.

Drawer Exploded View

Drawer Bottom Groove
(Section View)

33 — 32
1/4"
1/4"

30

32

33

30

39

32

35

30

Drawer Joint Detail
(Top View)

1/4" 1/4" 1/4"

Three Drawers for Storage

Our bed features three 12"-deep drawers, two of which are ideal for storing stationery and reading materials. The third, smaller drawer is designed for reading glasses, pens and similar items.

Cut the drawer fronts, backs and sides (pieces 30 through 32) to size, then chuck a 1/4" straight bit in the router table. Plow a through-groove in each part for the drawer bottoms (pieces 33 and 34), as shown above. Next, mill a vertical dado in the drawer sides near each end on the same face as the drawer bottom groove. Each dado is 1/4" square and located 1/4" from the end.

Use the same 1/4" router bit to cut rabbets on the ends of the drawer fronts to make a slick, locking corner joint. Dry-fit the drawers together. When everything works, assemble the drawers with glue and clamps. Make sure they're flat and square.

Solid-Hardwood Drawer Faces

You'll give your bed a great look if you arrange a continuous grain pattern through the hardwood drawer faces (pieces 35 and 36) and the tilting doors above them (pieces 37 and 38). If you edge-glue stock to produce this effect, match the grain along the joint so it looks as though all six parts were cut from the same board.

Following the manufacturer's instructions, use heavy-duty, full-extension drawer slides (pieces 39) to install the three drawers in their openings. Full-extension slides allow the drawers to pull out far enough to support the doors above them. The heavy-duty rating means that even an unabridged edition of *War and Peace* won't cause them to sag. Hold off on mounting the drawer faces until the doors are in place.

Uniquely Designed Tilting Doors

The three tilting doors in the headboard are what really fulfill a reader's dreams. All three conceal cavities large enough to store plenty of printed matter, while either of the larger doors drops down to become an instant desk (depending on which side of the bed you prefer). The smaller, middle door transforms into a shelf for popcorn or a remote control.

You have already glued up stock for the doors. Now cut them to size. Rip and crosscut first, then arch the tops on the band saw. Belt-sand the

saw marks away, then sand all three doors and break their edges gently with 180-grit sand paper.

Mount the doors using heavy-duty piano hinges (pieces 40). Mark the locations of the hinges on the doors and the head-board. Install just a couple of screws per hinge to assure you have the alignment right. Once you're sure all is correct, install the remaining screws. When the doors fit nicely, mount the magnetic door catches (pieces 41) to keep the doors from accidentally opening. With all three drawers mounted in their openings and fully extended, open the tilting doors. Locate the drawer faces so they'll support the doors at a true 90°.

Use double-sided tape or hot-melt glue to temporarily locate and attach the drawer faces and make sure they're properly spaced left to right. Remove the drawers and secure the faces with screws, working from inside the drawers. Predrill and countersink for your screws. When the holes are all drilled, remove the faces and use a 3/4" corebox bit mounted in your router table to create the finger pulls. Clamp stops to the fence to keep the recesses spaced about 1" in from each end.

Final Touches and Finishing

The only thing left to do before you pull out the mattress and take a nap is to apply a finish. Remove the drawers, then sand everything down to 220 grit. Use a tack cloth to remove the dust, and apply a coat of clear sanding sealer. Follow this with three coats of satin polyurethane, sanding lightly between each coat with 400-grit wet/dry paper.

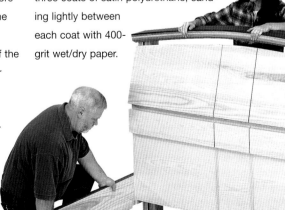

As you open the door on the desk, door supports slide smoothly out into position to support it.

Specialty brass hardware combines with classic inlay and dovetail details on this Federal-style Secretary Desk.

Federal Secretary Desk

Federal styling, an American response to various European influences, relies on a combination of simple elements to create an elegant complete design. With that goal in mind, our secretary features oval inlays and book-matched burl veneer, together with tapered legs and slender, light-colored inlay strips.

On a project like this, with so many details and complicated steps, you'll need to be organized. Two good pieces of advice before you start: First, work from the floor up. Second, have all your materials, including the burl veneer and specialty hardware, on hand before you make your first cut.

Take your time when choosing stock for the four legs (pieces 1). They'll look best if there are no cathedral spikes in the grain, especially after the inlay is applied. To keep a uniform appearance, use stock with growth rings running at a 45° angle across the bottom face.

After cutting the legs to the dimensions shown in the *Material List* on page 97, orient them so the best color and figure face forward. Then follow the *Technical Drawings* on page 102 and the *sidebar*, at right, to lay out and cut the tapers. Note all eight tapers stop shy of the top of the legs where the desk aprons (pieces 2 and 3) will be attached.

Rip the aprons to size from walnut

veneered plywood. The bottom of the aprons are accented with a solid piece of 3/8" molding (piece 4). Glue it in place and shape the bead profile on your router table, as shown in the *Bead Molding Detail* on page 97.

Making Floating Tenon Joinery

The aprons are secured to the legs with mortise and tenon joinery, but in this case

QUICK AND EASY LEG TAPERING

Make a bed from 3/4" plywood, 10" longer than your workpiece and wide enough to accommodate a toggle clamp. Rip another 4"-wide piece for the jig's fence and cut two small pieces to make a stop for the jig bed and a mounting block for the toggle clamp. Mark the starting and finishing points for a taper on one leg (see *Technical Drawings*), and place it on the bed with the stock you wish to remove hanging over the edge. Mount the fence and stop block against the edge of the leg (the fence will be positioned at an angle, relative to the jig bed). Toggle-clamp the leg in place and raise the blade up high. Set the jig against you saw's rip fence, and align the fence as necessary. Slide the jig along the fence to cut the tapers.

The nicely tapered legs on this classic design were produced using this simple jig.

FORMING THE OVAL ACCENTS

Federal styling relies on simple elements combined to create an elegant, complete design. To that end, our secretary uses oval inlays together with tapered legs and slender, light-colored inlay strips. The key to getting the ovals and strips to fit well is to use a template to guide your router. However, the space between the outside edge of the rub collar and the router bit must be accommodated (see inset). One trick is to use a machine nut to offset your pencil as you trace a line around the outside of the oval. Cut the template opening on your scroll saw and rout a few oval shapes with your new template and rub collar to test the fit. Expect to make a few adjustments — and possibly even a few templates — before your oval inlay fits perfectly. It's worth the effort to be precise.

To allow for the offset of the router bit and rub collar, use a small machine nut as a guide when tracing around the oval inlay.

After a few adjustments to the template, the ovals should fit perfectly in the scrap wood test piece. A precisely-made template is imperative here.

the tenons (pieces 5) float — that is, they aren't an integral part of either piece. As such, it is necessary to form matching mortises in both the legs and aprons.

Follow the *Technical Drawings* to lay out the mortises. Now, install a 3/8" straight bit in your router table and set the fence to the dimensions shown on the *drawings*. Use a stop block and a piece of masking tape to give you the proper size mortise (as shown in *Figure 1*), then test your set-up on some

scrap before milling the leg and apron mortises in several passes. Make the floating tenons to snugly fit the mortises. Next, use a pocket hole jig and bit to drill pocket holes in the top edges of the aprons (see *Technical Drawings* for locations). These holes will eventually hold face frame screws (pieces 6) to attach the legset to the rest of the desk. With this done, complete the inlay and stringing (pieces 7 and 8) in the legs, following the *sidebars* shown here.

Building the Legset Assembly

With the inlay and decorative stringing completed, sand the aprons and legs, starting with 100-grit and finishing with 220-grit papers. Dry-fit and temporarily clamp the legs and aprons together. With the assembly square and plumb, cut the corner braces (pieces 9) to size and predrill and countersink for their screws (pieces 10). When everything fits, remove the clamps and glue and screw the legset together.

LEG, DOOR AND DRAWER INLAYS

As with the decorative ovals, above, forming the grooves for the slender inlays is easy with a router, rub collar and a jig. Use the *Technical Drawings* to make jigs for all of the inlays. To form the long thin inlays, start with a piece of 3/4" stock, slicing it on your table saw a hair wider than the groove it will fill. Lower the blade and rip strips to the depth of the groove, test fitting as you go. It is imperative to use a zero-clearance insert in the table saw for this operation. Anytime you fit a strip of inlay into a tiny groove, try slightly tapering the edges of the strips to ensure a better fit. Use a file to remove just a bit of wood.

Use a router bit with a rub collar and a template to form the grooves on the tapered legs, drawer and door. Make some test cuts on scrapwood first to verify your set-up.

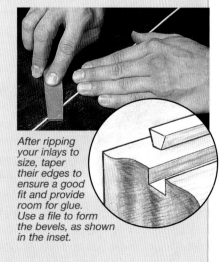

After ripping your inlays to size, taper their edges to ensure a good fit and provide room for glue. Use a file to form the bevels, as shown in the inset.

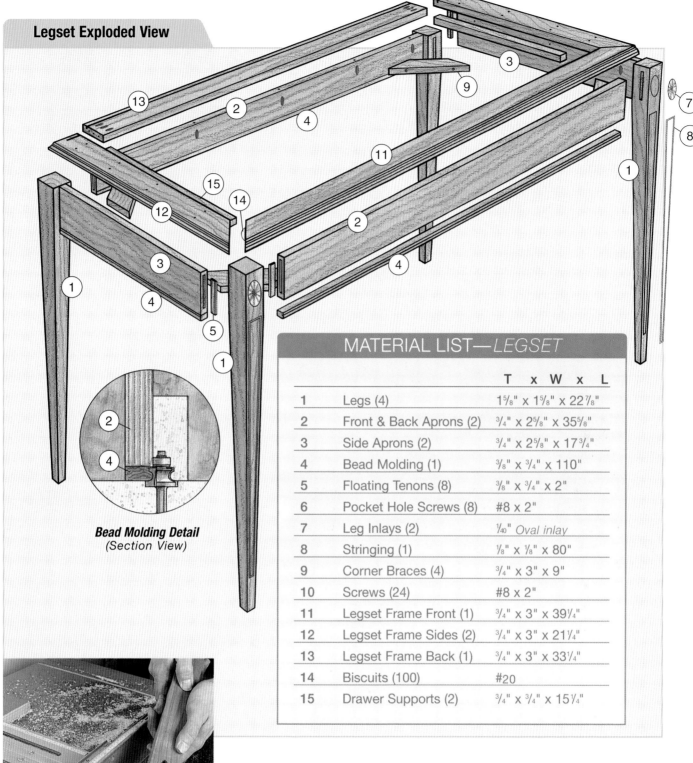

Bead Molding Detail
(Section View)

MATERIAL LIST—*LEGSET*

		T x W x L
1	Legs (4)	1⅝" x 1⅝" x 22⅞"
2	Front & Back Aprons (2)	¾" x 2⅝" x 35⅝"
3	Side Aprons (2)	¾" x 2⅝" x 17¾"
4	Bead Molding (1)	⅜" x ¾" x 110"
5	Floating Tenons (8)	⅜" x ¾" x 2"
6	Pocket Hole Screws (8)	#8 x 2"
7	Leg Inlays (2)	1/40" *Oval inlay*
8	Stringing (1)	⅛" x ⅛" x 80"
9	Corner Braces (4)	¾" x 3" x 9"
10	Screws (24)	#8 x 2"
11	Legset Frame Front (1)	¾" x 3" x 39¼"
12	Legset Frame Sides (2)	¾" x 3" x 21¼"
13	Legset Frame Back (1)	¾" x 3" x 33¼"
14	Biscuits (100)	#20
15	Drawer Supports (2)	¾" x ¾" x 15¼"

Figure 1: Floating tenons are a unique feature in this design. Use a stop block and masking tape to start and stop your mortises.

Making the Walnut Frame

A flat frame (pieces 11, 12 and 13) serves as a transition between the base and desktop. The front joints are mitered, while the back ones are simple butts held with screws. The miter joints are reinforced with #20 biscuits (pieces 14). Dry-fit the frame, then glue and clamp it together. Now add the drawer supports (pieces 15) with glue

and clamps (see *Exploded View*).

With a belt sander, smooth the frame to 220 grit before routing the ogee profile on the front and side edges. Set the frame upside down on the workbench and center the legset (side-to-side) on it. Align the back edges so they're flush with each other, then extend the pocket screw holes into the frame and set this assembly aside for now.

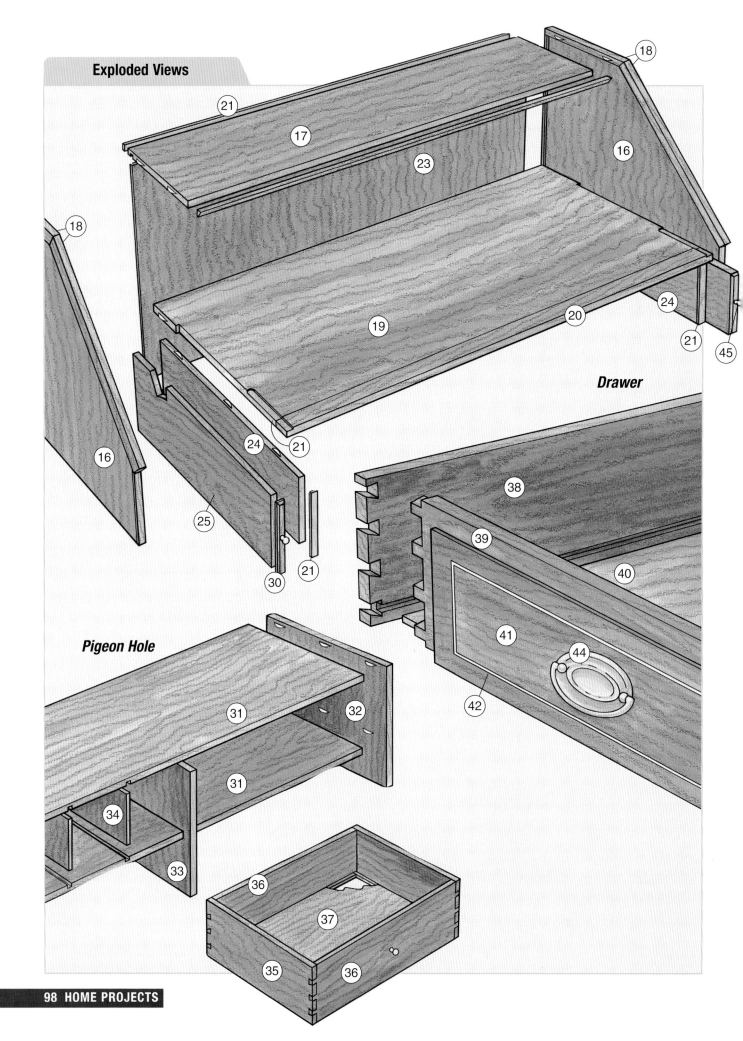

Drawer

Pigeon Hole

MATERIAL LIST—*CARCASS*

		T x W x L
16	Carcass Sides (2)	3/4" x 203/8" x 131/2"
17	Carcass Top (1)	3/4" x 113/8" x 363/4"
18	Carcass Edge Banding (1)	3/4" x 3/4" x 96"
19	Carcass Writing Top (1)	3/4" x 18" x 363/4"
20	Brace (1)	3/4" x 2" x 361/4"
21	Banding (1)	1/8" x 3/4" x 60"
22	Specialty Door Hardware (1 Set)	Brass
23	Carcass Back (1)	1/4" x 141/2" x 371/4"
24	Drawer Cavity Dividers (2)	3/4" x 4" x 197/8"
25	Door Supports (2)	3/4" x 315/16" x 20"
26	Door Edge (1)	3/4" x 3/4" x 124"
27	Door (1)	3/4" x 115/16" x 355/16"
28	Burl Door Veneer (2)	1/32" x 13" x 19"
29	Plain Door Veneer (1)	1/32" x 13" x 37"
30	Door Support Endcaps (2)	1/4" x 3/4" x 315/16"

MATERIAL LIST—*PIGEON HOLE UNIT*

		T x W x L
31	Pigeon Hole Top & Shelf (2)	1/2" x 10" x 351/8"
32	Pigeon Hole Sides (2)	1/2" x 10" x 813/16"
33	Pigeon Hole Large Dividers (2)	1/2" x 10" x 85/16"
34	Pigeon Hole Small Dividers (3)	1/4" x 10" x 43/8"
35	Pigeon Hole Drawer Sides (4)	1/2" x 37/8" x 10"
36	Pigeon Hole Drawer Frt & Bk (4)	1/2" x 37/8" x 115/16"
37	Pigeon Hole Drawer Bottoms (2)	1/4" x 95/8" x 11"
38	Large Drawer Sides (2)	1/2" x 37/8" x 197/8"
39	Large Drawer Front & Back (2)	1/2" x 37/8" x 3311/16"
40	Large Drawer Bottom (1)	1/4" x 333/16" x 193/8"
41	Large Drawer Face (1)	3/32" x 4" x 337/8"
42	Large Stringing (1)	1/8" x 1/4" x 168"
43	Key Pull (1)	Brass
44	Drawer Pulls (2)	Brass, 5/8" Dia.
45	Drawer Support Pulls (2)	Brass, 3/8" Dia.

Building the Carcass Sides

Cut the carcass sides (pieces 16) and top (piece 17) from a single sheet of veneered plywood, to preserve their grain pattern. Use a plywood-cutting blade in your table saw to cut these parts to shape (see *Technical Drawings*), following the dimensions provided in the *Material List*, above.

Use double-sided tape to temporarily hold the sides together, taping them in the same orientation they will appear on the desk. Now make the angled front edge cuts on the sides (see *Technical Drawings*).

Adding Solid-Hardwood Edges

The exposed edges of the top and angled edges of the sides are covered with hardwood banding (piece 18) that is mitered to length (see *Technical Drawings*) and applied with glue and clamps. Stretchable plastic packing tape makes a great clamp here. After spreading glue on the parts, wrap one edge of the tape around the opposite edge of each panel and press the first few inches firmly so it gets a good grip on the plywood. Stretch the tape tightly as you apply it across the face, over the banding and down the other face of each piece. When the glue dries, trim the banding flush with the plywood. Use a sharp cabinet scraper to shave the banding edges flush. Then cut the proper angle on the front edge of the top.

Time for Some Minor Milling

The sides are attached to the legset frame with screws. The writing top (piece 19), and the carcass top are joined to the sides with biscuits. Refer to the *Technical Drawings* before laying out and machining these biscuit slots, then apply a hardwood brace (piece 20) to the front edge of the writing top with glue and biscuits. Then apply hardwood banding (piece 21) to all the exposed edges of the walnut plywood.

You'll find dimensions on the *Technical Drawings* for making a notch in each side of the writing top: these notches are for the door hardware (pieces 22), and they can be cut on the band saw. Apply hardwood banding to the sides of these slots too, then machine biscuit slots in the ends of the writing top. The last bit of machining for the writing top is to rout mortises for the door hinges. You will also need to pare a chamfer into the leading edge directly in front of the hinge mortise. Check the *Technical Drawings* for more details.

We recommend walnut plywood for the carcass back (piece 23). It may be undersize in thickness, so select an undersized straight router bit to match. Refer to the *Technical Drawings* to find the groove locations and dimensions, then mill them in the carcass sides and top, and also in the frame for the back panel. Make sure to end the stopped grooves at the correct locations.

Carrying Out the Dry Assembly

Cut the drawer cavity dividers (pieces 24) and door supports (pieces 25) to size. In order to mount the door hinge hardware to the door supports, you need to drill a shallow mortise into the sides of the supports with a large Forstner bit (this will create right and left pieces) and finish by cutting the shaped notch onto each support (see *inside back cover*). Now you're almost ready to start dry-assembling the carcass.

The drawer cavity dividers are joined to the writing top by biscuits. Use the *Technical Drawings* to locate and cut the biscuit slots in the drawer cavity dividers, writing top and the carcass sides and top.

Final-sand all the inside surfaces, then dry-fit and clamp the carcass together. It's a good idea to apply finish to the inside surfaces before gluing up the carcass. Be sure not to get stain or finish on any area you will need to glue up later. After a dry-fit, glue and clamp the carcass together, checking for squareness. When the glue cures, secure the carcass to the frame by extending the frame's pilot holes into the sides and drawer cavity dividers.

Making the Door

The door is the most difficult and time-consuming part of this project, especially when you consider the veneer work involved. You don't want to make any mistakes here, so make a 6"-wide template the same dimension as the door from the writing top to the carcass top. This piece will help you test the fit of the hinge leaf and the lid support linkage before you get started on your burl-veneered masterpiece.

Apply solid-hardwood door edging (piece 26) to the edges of the door blank (piece 27), securing it with glue and clamps. Miter the corners of this banding so no end grain shows. Flush up the banding with the plywood after the glue dries, using scrapers and a sanding block to avoid rounding over the edges. The veneer will telegraph any

errors, so take your time. Leave the lid over-sized by 1/16" all around (that's the way it's listed in the *Material List*), for final trimming after the veneer work is completed. Your final trim will leave a 1/16" gap on each side.

Balance the door construction by gluing veneer (pieces 28 and 29) to both sides of the plywood. It's best to do this clamping with a veneer press (see sidebar page 101), or you can use bricks or sand bags on top of scrap plywood to apply even pressure to the panel and veneer. Cover the door with a sheet of wax paper to keep the veneering glue from sticking to things it shouldn't.

If you use a veneer press for this operation and glue both veneer faces at once, be sure to apply equal pressure to all areas of the panel. As you tighten your clamps, work from the center out to the edges to eliminate any air pockets or pooled glue. Scrap-wood crossbearers with curved bottom edges will help you keep the pressure evenly applied.

Use a Keller Dovetail jig or similar jig to create the dovetails on the drawers. Be sure to use different size dovetail bits on the large and small drawers.

Both drawers have through dovetails and plywood drawer bottoms. Test your set-up on scrap lumber of the same dimensions.

Prepping for the Hardware

After the veneering glue is dry, flush-trim the veneer with an ultra sharp knife. Set your table saw to 22½° to trim the top edge and 90° to trim the sides. Then sand the edges smooth with just a hint of a roll back where the veneer meets the edge.

Using the scrap template you made earlier as a guide, trim the sides of the door for the door hinge support hardware (piece 22), as indicated on the *Technical Drawings*. Cut the rabbets for the support linkages on your router table, using an extra-tall fence for good support. Use a sharp chisel to pare out the recess to 30° from vertical, (providing clearance for the hinge knuckle when the door closes). Connect the hardware to the door support pieces you prepared earlier. There is a bit of hand work involved when final-fitting the hinge support hardware, so dry-fit the hinges as you go.

Cut the door support endcaps (pieces 30) to size and sand them. Use two-sided tape to temporarily attach each endcap to a large piece of scrap while you mill the cove profile (see *inside back cover*) on their front faces. Do this on the router table with a bearing-guided bit. When they're completed, epoxy the two endcaps in place.

Making the Pigeon Hole Unit

Most of the pigeon hole assembly elements (pieces 31 through 34) are joined with lap joints in the center and simple butt joints and biscuits at the ends and top. The three small dividers are contained in small dadoes. Use your table saw to nibble out the six dadoes that hold the small dividers in place and your router table to mill the interlocking slots. Before moving on, cut the biscuit slots. All these dimensions are shown on the *Technical Drawings*. Again, it is a good idea to pre-finish this unit before you glue it up (mask off the joints). When the finish is dry, glue the assembly together, checking for squareness as you tighten the clamps. Give the outside a final sanding, then apply finish.

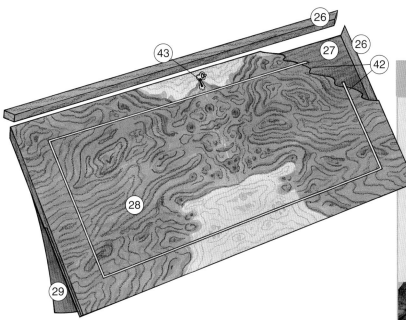

Building the Drawers

Cut stock for the drawers (pieces 35 through 40) and join the sides to the fronts and backs with through dovetails. We used a Keller Dovetail jig with two different sizes of bits (see the *Technical Drawings* for the dimensions and the *photos* on the facing page for milling details), but any similar dovetailing jig will work just as well. If you don't own a dovetail jig, you can cut them by hand. Use a 1/4" bit in your router table to cut stopped grooves for the bottoms (see the *Technical Drawings*), then glue up and clamp all three drawers.

For aesthetic reasons, we decided to cover the dovetails on the front face of the large drawer. After planing some walnut (piece 41) to 3/32" thickness, center it on the drawer front before gluing and clamping it in place. When the glue dries, use a flush-trim bit to clean the edges.

Adding Final Touches and Finish

To continue the striping theme established on the front faces of the legs, follow the same technique used there to apply stringing (piece 42) to the door face and the face of the large drawer. All the locations and dimensions are shown on the *Technical Drawings*.

Now you're ready to finish the rest of the bare surfaces. Remove all the hardware and thoroughly sand the project. Apply three coats of finish, sanding between coats with 400-grit wet/dry paper. Either lacquer or satin varnish would make a durable and attractive topcoat for this desk.

When the finish is dry, locate the key pull according to the *Technical Drawings* and follow the manufacturer's instructions to install it. Drill pilot holes for the key pull, the drawer support pulls and the drawer pulls (pieces 43, 44 and 45), and screw them in place at the locations shown on the *Technical Drawings*. Finally, apply a little wax to the door supports so they slide easily. Then breathe a big sigh of relief at completing such an ambitious project! This one is sure to become a family heirloom.

BURL VENEER

If this is the first time you've ever ordered burl veneer, you'll be surprised when you receive it. Burl veneer is definitely not ready to use right out of the box. Because of the many different grain directions, there's a tremendous amount of stress in the veneer. Never fear — waves, and even holes, are quite acceptable. But the first step in readying the veneer for use is to get it flat.

Do this by soaking your wavy panels in glycerine-based veneer treatment. Once it's saturated, start forming a big sandwich. This begins with a

piece of flat 3/4" melamine-covered MDF, cut at least 1/8" bigger all around than the sheet of veneer. On top of this, place a sheet of Fiberglas™ window screen and six sheets of newspaper to prevent bonding between the paper and burl. Place the wet veneer on the screen, then complete the sandwich with

Fill larger holes in the burl veneer with cut-outs of similarly colored veneer. Place a piece of masking tape behind the hole and glue the new piece in place.

more screen, newspaper and plywood. Clamp everything tight with a set of curved cauls to form a press.

Replace the newspaper after four hours and again after another eight. Do this twice a day for about a week. In extreme cases, you may have to go through this entire process twice, but it's well worth the effort as it makes the rest of the veneering work much easier.

A slick way to book-match the veneer with a straight, clean joint is to sandwich the two pieces between MDF panels. Hold them tightly together and slice them off on the table saw.

When the veneer is dry, fill any holes, holding your piece up to the light to spot them. Filling them now prevents them from trapping gobs of glue later. On larger holes, take trimmings from the edge of the sheet where it will be cut off, and place them on your bench. Align the hole over them, match the colors and trim to fit. Use masking tape on the top side to hold these trimmings in place.

Now clamp the veneer back in its press and keep it there until you're ready to glue the veneer to the plywood panel.

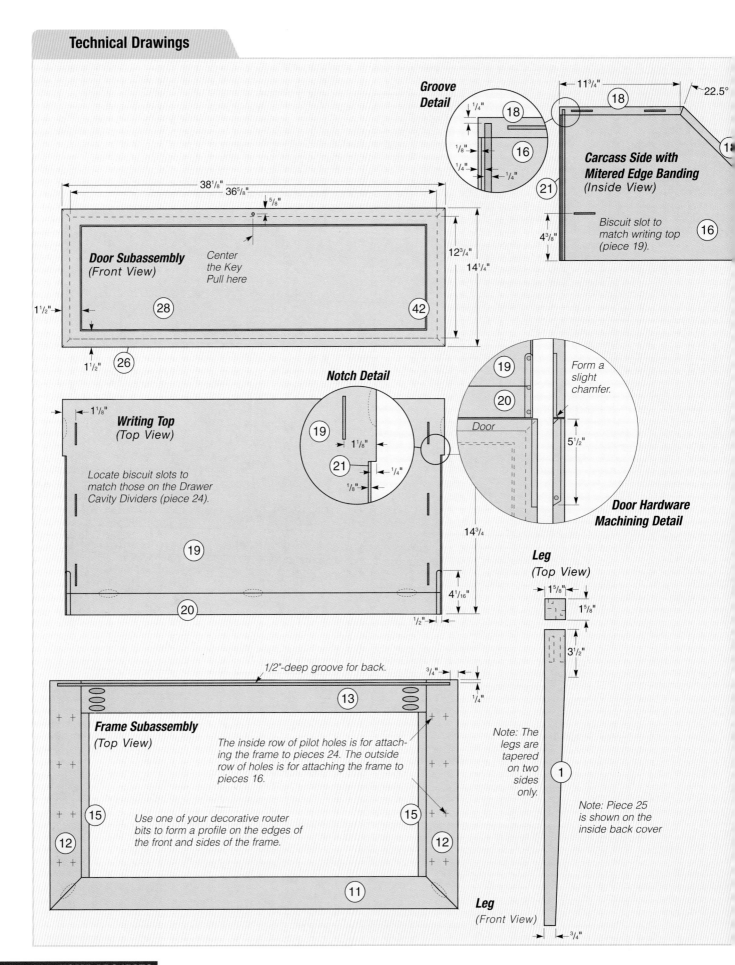

Groove Detail

1/4"

18

1/8"

16

1/4"

1/4"

11 3/4"

18

22.5°

18

Carcass Side with Mitered Edge Banding
(Inside View)

21

4 3/8"

Biscuit slot to match writing top (piece 19).

16

38 1/8"

36 5/8"

5/8"

Door Subassembly
(Front View)

Center the Key Pull here

12 3/4"

14 1/4"

28

42

1 1/2"

1 1/2"

26

19

20

Form a slight chamfer.

Door

5 1/2"

Door Hardware Machining Detail

Notch Detail

19

21

1 1/8"

1/4"

1/8"

1 1/8"

Writing Top
(Top View)

Locate biscuit slots to match those on the Drawer Cavity Dividers (piece 24).

19

20

14 3/4

4 1/16"

1/2"

Leg
(Top View)

1 5/8"

1 5/8"

3 1/2"

Note: The legs are tapered on two sides only.

1

Note: Piece 25 is shown on the inside back cover

1/2"-deep groove for back.

3/4"

13

1/4"

Frame Subassembly
(Top View)

The inside row of pilot holes is for attaching the frame to pieces 24. The outside row of holes is for attaching the frame to pieces 16.

15

15

12

12

Use one of your decorative router bits to form a profile on the edges of the front and sides of the frame.

11

Leg
(Front View)

3/4"

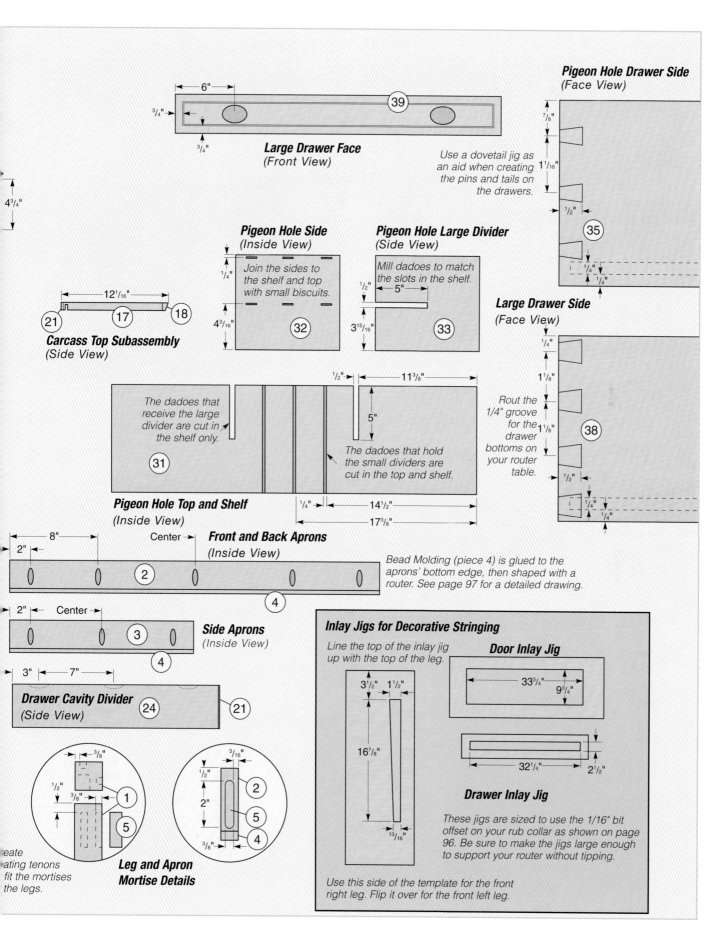

Pigeon Hole Drawer Side
(Face View)

7/8"

1 1/16"

1/2"

(35)

1/4"

1/4"

Use a dovetail jig as
an aid when creating
the pins and tails on
the drawers.

6"

3/4"

(39)

3/4"

Large Drawer Face
(Front View)

4 3/4"

Pigeon Hole Side
(Inside View)

Pigeon Hole Large Divider
(Side View)

1/4"

Join the sides to
the shelf and top
with small biscuits.

4 3/16"

(32)

Mill dadoes to match
the slots in the shelf.

1/2"

5"

3 15/16"

(33)

Large Drawer Side
(Face View)

1/4"

1 1/8"

1 1/8"

(38)

Rout the
1/4" groove
for the
drawer
bottoms on
your router
table.

1/2"

1/4"

1/4"

12 1/16"

(21) (17) (18)

Carcass Top Subassembly
(Side View)

1/2"

11 3/8"

5"

The dadoes that
receive the large
divider are cut in
the shelf only.

(31)

The dadoes that hold
the small dividers are
cut in the top and shelf.

1/4"

14 1/2"

17 3/8"

Pigeon Hole Top and Shelf
(Inside View)

8"

2"

Center

Front and Back Aprons
(Inside View)

(2)

(4)

Bead Molding (piece 4) is glued to the
aprons' bottom edge, then shaped with a
router. See page 97 for a detailed drawing.

2"

Center

(3)

Side Aprons
(Inside View)

(4)

3"

7"

Drawer Cavity Divider
(Side View)

(24)

(21)

3/8"

1/2"

3/8"

(1)

(5)

3/16"

1/2"

2"

3/8"

(2)

(5)

(4)

...eate
...ating tenons
...fit the mortises
...the legs.

**Leg and Apron
Mortise Details**

Inlay Jigs for Decorative Stringing

Line the top of the inlay jig
up with the top of the leg.

Door Inlay Jig

33 3/4"

9 3/4"

3 1/2"

1 1/2"

16 7/8"

13/16"

32 1/4"

2 1/2"

Drawer Inlay Jig

These jigs are sized to use the 1/16" bit
offset on your rub collar as shown on page
96. Be sure to make the jigs large enough
to support your router without tipping.

Use this side of the template for the front
right leg. Flip it over for the front left leg.

Entry Bench

Each sloppy winter day, wouldn't it be great to have a place to sit down while you pull on your boots or galoshes?" If you've seen plenty of winters already, the need probably grows as you age. And what about extra storage — wouldn't it be wonderful to have a spot for gloves and hats, too? Maybe this is the year to do something about it. Here's a handy little entry bench that will meet all your needs and then some — and it's a gem of a project to work on. The front and sides are standard raised panels, the lid opens for storage, and the bench is a perfect fit for any busy foyer, large or small.

Building the Frames First

The most logical starting point for this project is to create the raised panel frames, as these form the skeleton of the bench. For this operation, you'll need to borrow or invest in a stile and rail set. That's a router bit (or a matched pair of router bits) that mills perfectly mated profiles on stiles and rails. You can find them in beading, ogee, chamfer or concave profiles.

Rip stock for all the stiles and rails (pieces 1 through 8) about 1/16" larger in each dimension than the specific measurements shown in the *Material List* on page 108. Joint the stock to final dimensions, then trim the ends to length.

Using the Stile and Rail Set

Lay out your stiles and rails on the workbench (just butt them together for now), and mark the matching pairs where they meet. We like to use AA, BB and so on, to keep the parts oriented correctly during the milling process.

Chuck what we call the bead and

SHOULD YOU MAKE OR BUY RAISED PANELS?

We'll confess a temptation to buy raised panels for this entry bench rather than build them. Depending on where you shop, you can have your panels made by a custom cabinet shop for not much more than the cost of materials — especially when you factor in around $200 for buying the raised panel and rail and stile bit sets to do it yourself. If you're just getting into woodworking, or if you don't own a router table and mid-size or larger router yet, buying the panels is wise. However, if you're wondering if making the panels and frames is worth the fuss, we'll definitely say yes! This may be because we're really purists at heart and just plain enjoy the process of making a project from beginning to end. There's also something to be said for trying out new bits and techniques now and again. That's what keeps woodworking fresh and interesting. And, using bits for building raised panels doesn't require nerves of steel. Just follow the bit manufacturer's instructions carefully and work safely.

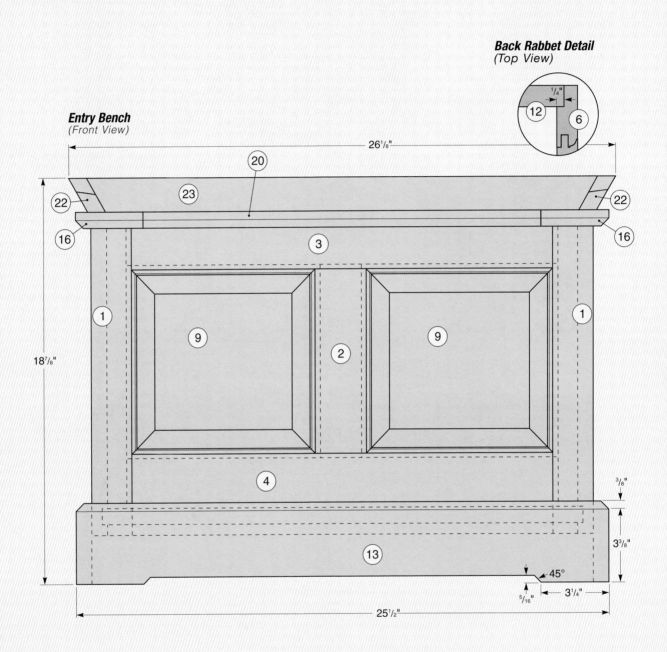

Back Rabbet Detail
(Top View)

Entry Bench
(Front View)

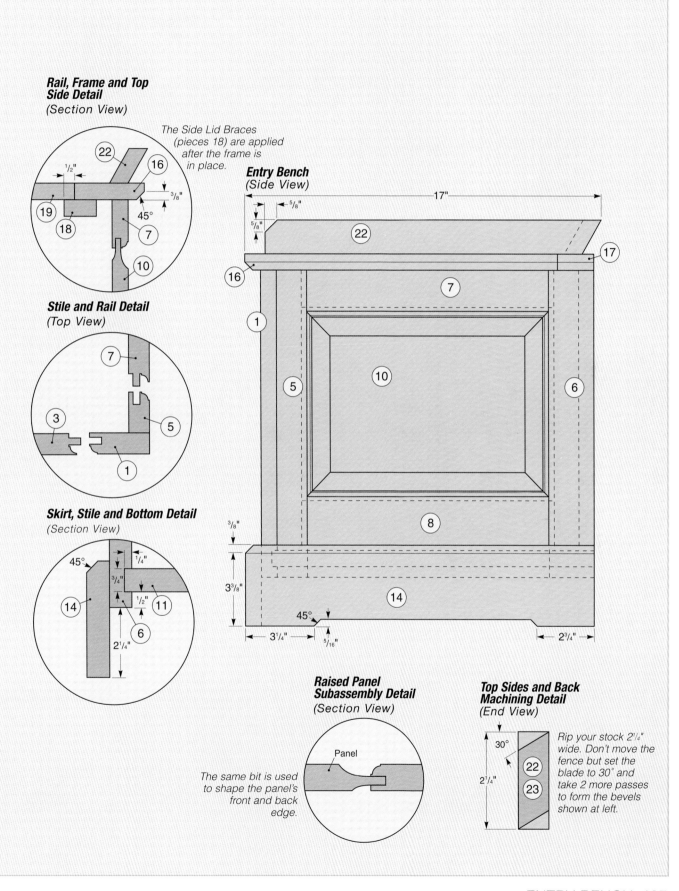

Rail, Frame and Top Side Detail
(Section View)

The Side Lid Braces (pieces 18) are applied after the frame is in place.

Stile and Rail Detail
(Top View)

Skirt, Stile and Bottom Detail
(Section View)

Entry Bench
(Side View)

Raised Panel Subassembly Detail
(Section View)

The same bit is used to shape the panel's front and back edge.

Panel

Top Sides and Back Machining Detail
(End View)

Rip your stock 2¹/₄" wide. Don't move the fence but set the blade to 30° and take 2 more passes to form the bevels shown at left.

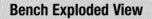

groove cutter (see *Figure 1*) into your router and set the bit height. Practice on a piece of scrap (the exact dimensions as your actual stock) until the profile matches the elevations shown in the *Technical Drawings* on the preceding two pages. This cutter will create the bead on the edge of the stile, plus the groove for the panel. It's a good idea to make these cuts in two or three passes, to get a clean profile safely. Mill one edge of each rail and the six outer stiles, and both edges of the front center stile. Then install the cope and tenoning cutter (see *Figure 2*): This might be a separate bit, or a rearrangement of your first set-up. Look at the manufacturer's instructions for details. Use some scrap to set the height and test your fit, then mill both ends of the front center stile and both ends of each of the rails.

Making the Panels

Glue two or three well-matched boards together for each panel (pieces 9 and 10). Make sure to select stock with color and grain that is so similar the final joint becomes almost invisible. After cutting the panels to size, you can mill both the front and back profiles with the same router bit as shown on page 110. We used a vertical panel raising bit because its cutting edges are closer to the shaft than traditional horizontal bits, which makes it more stable: the tip of the bit actually travels at a slower speed. You can also use a vertical bit safely in a mid-size router.

Make each profile in several passes, with your router set to an appropriate speed. Machine the panels across the grain first, to minimize tearout, and clamp a high auxiliary fence to your router table fence to stabilize the workpiece.

MATERIAL LIST

		T x W x L
1	Front Outer Stiles (2)	$^3/_4$" x $2^3/_{16}$" x $14^1/_4$"
2	Front Center Stile (1)	$^3/_4$" x $2^7/_{16}$" x $8^{13}/_{16}$"
3	Front Top Rail (1)	$^3/_4$" x $2^3/_{16}$" x $20^1/_8$"
4	Front Bottom Rail (1)	$^3/_4$" x $3^3/_4$" x $28^1/_2$"
5	Side Front Stiles (2)	$^3/_4$" x $1^7/_{16}$" x $14^1/_4$"
6	Side Back Stiles (2)	$^3/_4$" x $2^3/_{16}$" x $14^1/_4$"
7	Side Top Rails (2)	$^3/_4$" x $2^3/_{16}$" x $12^1/_8$"
8	Side Bottom Rails (2)	$^3/_4$" x $3^3/_4$" x $12^1/_8$"
9	Front Panels (2)	$^3/_4$" x $8^7/_8$" x $8^{11}/_{16}$"
10	Side Panels (2)	$^3/_4$" x 12" x $8^{11}/_{16}$"
11	Bottom (1)	$^3/_4$" x $15^5/_8$" x $23^1/_4$"
12	Back (1)	$^3/_4$" x 13" x $23^1/_4$"
13	Front Skirt (1)	$^3/_4$" x $3^3/_4$" x $25^1/_2$"
14	Side Skirts (2)	$^3/_4$" x $3^3/_4$" x $16^3/_4$"
15	Lid Brace, Front (1)	$^3/_4$" x $^1/_2$" x $22^1/_2$"
16	Top Frame, Sides (2)	$^3/_4$" x $3^1/_4$" x 15"
17	Top Frame, Back (1)	$^3/_4$" x $1^3/_4$" x $25^1/_2$"
18	Lid Brace, Sides (2)	$^3/_4$" x $1^1/_2$" x 14"
19	Lid (1)	$^3/_4$" x $12^7/_8$" x $18^7/_8$"
20	Lid Cap (1)	$^3/_4$" x 2" x $18^7/_8$"
21	Lid Hinge (1)	$1^1/_2$" *Brass piano*
22	Top Sides (2)	$^3/_4$" x $2^1/_4$" x $16^1/_8$"
23	Top Back (1)	$^3/_4$" x $2^1/_4$" x $26^1/_8$"

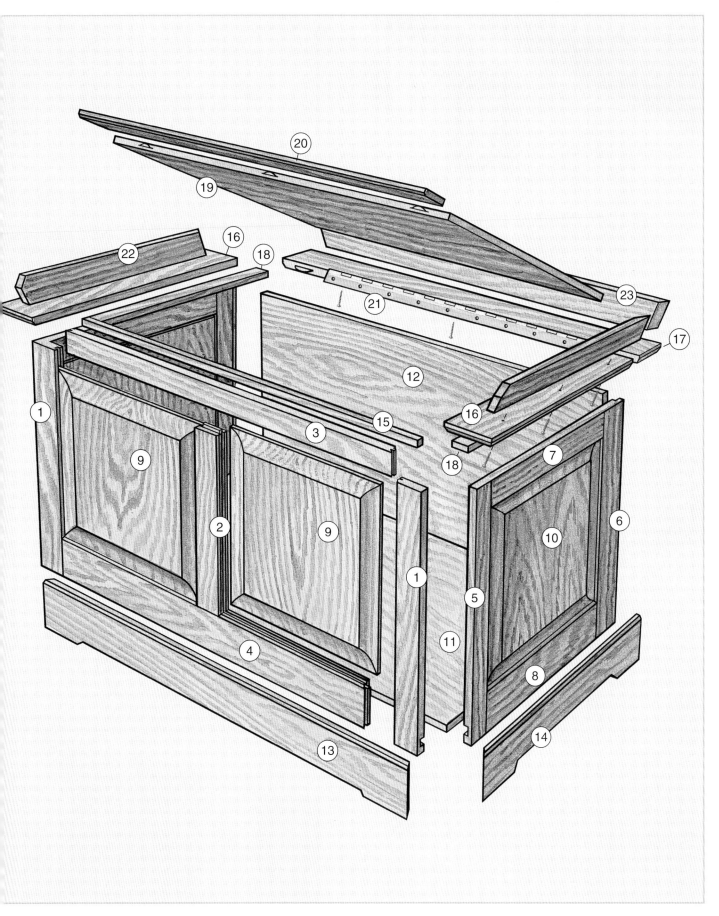

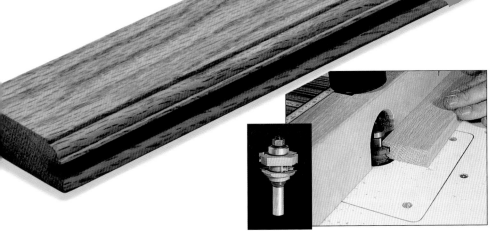

Assembling the Frames and Panels

Sand the frame elements and apply stain (if you plan on staining your bench) to the panels; this will prevent color gaps later if the panels move after finishing. Glue and clamp the frames together, with the panels floating freely in their grooves. If you glue the panels in place, they may split as the wood reacts to changes in humidity.

Make sure the assemblies are flat and square as you apply the clamps. You can add a sandbag, if needed. When the glue has set, plow dadoes for the bottom (piece 11) and rab-

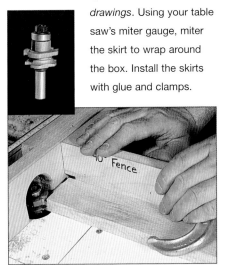

Figure 1: Stile and rail bits are the best way to create the mating joints characteristic of frame and panel construction. With your first pass you'll form a bead and groove.

Adding the Skirt and Top

When the carcass glue is dry, rip and joint a board that's long enough to yield the front and side skirts (pieces 13 and 14). Mill a chamfer on its top edge (see *Technical Drawings*) using a router bit. Machine the three skirts to length, then band-saw reliefs on their bottom edges as shown on the drawings. Using your table saw's miter gauge, miter the skirt to wrap around the box. Install the skirts with glue and clamps.

bets for the back panel (piece 12). Their dimensions and locations are shown on the *Technical Drawings*.

Glue and clamp the side frames to the front frame as shown in the *Exploded View* on page 109. While a simple butt joint is quite adequate here, you might want to use biscuits to help align the parts. Slide the bottom into its dado to help keep things square, then predrill for a couple of 4d finish nails in each side, to hold the back in place while it's being glued and clamped. (For stability, we used oak veneered MDF for the bottom and back.) Set and fill the nail heads and sand the filler smooth when it's dry.

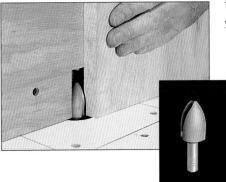

Figure 2: The rail ends are machined to fit into the grooves formed by the first cutter. Then use a raised panel bit (below) to shape both sides of the panels.

Temporarily clamp a plywood straight-edge to the carcass to keep the skirts aligned as you clamp them in place. Glue and clamp the front lid brace (pieces 15) in place next. Move on to the top frame (pieces 16 and 17). The bottom edge of this frame is chamfered to match the top edges of the skirts. Chamfer the ends of the frame back, then glue it to the carcass. With the frame back already in place, it's a little easier to locate the chamfers on the edges of the top frame sides for a perfect fit. Use biscuits on the ends of the frame sides to help glue and clamp them into place. Now, position and glue the lid side braces (pieces 18) under the frame sides.

Installing the Lid

The lid is a panel of veneered MDF (piece 19) with a strip of solid oak (piece 20) edge-glued to it. Pick up the skirt's chamfer on the front edge of this edging, then dry-fit the seat (allow for the depth of the hinge as you do). Trim the hinge (piece 21) to length, then predrill for its screws and install it.

Follow the directions in the *sidebar* on the next page to make the top sides and back (pieces 22 and 23), then glue and screw these pieces in place. Predrill for the screws and countersink their heads.

Finishing Up

Remove the lid hinge and sand all parts down through the grits to 220. Apply the stain of your choice (we used a red oak tint, to even out the wood's natural colors), followed by three coats of clear finish. Reinstall the hinge, and you're finally ready to put on your boots in comfort.

MAKING SHADOWBOX MITER CUTS

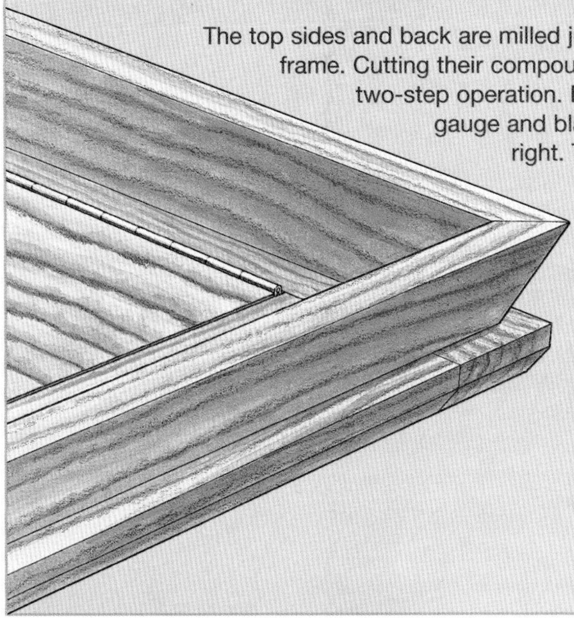

The top sides and back are milled just like a shadowbox picture frame. Cutting their compound miters on a table saw is a two-step operation. Begin by adjusting the miter gauge and blade angles using the chart at right. The Desired Angle is the angle the seat side makes with the top (in this case, 60°). Cut one end of each frame piece with the miter gauge set for a left-to-right downward slope. Then reverse the miter gauge exactly 90° and reposition the frame segment for the cut at the other end. Make sure the piece is oriented with the toe of the miter ahead of the heel, then make your cuts.

Desired Incline	Blade Angle	Miter Gauge Angle
5°	43¾°	85°
10°	44¼°	80¼°
15°	43¼°	75½°
20°	41¾°	71¼°
25°	40°	67°
30°	37¾°	63½°
35°	35¼°	60¼°
40°	32½°	57¼°
45°	30°	54¾°
50°	27°	52½°
55°	24°	50¾°
60°	21°	49°

Quick Tip

Three-spoke Clamp Pads

Positioning a pad between the jaw of a bar clamp and the assembly you're building can be tricky. Trying to keep the clamps in position — especially when you're at the other end of a large cabinet or paner — can be downright frustrating. These three-spoke pads solve both problems at once. Two of the three spokes become the stand's legs (they even allow for uneven surfaces), while the third spoke automatically centers itself as a hands-free pad between the metal of the clamp jaw and the workpiece being glued up. No more pads slipping out of place, and these will never get lost.

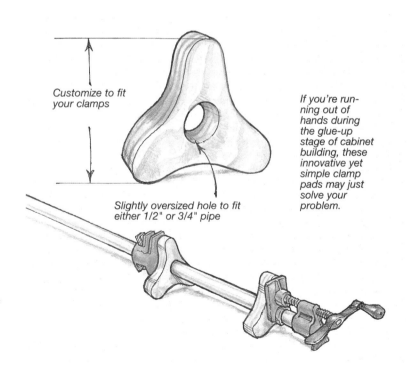

Customize to fit your clamps

Slightly oversized hole to fit either 1/2" or 3/4" pipe

If you're running out of hands during the glue-up stage of cabinet building, these innovative yet simple clamp pads may just solve your problem.

Rock-Solid Trestle Table

Contributing editor Rick White's neighbor Roger once commissioned him to replace the family's three-generation-old dining room table. Despite being a smart guy, Roger apparently had spent most of fifty years banging his shins on the low beam that held the table's legs in place. A half century of accumulated wisdom — and bruises — finally prompted a change. The result of Rick's efforts is the trestle table you see here. Its sensible design continues to put distance between Roger and his table pains.

Rick's trestle table incorporates several design elements the original lacked. It had to be large enough to seat six comfortably — eight in a pinch. The neighbors also wanted a table that would come apart and go back together easily (since their dining room doubles as a dance floor on Thursday nights).

Roger wasn't ready to move away from the solid-oak trestle style he was so accustomed to, but his wife Joan wanted a top that wouldn't feature "crumb catchers" and a slightly fancier look. Of course, both wanted to keep the cost way down. This last directive probably sounds familiar if you've ever built a project for a neighbor!

The first thing Rick recommended was breadboard ends, for two reasons. First, the breadboard ends add a few inches of depth

Figure 1: Use your table saw to make the straight cuts in the feet, then switch to the band saw to complete the curved cuts.

to the ends of the tables — additional leg clearance for anyone seated there — but more important, breadboard ends allow the legs to be moved further in without risking cupping at the ends. To address Joan's concern, they (along with a little extra router work) tend to upscale the overall appear-

ance. Rick also kept the costs down by specifying readily available, 3/4"-thick hardwood stock. If there's a lumberyard of any consequence near you, finding material for this table should pose no difficulties.

Starting with the Feet

When it came to the large mortises in the feet, the decision to build with 3/4"-thick stock made for easier work. The feet consist of three thicknesses of wood face-glued together, so making the large bottom mortises meant simply leaving a hole in the middle of each foot, as shown in the *Foot Mortise and Leg Tenon Detail* on page 117.

Start building the feet by cutting six laminations (pieces 1) to shape. Make the straight cuts on your table saw, as shown in *Figure 1*, then finish up each cut by bandsawing the curves to shape.

After the laminations are cut to shape,

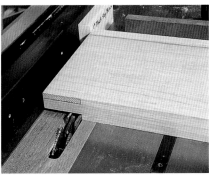

Figure 2: A spacer clamped to the fence lines up the legs for tenoning and prevents binding by keeping the work away from the fence.

Table Exploded View

Beading Detail

18
18

18

18

18

10

11

9

19

12

16

17

4

4

15

14

16

7

16

13

12

Roundover and Glue Trap Detail

6

8

7

3

2

2

3

2

Beam Subassembly Detail

6   6

7

8

2

1

1

5

MATERIAL LIST

		T x W x L
1	Feet Laminations (6)	$\frac{3}{4}$" x 4" x 38"
2	Leg Laminations (4)	$\frac{3}{4}$" x 8$\frac{1}{2}$" x 26$\frac{3}{4}$"
3	Leg Moldings (4)	$\frac{3}{4}$" x 1$\frac{1}{2}$" x 18$\frac{1}{2}$"
4	Tabletop Support Laminations (4)	$\frac{3}{4}$" x 4$\frac{7}{8}$" x 24"
5	Leg Dowels (2)	$\frac{3}{8}$" *Dia.* x 1$\frac{1}{4}$" "
6	Beam Laminations (2)	$\frac{3}{4}$" x 5$\frac{1}{2}$" x 43$\frac{3}{8}$"
7	Beam Moldings (2)	$\frac{3}{4}$" x 1$\frac{1}{2}$" x 43$\frac{3}{8}$"
8	Tapered KD Fittings (2)	6" *Steel*
9	Tabletop (1)	$\frac{3}{4}$" x 40" x 74$\frac{7}{8}$" *(includes tongues)*
10	Tabletop Cleats (2)	$\frac{3}{4}$" x $\frac{3}{4}$" x 68$\frac{7}{8}$"
11	Tabletop Moldings (2)	$\frac{3}{4}$" x 1$\frac{1}{2}$" x 68$\frac{7}{8}$"
12	Support Bracket Sides (4)	$\frac{3}{4}$" x 3" x 38$\frac{1}{4}$"
13	Support Bracket Bases (2)	$\frac{3}{4}$" x 3$\frac{3}{8}$" x 38$\frac{1}{4}$"
14	Support Bracket Screws (20)	#6 x 1$\frac{1}{8}$"
15	Support Bracket Washers (20)	*Countersunk*
16	Swivel Mirror Screws (4)	$\frac{3}{8}$" *Brass (with threaded inserts)*
17	Alignment Blocks (4)	$\frac{3}{4}$" x 1$\frac{1}{2}$" x 2"
18	Endcap Laminations (4)	$\frac{3}{4}$" x 5$\frac{7}{8}$" x 41$\frac{3}{4}$"
19	Endcap Dowels (6)	$\frac{3}{8}$" *Dia.* x 1$\frac{1}{4}$"

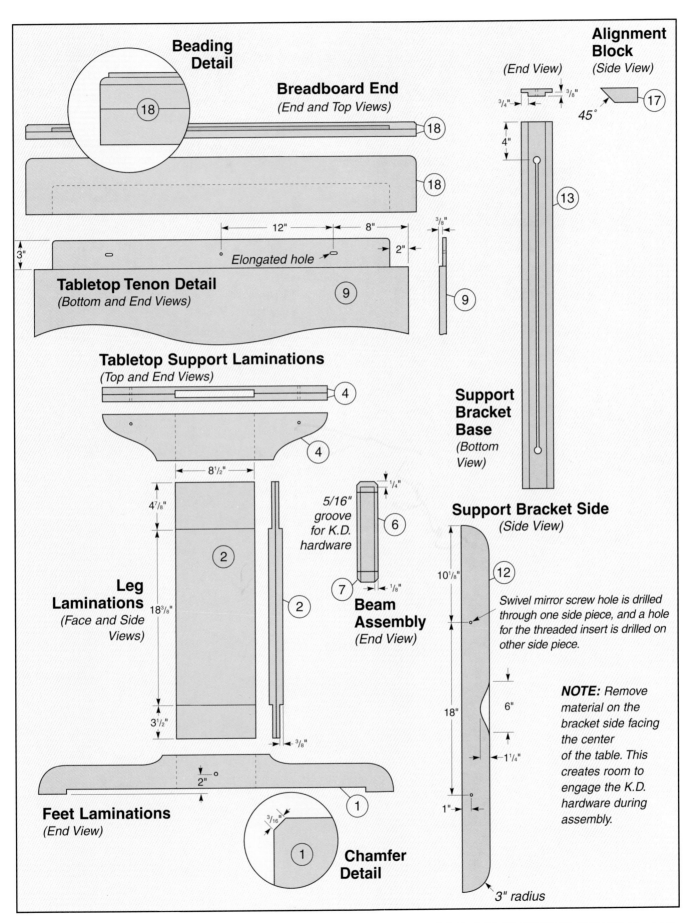

Beading Detail

(18)

Breadboard End
(End and Top Views)

(18)

(18)

Alignment Block
(Side View)

(End View)

3/4" 3/8"

4"

45°

(17)

(13)

12"   8"

3/8"

3"

Elongated hole

2"

Tabletop Tenon Detail
(Bottom and End Views)

(9)

(9)

Support Bracket Base
(Bottom View)

Tabletop Support Laminations
(Top and End Views)

(4)

(4)

8 1/2"

4 7/8"

(2)

(2)

18 3/8"

3 1/2"

Leg Laminations
(Face and Side Views)

5/16" groove for K.D. hardware

1/4"

(6)

(7)

1/8"

Beam Assembly
(End View)

Support Bracket Side
(Side View)

10 1/8"

(12)

Swivel mirror screw hole is drilled through one side piece, and a hole for the threaded insert is drilled on other side piece.

18"

6"

1 1/4"

NOTE: *Remove material on the bracket side facing the center of the table. This creates room to engage the K.D. hardware during assembly.*

3/8"

2"

Feet Laminations
(End View)

3/16"

(1)

(1)

Chamfer Detail

1"

3" radius

Figure 3: After rounding over all four long edges of the leg moldings, create two V-shaped glue control grooves in each back face.

remove the center sections of two of them (see *inside front cover*). These instant mortises will be a bit wider than the leg tenons, which allows the laminated legs to shrink and expand with seasonal changes in humidity.

Glue and clamp the feet together, making sure the ends and the top edges are flush as you tighten your clamps. When the glue is dry, scrape off any excess before jointing the top and bottom edges and drum-sanding the curved areas. Then run a bearing-guided chamfering bit along the top edge of each foot.

Making the Tenoned Legs

Each of the legs (pieces 2) is made from a pair of face-glued boards, edged with a custom molding. After cutting and jointing

the boards to size, glue and clamp the bark sides together, as discussed in the *sidebar, below*. After the glue sets, joint the edges before rounding over the vertical edges of each leg with a 1/4"-radius roundover bit.

Now lay out the tenons on the ends of the legs (the top and bottom are different thicknesses). Cut them with a dado head, using your table saw's miter gauge and a spacer block (see *Figure 2*).

Rip and joint the leg moldings (pieces 3) to dimension, then use the same roundover bit you used on the legs to shape all four of its long edges. Stay at the router table a minute longer to mill two glue traps in the back face of each piece of molding (see *Figure 3*), using the tip of a V-groove bit.

Forming the Tabletop Supports

While the table's feet are three laminations thick, there is no structural or aesthetic reason for such a large build-up in the tabletop supports. To save time and materials, Rick went with just two laminations here.

Creating the tenons in these supports is a simple matter of cutting a 3/8"-deep dado in each lamination (piece 4), then gluing two pairs together (see *inside front cover*). Use the same table saw technique you used for the leg tenons to create these dadoes. Dry-fit them to the legs as you go, to ensure a correct fit.

Figure 4: After cutting the glued-up tabletop supports to shape, drum-sand the curved edges smooth and even.

Transfer the Scaled Pattern from the *inside front cover* to each support lamination, then band-saw all of them to shape. Do this after cutting the dadoes, because this step is more forgiving — a slip here is easier to repair than a crooked mortise.

Glue and clamp the two sets of support laminations together in the correct orientation. After the glue dries, use your drum sander to remove the band saw marks, as shown in *Figure 4*.

Assembling the Legs

Dry-fit the leg tenons in the feet and tabletop support mortises. The fit should be snug on the wide faces and leave a 1/16" gap at either end to allow for movement (see *Figure 5*). When you're satisfied with the fit, glue the feet to the legs.

GRAIN ORIENTATION IN FACE-GLUED BOARDS

Through the ages, countless woodshop students have discovered, (often to their dismay), that wood retains a tendency to curl away from the center of the tree.

Christian Becksvoort explained this best in his excellent book, *In Harmony with Wood*: "On a plain sawn board, [cupping] is usually manifested in the concave surface forming away from the tree."

So, to put it simply, gluing the bark sides together, as shown here, will decrease the chance that the edges will peel apart later. For rift- or quartersawn lumber, grain orientation is less of an issue for face-gluing because the growth rings run nearly perpendicular to the board faces.

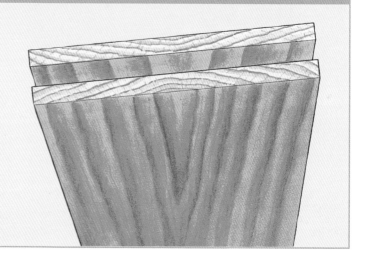

While the glue is wet, lock each tenon into its mortise with a 3/8"-diameter dowel (piece 5: See *inside front cover* for hole and dowel locations). Each dowel should penetrate the inside foot lamination as well as the leg tenon laminations.

Before gluing the tabletop supports in place, trim the moldings to length. Glue and clamp them in place, keeping the glue between the traps you milled earlier. When the glue is dry, install the tabletop supports with glue and clamps.

Milling the Beam

Remember poor old Roger's shins? The beam on this table is located high enough to avoid even the tallest diner's ankles. It is made from two face-glued laminations (pieces 6) that are edged with square moldings (pieces 7). Glue and clamp all four elements together. After the glue dries, ease the long edges with your chamfering bit (see *page 115*).

Stay with the router to cut mortises in the ends of the beam for the tapered steel knock-down fittings (pieces 8) that hold the beam to the legs. Use a bearing-guided rabbeting bit to make these mortises, as shown in *Figure 6*. Their dimensions can be found on *page 115*. To center the tapers

Foot Mortise and Leg Tenon Detail

in the mortises, Rick found that pairs of thin drill bits made perfect spacers (*Figure 6, inset*) while predrilling for the screw holes.

Making the Tabletop

While veneered plywood is one choice for the tabletop (piece 9), Rick's neighbors opted for traditional solid oak. For a stable top, alternate the end grain of each board — but don't get religious about it. There's nothing sadder than an exquisite face of a board staring at the floor for a couple of generations because someone got carried away on a simple rule of thumb. After the glue has dried, scrape the excess and sand thoroughly. Use a straightedge and a straight bit in your router to trim the tabletop to its exact width and length, making each cut in several passes. To minimize tearout, use a fresh straight or spiral carbide bit.

Stay with your straightedge and router to cut the 3/8"-thick tenons on the ends of the tabletop (see *page 115*). Then remove 2" from the end of each tenon with your jigsaw, and smooth any tearout with a file.

Build up the tabletop's edges by gluing and clamping 3/4"-square cleats (pieces 10) along each long edge. While the glue dries, use a beading bit to form the edge of the moldings (pieces 11) as shown in the drawing on *page 118*. Glue and clamp these moldings in place, and, when the glue

dries, scrape off the excess and belt-sand them flush. Before you leave the tabletop, sand a 3/8" radius on each of the four tenon corners.

Forming the Tabletop Cleats

Use a pair of U-shaped support brackets to lock the top to the legsets. Each bracket is made up of two sides (pieces 12) and a base (pieces 13). Following the dimensions shown on *page 115*, use a dado head in your table saw to create rabbets on the long edges of each base (see *Figure 7*).

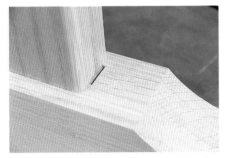

Figure 5: Leave 1/16" play on either side of the legs when you glue them into their mortises, to allow for wood movement. Leg moldings will eventually cover these gaps.

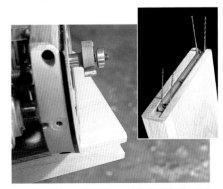

Figure 6: Use a bearing-guided rabbeting bit to cut mortises for the steel tapers. Pairs of matched drill bits help center the tapers while you predrill for their screws.

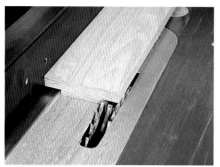

Figure 7: Use a dado head in your table saw to cut rabbets in the support bracket bases. Two support bracket sides will fit into the rabbets.

Band-saw and sand the ends of the support bracket sides to the shape shown on *page 115*, then glue and clamp the brackets together. Drill a 3/4" hole 4" from

the ends of each bracket base, then chuck a 1/4" straight bit in your router to cut a groove between these holes (see *Figure 8*). The large holes at the ends of the grooves will stop the base pieces from splitting.

Assemble the legs and beam and center them on the upturned top. Mark the locations of the legs (make sure they are perpendicular to the edges of the tabletop), then remove the legset. Use your marks to locate the support brackets, then predrill for ten screws (pieces 14) in each bracket base. Use washers (pieces 15) to seat the screws along the groove: the washers will accommodate expansion and contraction of the

40"-wide top through the seasons.

Replace the legset, this time seating it upside down in the support brackets and centering it side to side. Drill two holes (see *page 115*) in each of the outside support bracket sides, continuing through the tabletop supports (don't go all the way through the inside support brackets). Remove the legsets and enlarge the holes in them — but not in the brackets — to receive the threaded inserts that come with the swivel mirror screws (pieces 16). Screw the inserts home and tighten everything up with the swivel mirror screws. At this point, you can add the optional alignment blocks

AN EASY APPROACH TO BUILDING BREADBOARD ENDS

Breadboard ends are caps employing grain running perpendicular to a tabletop. This warp-fighting joint typically features a mortise slightly wider than its tenon to accommodate wood movement. Start by laying out the 3/8"-deep mortises (*pages 158-160*), and remove the waste with a straight bit chucked in your router. Clamp the two laminations (pieces 18) together, and dry-fit them to a tenon. When you've got a good fit, glue the laminations together. Be sure the mortises are perfectly aligned. After the glue dries, joint both long edges before sanding a 3/4" radius on the outside corners of each endcap. The endcaps are intentionally 1/4" longer than the tabletop is wide, to allow for expansion in the top. Shape the top outside edge of each breadboard end with the same beading bit you used on the tabletop edge molding. Then slide the ends onto the tabletop tenons and drill three 1/4" holes up from the bottom, at the locations shown on *pages 158-160*. Remove the endcaps and elongate the two outside holes in each tenon, as shown here. Reinstall the ends and secure them by gluing the three dowels (pieces 19) in place. The slotted holes allow the tenons to move a little inside the endcaps' mortises.

Remove the endcaps and elongate the two outside holes in each tenon (see details on *pages 158-160*).

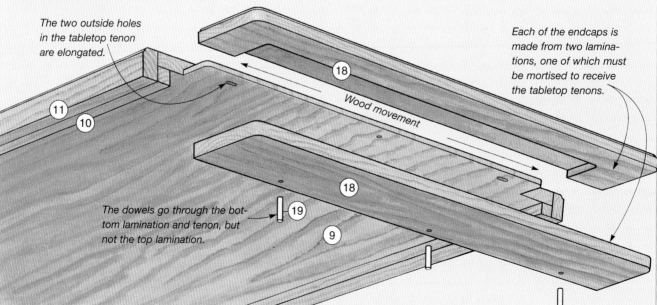

The two outside holes in the tabletop tenon are elongated.

Each of the endcaps is made from two laminations, one of which must be mortised to receive the tabletop tenons.

Wood movement

The dowels go through the bottom lamination and tenon, but not the top lamination.

Figure 8: Create the screw slots in the cleat bases in several passes, raising the 1/4" bit 1/8" with each pass.

(pieces 17, see *page 115*). They're handy for quickly lining things up if you'll be knocking down the table often. All that really remains now is the breadboard ends, and those are described on the preceding page.

Finishing Up

Roger and Joan wanted a clear finish that would showcase the white oak and still be impervious to spills, dropped silverware and other dining room hazards. In the end it came down to satin polyurethane or Danish oil. While everyone loved the look and feel of the oil, Rick still advised the poly finish for its harder finish and greater durability.

Rick applied five coats of finish to the top and three to the legset. The top's underside received two coats — it's always smart to coat both faces of a top to keep moisture moving in and out of both faces evenly. First coats of finish on all the surfaces were cut with 25% thinner to act as a sanding sealer, and all but the topcoat were steel-wooled between applications. The end result was a smooth low-luster finish that was exactly what the clients were looking for: A classic piece of furniture completely at home in a 100-year-old rural farmhouse.

This sturdy trestle table is ready to knockdown in minutes: it comes apart and sets up without tools.

Quick Tip

End Caps Keep Panels from Buckling

Here's a way to keep solid-wood panels from buckling when they're edge-glued and clamped. Make custom end caps by plowing grooves the same dimension as the panel stock in a couple of 2x4s. Apply a strip of tape in each groove or use paste wax to prevent any glue squeeze-out from bonding the caps to the panel. Then, fit the end caps over the panel ends to keep everything lined up.

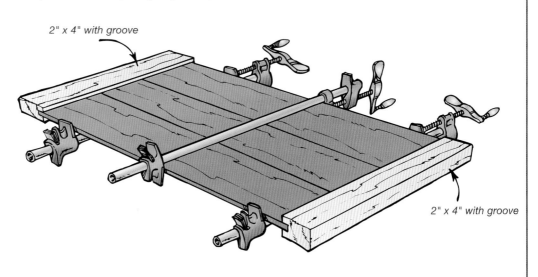

2" x 4" with groove

2" x 4" with groove

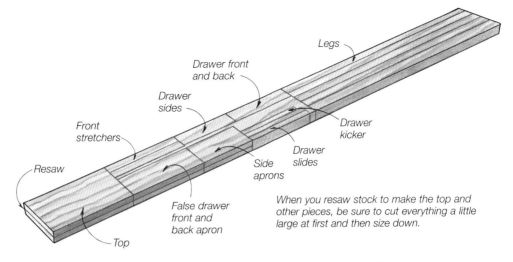

Legs

Drawer front
and back

Drawer
sides

Drawer
kicker

Front
stretchers

Drawer
slides

Side
aprons

Resaw

False drawer
front and
back apron

When you resaw stock to make the top and
other pieces, be sure to cut everything a little
large at first and then size down.

Top

One Board Hall Table

O ne board doesn't actually describe the style or look of this table, but it is a pretty
complete description of the material that goes into it. If you haven't been hoard-
ing special pieces of stock (maybe you're just getting started with this hobby or haven't
yet become a "wood-aholic") then shopping is really simple. A seven-inch-wide, eight-foot-
long piece of 8/4 stock is all you will need. This one board approach creates a beautiful
table with consistent figure and color. We made our version of this project from a wonderful
piece of Lake Superior flame birch.

Dividing and Cutting

Take a look at the "one board" diagram,
above, and begin cutting the longer pieces of stock
to their rough lengths, but a little oversized to start.
Cut the legs (pieces 1) into squared-up full leg
blanks for tapering later and, using the *Material List*
on page 123 as a guide, cut the rest of the pieces
to size. Some pieces will need to be resawn and
planed to their proper dimensions.

Arrange the leg pieces so the best faces will
be viewed on the table. Mark the tops of the legs to
keep this orientation. Lay out and cut the mortises
in the aprons and stretchers (pieces 2 through 4)
and matching mortises in the legs (check the
Elevation Drawings on page 122 for locations and
placement details). Use your drill press to remove
most of the waste and clean up the mortises with a
sharp chisel. On your dry fit, you'll notice that the
legs are offset from the aprons just a bit. Now size
and cut the large and small floating tenons (pieces
5 and 6) to fit the mortises you just made.

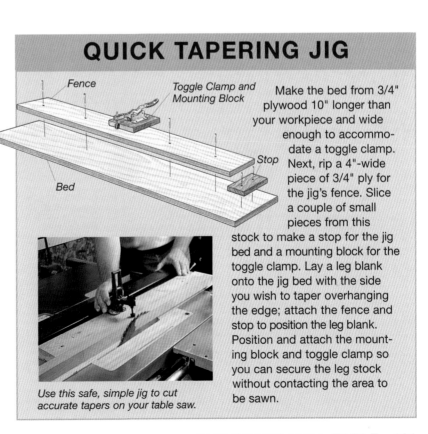

QUICK TAPERING JIG

Fence

Toggle Clamp and
Mounting Block

Bed

Stop

Make the bed from 3/4"
plywood 10" longer than
your workpiece and wide
enough to accommo-
date a toggle clamp.
Next, rip a 4"-wide
piece of 3/4" ply for
the jig's fence. Slice
a couple of small
pieces from this
stock to make a stop for the jig
bed and a mounting block for the
toggle clamp. Lay a leg blank
onto the jig bed with the side
you wish to taper overhanging
the edge; attach the fence and
stop to position the leg blank.
Position and attach the mounting block and toggle clamp so
you can secure the leg stock
without contacting the area to
be sawn.

*Use this safe, simple jig to cut
accurate tapers on your table saw.*

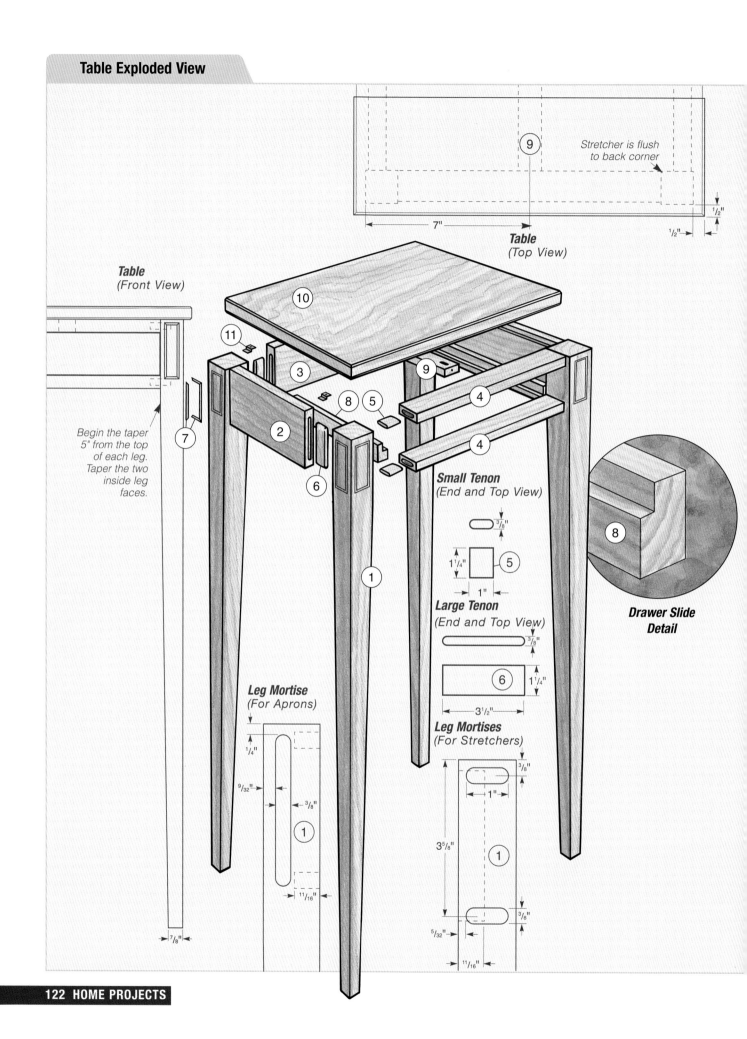

Table
(Top View)

Stretcher is flush
to back corner

7"

1/2"

1/2"

⑨

Table
(Front View)

⑩

⑪

③

⑨

④

④

Begin the taper
5" from the top
of each leg.
Taper the two
inside leg
faces.

⑦

②

⑧ ⑤

⑥

①

Small Tenon
(End and Top View)

3/8"

⑤

1 1/4"

1"

Large Tenon
(End and Top View)

3/8"

⑥

1 1/4"

3 1/2"

Drawer Slide
Detail

⑧

Leg Mortise
(For Aprons)

1/4"

9/32"

3/8"

①

11/16"

7/8"

Leg Mortises
(For Stretchers)

3/8"

1"

①

3 5/8"

3/8"

5/32"

11/16"

Stretcher
(End and Side View)

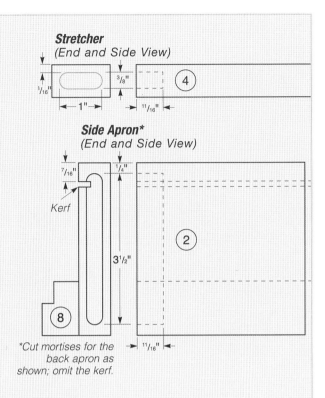

3/16" 3/8" (4)
1" 11/16"

Side Apron*
(End and Side View)

7/16" 1/4"
Kerf
(2)
3 1/2"
(8)
11/16"

*Cut mortises for the
back apron as
shown; omit the kerf.

Drawer Slide
(End View)

1/2"
9/32" (8)

MATERIAL LIST—*TABLE*		
		T x W x L
1	Legs (4)	1 3/8" x 1 3/8" x 35 1/4"
2	Side Aprons (2)	3/4" x 4" x 8 1/4"
3	Back Apron (1)	3/4" x 4" x 11 1/4"
4	Front Stretchers (2)	3/8" x 1 9/32" x 11 1/4"
5	Small Floating Tenons (4)	3/8" x 1" x 1 1/4"
6	Large Floating Tenons (6)	3/8" x 3 1/2" x 1 1/4"
7	Inlay (1)	1/8" x 1/8" x 72"
8	Drawer Slides (2)	7/8" x 1 1/4" x 8 1/4"
9	Drawer Kicker (1)	3/4" x 1" x 8 25/32"
10	Top (1)	3/4" x 12" x 15"
11	Tabletop Fasteners (4)	*Steel*

LOW-RISK INLAY JIG

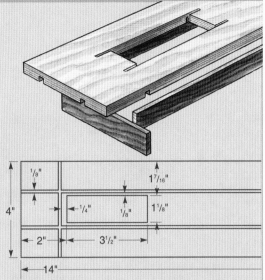

1/8" 1 7/16"
4" 1/4" 1/8" 1 1/8"
2" 3 1/2"
14"

Build this jig from 1/2" inch plywood to the
dimensions shown above. The opening is kept
close to one end of the jig to provide room to
clamp the fixture onto the leg blanks without
interfering with your router movement. Cut a
dado and two grooves on the underside to
locate the three cleats, as shown in the elevation and exploded views above.

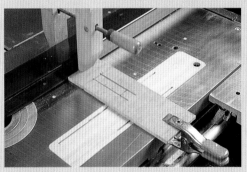

*To cut the jig opening, position the jig blank against
the rip fence on the table saw with the blade lowered below the table. Then carefully elevate the
blade to form the opening.*

*Use a homemade jig, a 3/8" O.D. rub collar and a
1/8" veining bit to cut the inlay slots. Plunge your
router and take a single lap around the jig opening.
Make sure the rub collar hugs the jig constantly.*

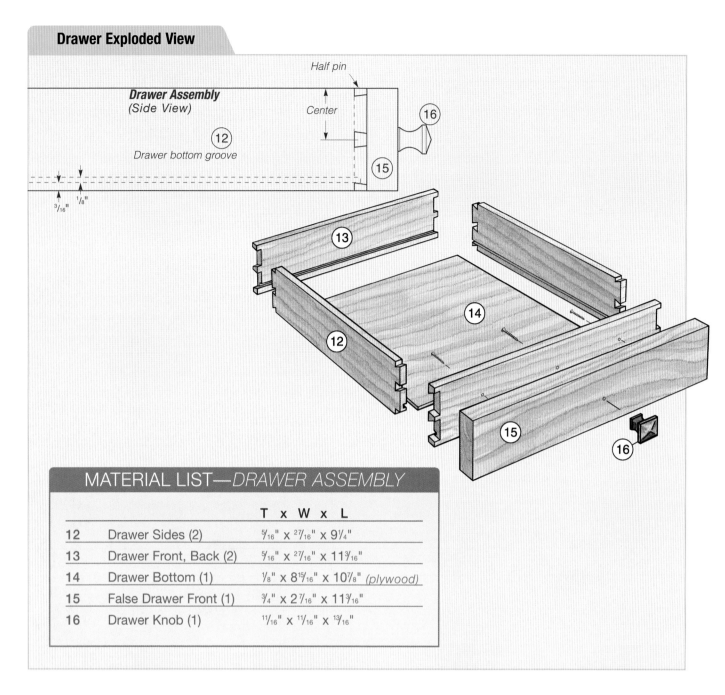

Half pin

Drawer Assembly
(Side View)

Center

⑫

Drawer bottom groove

⑯

⑮

³⁄₁₆" ¹⁄₈"

⑬

⑭

⑫

⑮

⑯

MATERIAL LIST—*DRAWER ASSEMBLY*		
	T x W x L	
12	Drawer Sides (2)	$\frac{5}{16}$" x $2\frac{7}{16}$" x $9\frac{1}{4}$"
13	Drawer Front, Back (2)	$\frac{5}{16}$" x $2\frac{7}{16}$" x $11\frac{3}{16}$"
14	Drawer Bottom (1)	$\frac{1}{8}$" x $8\frac{15}{16}$" x $10\frac{7}{8}$" *(plywood)*
15	False Drawer Front (1)	$\frac{3}{4}$" x $2\frac{7}{16}$" x $11\frac{3}{16}$"
16	Drawer Knob (1)	$\frac{11}{16}$" x $\frac{11}{16}$" x $\frac{13}{16}$"

Forming Tapers and Inlays

Lay out the taper on one of the legs. The outside two faces are straight and the insides have the taper. Start the taper 5" from the top and reduce the leg to 7/8" square on the bottom. Use the jig described on page 121 to slice tapers on the inside faces of each leg. Once all the tapers have been cut, move on to the decorative inlay (piece 7) on the outside faces at the top of each leg. Again, as with the tapers, the key to success with this task is to build the simple jig described on page 123. The jig is designed to work with a 3/8" O.D. guide bushing set in a plunge router base. Install a 1/8" router bit and set the bit height to cut just shy of 1/8" deep with the router sitting on the inlay jig. Make several test cuts in scrap cut to the size of the leg stock in order to get the feel of the procedure. Now position the jig on the end of a leg with the blank held tight against the jig's cleats, using two clamps to secure it properly. Start in one corner, plunge the bit, and continue around the opening in a clockwise direction. Lift the router when you get back to the starting point. Recutting may enlarge the groove and cause problems as you are fitting the inlay pieces. Repeat the process on all the faces where the inlay appears. Use a wide chisel to square up the corners. Hold the flat back of the chisel on the wall of the groove and rock it down into the uncut area to create perfectly square corners.

With the grooves cut, prepare some mahogany for the inlay. (You can also buy commercially available 1/8" inlay strips as well as more elaborate inlays with patterns.) Resaw your mahogany and plane it to 1/8"

MAKING DOVETAILS WITH A KELLER JIG

Some folks shy away from dovetail joints, thinking them too difficult and time-consuming. If your only option was to cut them by hand with a backsaw we'd probably agree, but with modern jigs and routers, this joint is within the scope of most woodworkers. We used the Keller Jig to cut dovetails in the drawer sides, front and back for this project. Always test your setup on scrap lumber dimensioned to the exact size of the stock used in your project. We find it useful to run the tails 1/32" long and sand them smooth.

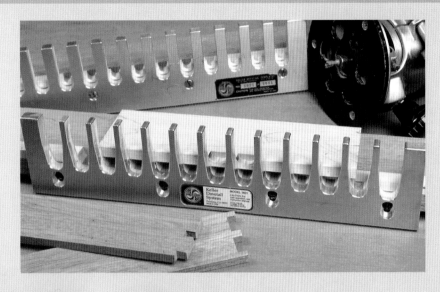

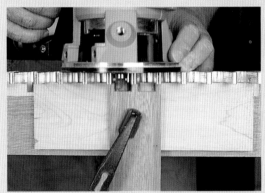

Use the Keller Jig to machine the drawer front and back first, forming the half pins at each end and then centering a pin in the middle.

Next, machine the tails on the drawer sides. Check each side for cupping, orienting any bow to the inside to prevent separation as the drawer ages.

thick. Put a zero-clearance insert in your table saw and use a sharp blade to rip 1/8"-wide inlay strips. Dry-fit the first strip you cut to ensure the rest will fit properly. Make the inlay pieces snug enough to just barely fit into the groove. If just the slightest tap with a hammer is needed to persuade them into place, you've got a perfect fit. Mitering the inlay to length is something of a challenge. The short pieces cause you to work close to the saw blade. A small extension on your miter gauge with a stop will safely cut the parts to their exact length. To be extra safe, use a piece of scrap or length of dowel to hold the small parts during cutting.

Wrapping Up the Legs and Aprons

Grab a knife or scraper to pare a slight chamfer on the back edges of the inlays. Run a small bead of glue in the bottom of the slot and tap them home. Or press the inlays into place using a wallpaper seam roller to help reduce the chance of breaking a delicate piece. When the glue securing the inlays has cured, you may have to carefully scrape the inlay flush.

Now use a 1/8" roundover bit in a trim router or medium-grit sandpaper to break all the edges of the legs fairly heavily, then finish-sand the legs to 220 grit. Run the tapered faces of the legs over the jointer, set

to a light pass, to remove the saw marks. A scraper also works for this clean-up if you don't have a jointer. Avoid using a power sander on the legs near the mortises. It can round over the surface and spoil the joint. It's better to use a scraper or hand-sanding block here.

Sand the apron and stretchers as well, and break just the bottom edges of these pieces. The ends and tops need to remain square — they butt against other parts. Now cut a kerf in the side aprons for tabletop fasteners. See the *Elevation Drawings* on page 123 for the proper kerf locations.

Starting the Assembly

Glue up the legs and aprons in two sub-assemblies: First, join the legs to the side aprons and then, when the glue has cured, attach those sub-assemblies to the back apron and stretchers. Be prudent with the amount of glue you use. It is important to avoid excess glue squeeze-out on the visible surfaces.

Machine the drawer slides (pieces 8) on your table saw by plowing rabbets as shown in the *Drawer Slide Detail* on page 123. Then turn to your drawer kicker (piece 9) and drill a pocket hole at each end of the piece.

Move to the table sub-assembly and glue and clamp the drawer guides in place against the side aprons (flush with the bottom stretcher). Install the drawer kicker (see the *Elevation Drawing* on page 122 for placement), using clamps to steady it as you drive the attachment screws home.

Topping It All Off

Glue up the top (piece 10) from the resawn pieces you cut earlier. Take care when you align the pieces to get a book-matched grain orientation. It is a great way to really show off the figure of the wood. After the glue has dried, size the top and use a belt sander to smooth the surfaces. Switch to a router and form 3/32" chamfers on the top and bottom edges. After sanding the top to 220 grit, attach it to the legs. To do this, place the top face down on a solid-padded work surface and set the leg sub-assembly in position. Fit tabletop fasteners (pieces 11) into the apron kerfs and drive the screws through their holes into the tabletop. With everything lined up, remove the top and set it aside until you've applied the finish.

Making the Drawer

Cut grooves in the drawer sides, front and back (pieces 12 and 13) to accept the drawer bottom (piece 14). We used a Keller Jig to cut through dovetails on the drawer

SHAPING A KNOB IN TWO STEPS

You could use a nice brass pull on this project, but we made a simple yet striking hardwood knob out of walnut. It's easy to make in just two steps and a perfect accent to a stylish table like this one.

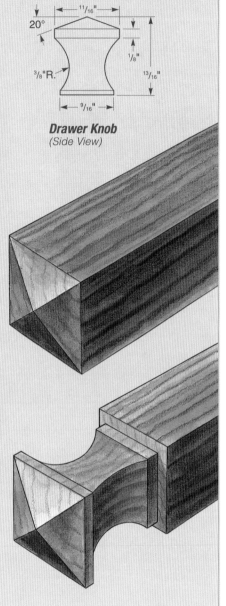

Drawer Knob
(Side View)

Disc-sand the top bevel angles holding the workpiece against a miter gauge.

Spindle-sand the the inner contours to shape, then bandsaw the knob free.

pieces, as shown in the *sidebar* on page 125. Dry-fit the drawer components and, once they all fit well, glue and clamp them together. Don't glue the drawer bottom in place: it must float freely. Size the false front (piece 15) to allow a 1/16" clearance all around the drawer opening.

Break all its edges with sandpaper and final-sand to 220 grit.

While a solid-brass knob would look good on this piece, we departed from the one board concept and designed an end grain knob from walnut (piece 16), as shown in the *sidebar* above.

Finishing and Final Assembly

Fit the drawer in the table. Finish sand all the parts and make a final check for glue squeeze-out by wiping with mineral spirits.

Apply three coats of polyurethane varnish, sanding after the second coat with 320-grit paper. Lay down the last coat, then final-sand with 600 grit. Buff with 0000 steel wool to create a soft, satiny sheen.

Predrill the false drawer front to center the knob. With the drawer in the table, position the false front in the opening, using shims to keep it centered. Temporarily drive a single screw through the predrilled hole in the false front and into the drawer. Open the drawer and make sure the alignment is correct. Then drive two #6 screws from inside to attach the false front. Remove the temporary screw and drive a #8 screw from the inside to attach the knob. (Be sure to predrill the knob first!) Reinstall the top and wax the drawer slides to complete this project.

This is not your normal hall table, but tucked discreetly beside a door, it makes an elegant place to set the mail or a purse while removing a coat.

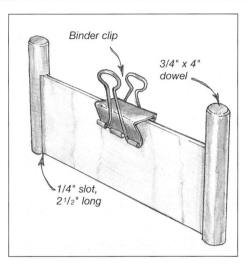
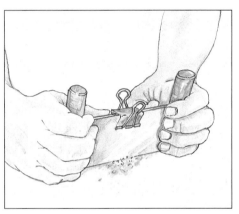

Keep in mind the time of year when making drawers. If you make a snug-fitting drawer during a Midwestern winter, don't expect to get it open on a humid day in August.

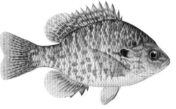

An Angler's Cabinet

Like contributing editor Rick White, our readers tell us they enjoy fishing as much as making sawdust. It was in the spirit of this sense of community that we asked Rick to share some of his favorite fishing hot spots. He flatly declined the request. Apparently, this is where fishing and woodworking part ways, because he was more than happy to share the design of this angler's cabinet instead.

Fishing is more than a hobby for Rick. When free time rolls around, you can generally find him in one of two places: His shop or his boat. One common denominator between fishing and woodworking for him is the absolute necessity of having the proper "tool" for the proper job. When he needs a mortising machine or maybe a Fenwick fishing rod, he buys what he needs. It gets troubling, however, when all those tools start to accumulate. Storing tools can be a challenge, whether it be in the workshop or in the den with those trophy fishing mounts.

Hence this storage cabinet, specifically designed to hide — er, store — his ever-growing collection of fishing tackle. Rick chose knotty pine lumber and plywood for this project to reflect his Northwoods heritage, and he even lined the interior of the cabinet with 1/4" tongue-and groove-pine paneling to add visual interest.

Storage is the Key

By making use of every inch of interior space, Rick is able to store a ton of stuff in this cabinet and retain a relatively small footprint. Each door is a swinging cabinet of its own, holding rods, reels, nets, stringers and other gear. The trade-off is that this unit is very tall — just a few inches short of an 8' ceiling. (Check your ceiling's height before you build; you may need to adjust the height.) The shelves are adjustable and include a couple of full-extension drawers for monofilament line (to keep it out of the light ... it can break down from ultraviolet rays) and other smaller items like special reels and tools. (Rick even bought a new drawer lock router bit to build the interlocking drawer joints — more about that on page 134.)

The casework design for this cabinet is basically two big boxes that share a base and decorative top. Heavy-duty wraparound

Fishing poles, gear and other essentials are out of sight but not out of mind in this project designed to blend two wonderful hobbies.

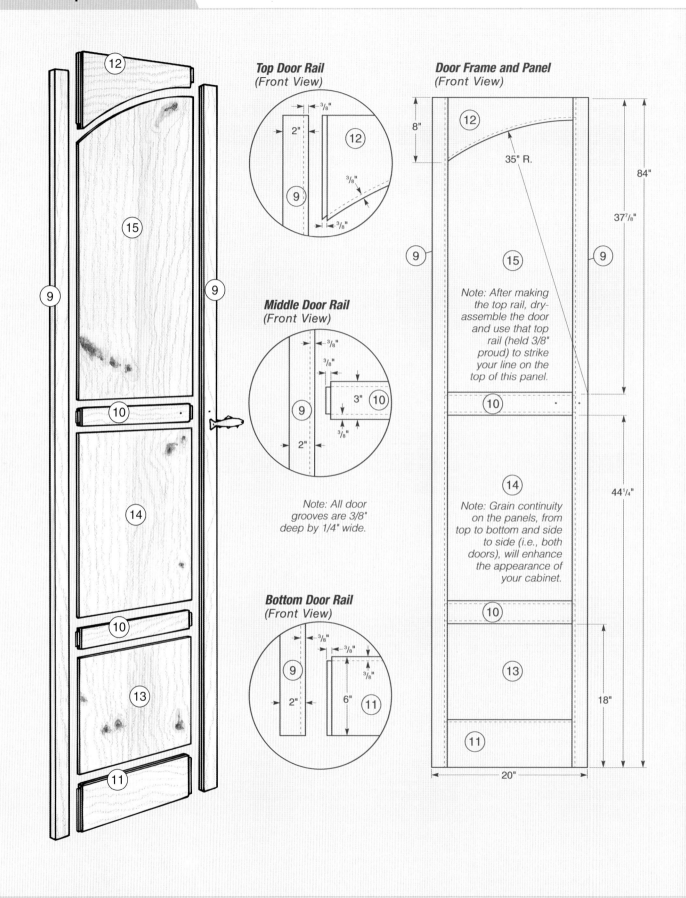

Top Door Rail
(Front View)

3/8"
2"
12
9
3/8"
3/8"

Middle Door Rail
(Front View)

3/8"
3/8"
9
3" 10
2"
3/8"

Note: All door
grooves are 3/8"
deep by 1/4" wide.

Bottom Door Rail
(Front View)

3/8"
3/8"
9
2"
6" 11
3/8"

Door Frame and Panel
(Front View)

8"
12
35" R.
9
15
9
Note: After making
the top rail, dry-
assemble the door
and use that top
rail (held 3/8"
proud) to strike
your line on the
top of this panel.
10
84"
37⁷/₈"
14
Note: Grain continuity
on the panels, from
top to bottom and side
to side (i.e., both
doors), will enhance
the appearance of
your cabinet.
44¹/₄"
10
13
18"
11
20"

MATERIAL LIST—*CARCASS & DOOR*

		T x W x L
1	Carcass Sides (4)	$3/4" \times 21^3/_{16}" \times 84"$
2	Carcass Tops and Bottoms (4)	$3/4" \times 21^3/_{16}" \times 19"$
3	Fixed Shelves (2)	$3/4" \times 18" \times 19"$
4	Divider Shelves (6)	$3/4" \times 17" \times 19"$
5	Rod Base Shelves (2)	$3/4" \times 10^5/_8" \times 19"$
6	Rod Divider Shelves (2)	$3/4" \times 10^5/_8" \times 19"$
7	Carcass Backs (2)	$1/4" \times 19" \times 83^1/_4"$
8	Pine Edging (1)	$1/8" \times 3/4" \times 75'$
9	Door Stiles (4)	$3/4" \times 2" \times 84"$
10	Middle Rails (4)	$3/4" \times 3" \times 16^3/_4"$
11	Bottom Rails (2)	$3/4" \times 6" \times 16^3/_4"$
12	Top Rails (2)	$3/4" \times 8" \times 16^3/_4"$
13	Bottom Panels (2)	$1/4" \times 17" \times 12^3/_4"$
14	Middle Panels (2)	$1/4" \times 17" \times 24"$
15	Top Panels (2)	$1/4" \times 17" \times 34^3/_4"$

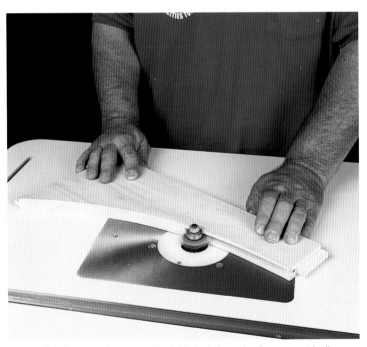

Use a 1/4" slot cutter in your router table to help make the symmetrically curved top door rails. The rails provide a nice bit of visual interest to this tall slender cabinet.

piano hinges support the doors and some fancy, fish-shaped pulls dress the unit. If you have a well outfitted shop and a measure of determination, you might be able to polish off this piece in a long weekend.

Constructing the Big Box

Slice up your sheet stock first, cutting the four sides and their tops and bottoms (pieces 1 and 2) from knotty pine plywood (see the *Cutting Diagram* on page 134). RIck chose to make one large box for each compartment of the cabinet. After you assemble each box, slice the door sections off the front of each one, ensuring perfectly matched doors and cabinet sections. Before you start assembly, look to the *Elevation Drawings* on the facing page for the locations of the dadoes and rabbets you'll need to plow for the shelves and back, and the tops and bottoms.

Be sure to check the actual thickness of your lumber and plywood before you start the various machining operations — even manufactured stock can vary in thickness. Once you've completed your machining, join the sides, tops and bottoms with glue and screws set into counterbored holes. (Plug the holes later with flat-topped pine plugs.) Now make the fixed shelves and divider shelves (pieces 3 and 4) that go into the gear storage side of the cabinet. On the rod-holding side you will need to make matching pairs of rod divider and rod base shelves (pieces 5 and 6). The *Scaled Drawings* on page 134 show the shapes and machining details for these solid-lumber pieces. Lastly, mount the plywood backs (pieces 7) into each compartment, making sure the units are square before the glue cures.

More Than Just Making Making the Doors

When it comes time to cut the door sections off the large boxes, ask a friend to lend a hand (see *photo*, next page). It's safer and easier than doing it yourself. Making the doors this way not only ensures a perfect fit to the carcass, but it also keeps the grain pattern intact on the side panels. After the door sections are removed, glue the fixed shelves and the rod holders in place. Then apply 1/8"-thick pine edging (piece 8) to hide the exposed edges of the plywood.

The front of each of the door sections is closed up with a classic frame-and-panel assembly, accented with symmetrically arched top rails. Make the flat door

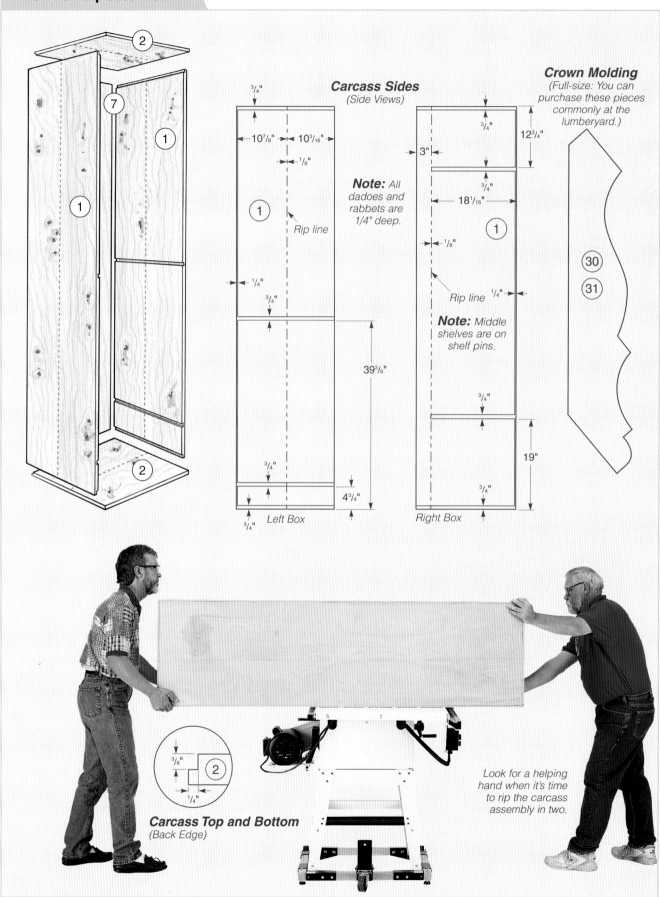

② ⑦ ① ①

Carcass Sides
(Side Views)

3/4"

10⁷/₈" 10³/₁₆"

1/8"

①

Rip line

1/4"

3/4"

39³/₈"

3/4"

4³/₄"

3/4"

Left Box

Note: All dadoes and rabbets are 1/4" deep.

3/4"

12³/₄"

3"

3/4"

18¹/₁₆"

①

1/8"

Rip line

1/4"

Note: Middle shelves are on shelf pins.

3/4"

19"

3/4"

Right Box

Crown Molding
(Full-size: You can purchase these pieces commonly at the lumberyard.)

③⓪
③①

3/8"
②
1/4"

Carcass Top and Bottom
(Back Edge)

Look for a helping hand when it's time to rip the carcass assembly in two.

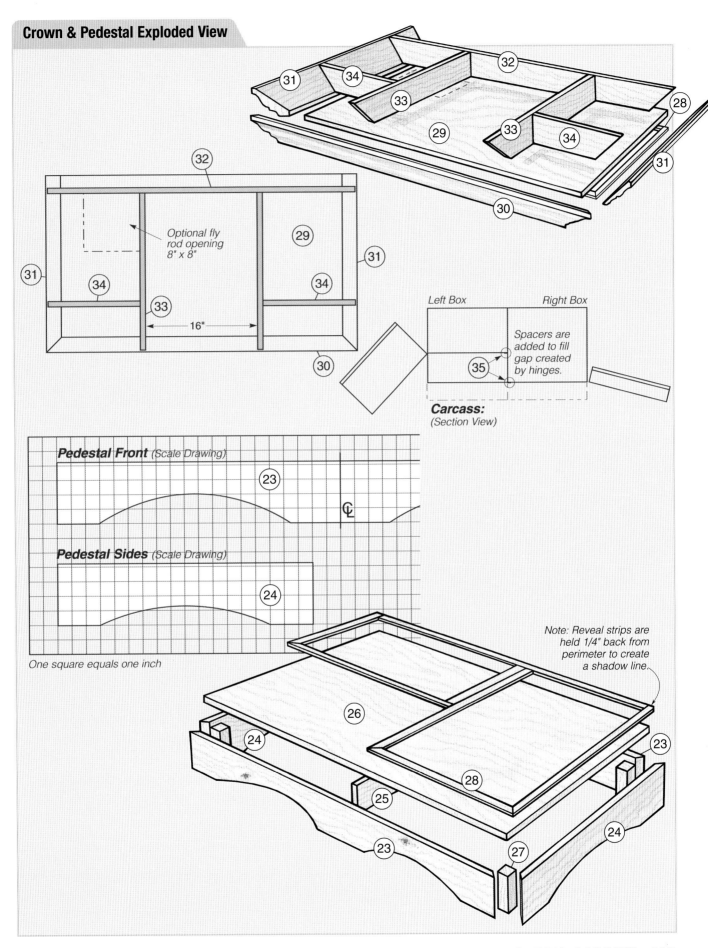

Optional fly
rod opening
8" x 8"

16"

Left Box

Right Box

Spacers are
added to fill
gap created
by hinges.

Carcass:
(Section View)

Pedestal Front (Scale Drawing)

Pedestal Sides (Scale Drawing)

One square equals one inch

Note: Reveal strips are
held 1/4" back from
perimeter to create
a shadow line.

CUTTING DIAGRAM FOR 3/4" KNOTTY PINE PLYWOOD

Knotty pine plywood is a good choice for this cabinet because it has the stability of regular plywood combined with the beauty of knotty pine lumber. You will need to purchase this plywood at a full-service lumberyard — one that commonly deals with cabinet-grade hardwood and plywood. (While you're there, pick up the crown molding.) Use the cutting diagrams at right for sizing down each sheet of plywood.

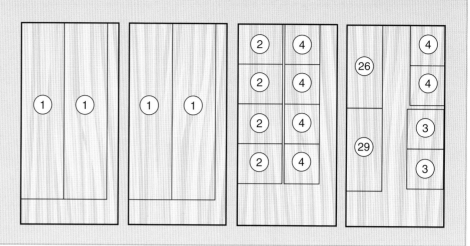

Drawer Exploded View

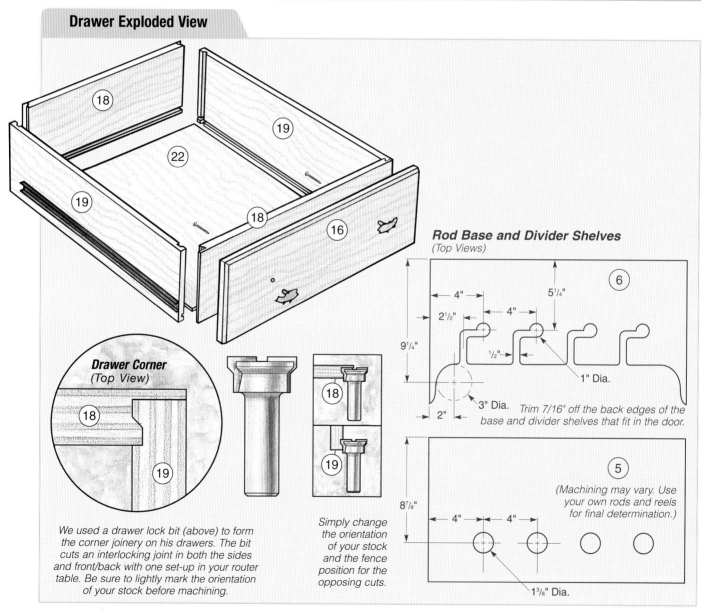

Drawer Corner
(Top View)

We used a drawer lock bit (above) to form the corner joinery on his drawers. The bit cuts an interlocking joint in both the sides and front/back with one set-up in your router table. Be sure to lightly mark the orientation of your stock before machining.

Simply change the orientation of your stock and the fence position for the opposing cuts.

Rod Base and Divider Shelves
(Top Views)

Trim 7/16" off the back edges of the base and divider shelves that fit in the door.

(Machining may vary. Use your own rods and reels for final determination.)

panels with 1/4" knotty pine plywood.

Select straight pine lumber to make the stiles and rails (pieces 9 through 12) and cut these pieces to size. Tight knots are acceptable, as they add to the overall rustic look of the cabinet. Start the machining by plowing a 1/4"-wide by 3/8"-deep groove down the length of the stiles' inside edges, using a 1/4" dado head. Do the same to the appropriate edges of the middle and bottom rails. Now set up your miter gauge and employ the same dado head to form the full-width tenons at the ends of all the rails. (The top rails remain rectangular for the moment.)

On a large, flat work surface, temporarily clamp the stiles and rails together as they will appear on the front of the cabinet. (You don't need the panels during this test assembly.) Make sure the clamp-up is square and true. At the center seam, measure down 37⅞" and strike a 35" radius across the top rails to create their gentle curve. Disassemble the clamp-up and take the top rails over to your band saw. Cut the arcs and then sand the rough saw marks smooth while holding the rails together as a

pair. Chuck a 1/4" bearing-guided slot cutter in your router table and plow a groove centered along the curved edge of each rail, as shown in the *photo* on page 131.

With that done, you're ready to cut up your 1/4" knotty pine plywood to form the flat panel sections (pieces 13, 14 and 15) of the door. The key here is to select material in such a way that the grain flows visually across the front of both doors and through the rails. Test-fit the door assemblies together, leaving off the curved top rails. Lay the curved rails on top of the assemblies (but hold them 3/8" proud of the top of the door stiles), and use the curved bottom edge to strike a pencil line onto the upper door panel. Take the top panels to the band saw and cut the curve right on the pencil line. You may want to scribe the line with a shop knife to prevent grain tear-out. Do one final test-fit before you glue and clamp the door subassemblies together. Then secure the door fronts to the cut-off door assemblies with glue and finish nails. Scrape and sand the doors smooth, and you're ready to move on to making the drawers.

A little hardware splurge adds a rustic touch and some identity to this angler's cabinet.

Making the Drawers, Index Holes and Top Opening

The two drawers are made mostly of 1/2" material (pieces 16 through 21) with 1/4" plywood bottoms (pieces 22). We used a drawer lock router bit (see *drawings* on the previous page) to form the drawers' corner joints. It works slick: Just cut the sides, fronts and backs to size, plow the 1/4" bottom dadoes (1/4" up from the bottoms), and use the bit to rout the corner joints on your router table. A little test-fitting on some scrap lumber is all the set-up that's required.

Once the drawer boxes are glued up, mount them in the cabinet on full-extension drawer slides and use double-sided tape to fit the faces to the front of each drawer. Nice and easy. With the drawers ready to go, move on to drilling the index holes for the shelf support pegs.

If you're a fly fisher, one last detail you may want to include is the opening at the top of the rod holder side the cabinet. Rick bored it so his fly rods could extend out through the top. You may not need this detail, as the interior height is sufficient for most ordinary fishing rods. Make this opening with a jigsaw, and cover the exposed plywood with your 1/8" pine edging.

Adding the Crowning Touches

This cabinet sits on a separate pedestal and is capped off with crown molding (purchased), held in place with some bracing. The pedestal is framed up with a front, back

Tongue-and-groove pine paneling is a final detail in this Northwoods fishing cabinet. Finished with orange shellac, this project will look great in your den, cabin or vacation home.

and two side pieces as well as a center support beam (pieces 23 through 25). See the *Exploded View Drawing* on page 133 for construction details. Band-saw the exposed front and side members of the pedestal with the decorative curves shown in the *Scaled Drawings* on page 133. Glue and screw the base together and drop the base top (piece 26) in place to square up the subassembly. Glue cleats (pieces 27) in each corner to provide a little extra support. Now trim out the pedestal with 1/4"-thick reveal strips (piece 28) mitered around the top edge, holding them back 1/4". These strips separate the carcass from the base (and, later, the crown molding), and create a pleasing shadow line. They also allow the large doors to swing freely.

Next, create the crown molding subassembly. Wrap the crown molding around a 3/4" plywood cap (pieces 29, 30 and 31). On the underside of the cap secure more of the reveal strip with glue and small brads. Next, cut an opening to match the fly rod hole in the top of the rod holder side the cabinet. (If you didn't include this detail, ignore this step.) Finally, install bracing (pieces 32 through 34) to add support to the top's crown molding (see *drawings*).

A word to the wise: Because the cabinet is so tall, install the base and top after you've placed the cabinet in your room. This will make it a lot easier to set the cabinet upright in a typical house with 8-foot ceilings. Mount the subassemblies prematurely and the cabinet may not fit.

Adding Some Fishy Hardware

With most of the work done, temporarily mount the pedestal and base to the cabinet. Then hang the doors, using wraparound piano hinges for strength and durability. You will have to notch the wrapping aspect of the hinges to fit around the fixed shelves. To accommodate the thickness of the hinges, glue several small spacers (pieces 35) in place.

Rick selected specialty fish-shaped pulls on the doors and drawers. You can buy it from Rockler (800-610-0883 or www.rockler.com). Then mount magnetic catches to hold the doors shut. Finally, to add to the Northwoods theme, cut and fit 1/4" pine tongue-and-groove paneling (piece 36) inside the cabinet and doors. Glue it in place (see photo on page 135) and use a few small brads for insurance.

Finishing Up with Shellac

After the paneling is in place, it's time for a thorough sanding inside and out (always a pain!) followed by several coats of orange shellac (see the *tip* on mixing shellac on the next page). Sand lightly after the first coat to remove any dust nibs. After that, you can apply the remaining coats without sanding — shellac partially dissolves the layer of finish underneath and fuses to it for a good bond without sanding. You just can't beat orange shellac as a finish on pine lumber. It brings out the beauty of the grain and knots and adds a real warmth to the wood.

Now, all you have to do is figure out a way to quietly get all your fishing gear into the cabinet without anyone noticing how much stuff you actually own!

MATERIAL LIST—*DRAWERS, PEDESTAL & CROWN*

		T x W x L
16	Small Drawer Face (1)	1/2" x 6" x 18 1/4"
17	Large Drawer Face (1)	1/2" x 12" x 18 1/4"
18	Sm. Drawer Front and Back (2)	1/2" x 6" x 17 1/4"
19	Sm. Drawer Sides (2)	1/2" x 6" x 17"
20	Lg. Drawer Front and Back (2)	1/2" x 12" x 17 1/4"
21	Lg. Drawer Sides (2)	1/2" x 12" x 17"
22	Drawer Bottoms (2)	1/4" x 16 1/2" x 17"
23	Pedestal Front and Back (2)	3/4" x 4 1/4" x 40"
24	Pedestal Sides (2)	3/4" x 4 1/4" x 18"
25	Pedestal Support Beam (1)	3/4" x 3 1/2" x 16 1/2"
26	Pedestal Top (2)	3/4" x 16 1/2" x 38 1/2"
27	Support Cleats (4)	3/4" x 3/4" x 3 1/2"
28	Reveal Strip (1)	1/4" x 3/4" x 250"
29	Crown Cap (1)	3/4" x 21 11/16" x 39 1/2"
30	Crown Front Molding* (1)	3/4" x 3 5/8" x 45"
31	Crown Side Molding* (2)	3/4" x 3 5/8" x 22"
32	Crown Long Brace* (1)	3/4" x 2" x 43 3/4"
33	Crown Medium Braces* (2)	3/4" x 2" x 21 7/8"
34	Crown Short Braces* (2)	3/4" x 2" x 13 3/16"
35	Door Spacers (6)	1/8" x 3/4" x 2"
36	Pine Paneling (1)	1/4" x 40 *sq. ft.*

Floor Kill Switch

If you frequently cut large sheets of plywood for casework, you know how hard it is to reach the table saw's switch when something goes wrong. Many catalog and retail outlets sell a foot-operated switch that is plugged into the wall, then the saw is plugged into the switch. By placing the switch a couple of feet in front of the saw, but a little to one side, you can easily reach it in an emergency, yet avoid accidentally turning off the saw in the middle of a cut.

Mixing and Storing Shellac

Shellac flakes are mixed with denatured alcohol in various ratios, or cuts. One pound of shellac mixed with one gallon of alcohol produces what is called a "one-pound cut." A three-pound cut would still only have one gallon of alcohol, but three pounds of flakes. The lower the cut, the thinner the mix. That means more coats, but a smoother application. It's all a matter of personal preference. Either way, make sure you buy fresh flakes, as older stock will give you some serious application headaches. You can also buy shellac as premixed liquid in a can, but it will typically be closer to a three-pound cut. Thin it with denatured alcohol, just as do with flake shellac.

Even fresh flake shellac can take several hours to dissolve in alcohol. You can speed up the process by pulverizing the flakes in a plastic freezer bag with a rolling pin or by chopping them up in a coffee grinder.

Whether you mix flakes or liquid shellac to your desired cut, be sure to do the mixing in a clean, plastic or glass container. Shellac will react with metal — be it a coffee can or metal lid — which will change its color. Store mixed shellac for no more than six months, and test it before you use it on scrap. If the shellac doesn't cure to a hard film in a few hours, it's too old and should be discarded.

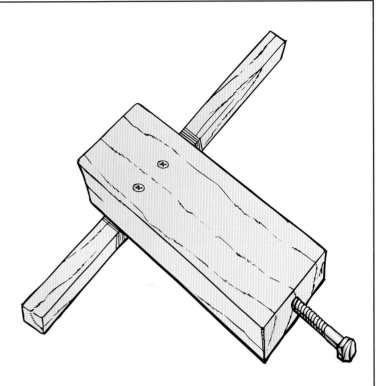

Table Saw Blade Alignment Jig

This little jig (above and below) slides in the miter gauge slot on your table saw and makes it possible to align the blade perfectly with the slot. Make it from two pieces of scrap and drive a hex-head lag bolt into the end. To use it, set the head of the bolt so it just barely grazes the saw blade at the front of the blade, as close to the teeth as possible. Then slide the jig to the back of the blade and without moving the bolt, check again to see if any minor realignment is required. Most experts agree that both the front and the rear of the blade should be exactly parallel with the miter slot — as well as to the rip fence.

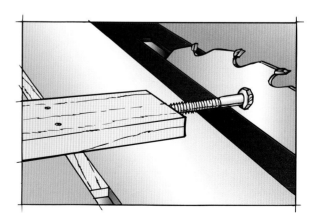

Building the barbecue cart will require about 50 hours of shop time. You'll need a table saw, portable and table-mounted routers and a drill. Use carbide bits and blades to mill the Corian.

- 20 board feet of 4/4 white oak
- 2 board feet of 8/4 white oak
- 56 lineal feet of 1x6 clear redwood
- 1 piece of Corian 1/2" x 15" x 32 3/4"

Backyard Barbecue Cart

Barbecuing is a great pastime, but the prep work is a chore — lugging everything from the utensils and hot pads to the charcoal and lighter fluid out to the grill. Build this barbecue cart as a way of saving some effort. It's sturdy enough to wheel around outside and large enough to store one or more bags of charcoal. We're sure it will prove to be a capable assistant to your family's chief outdoor cook—even if that person is you!

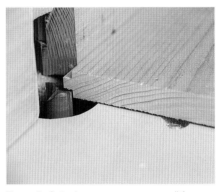

Figure 2: Cut a tongue or groove on all four edges of the redwood panel pieces, and follow up with a chamfering bit.

The cart you see here is made of soft clear redwood panels framed with hardy white oak. Both species stand up well to the elements. We also used stainless steel screws, waterproof polyurethane glue and some forged iron hardware with an exterior-grade finish. It's all topped off with Olympic WaterGuard wood sealant.

Figure 1: Just about all the tongues and grooves can be cut on the router table with a single fence adjustment.

A couple of notes about redwood: First, there are three grades: "Construction," "Construction Heart" and "All Heart." All Heart is the most expensive, but it's also knot-free. Second, 3/4" redwood is a nominal dimension — it's frequently 11/16" thick, sometimes even 5/8". So make sure you adjust your milling setups accordingly.

Starting with the Oak Frames

This project is primarily an exercise in frame and panel construction. Once the pieces are cut to size (see the *Material Lists*), all the remaining milling can be done with a table-mounted router.

The cart's carcass consists of a door frame, a top frame, and three frame and panel subassemblies: The back, the short end (near the wheels), and the long end (with the handle). All five carcass frames (pieces 1

through 8) and the door frames (pieces 27 through 29) are cut from white oak, while the panels (pieces 10 through 14, 30 and 31) are made of free-floating tongue and groove redwood boards.

Tongue and groove construction also holds the frames together. Begin them by cutting all the grooves first, because it's easier to adjust the thickness of the tongues than the width of the grooves. Install a 1/4" straight bit in your router table, locating its center 3/8" from the fence. This will center each groove in the edge of the stiles and rails. Set the depth of cut to 1/4", then consult the *Technical Drawings* on pages 144 and 145 for the locations of the grooves.

Several of the grooves in the frame pieces are stopped, while others run the full length of the piece. Cut all the grooves (see *Figure 1*), then follow up by making the

MATERIAL LIST—*CARCASS & DOORS*

#		T x W x L
1	End Rails (4)	¾" x 2" x 13¼"
2	Front & Back Rails (4)	¾" x 2" x 31"
3	Short End Stiles (2)	¾" x 1⅝" x 33½"
4	Long End Stiles (2)	¾" x 1⅝" x 34½"
5	Short Front & Back Stiles (2)	¾" x 2" x 33½"
6	Long Front & Back Stiles (2)	¾" x 2" x 34½"
7	Top Stiles (2)	¾" x 2½" x 36¾"
8	Top Rails (2)	¾" x 2½" x 15½"
9	Leg Braces (4)	¾" x 3" x 5¾"
10	Middle End Panels (2)	¾" x 2½" x 26"
11	Outer End Panels (4)	¾" x 5½" x 26"
12	Back Panel - A (1)	¾" x 4⅜" x 26"
13	Back Panels - B (6)	¾" x 4" x 26"
14	Back Panel - C (1)	¾" x 4⅛" x 26"
15	Bottom Stretchers (3)	¾" x 2" x 15"
16	Bottom Boards (3)	¾" x 5" x 32¾"
17	Wheels (2)	5½" Dia.
18	Axles (2)	⅜" x 2½" Carriage Bolts
19	Axle Nuts (2)	⅜" Dia. locking nuts
20	Cutting Board Panel (1)	¾" x 12¼" x 22½"
21	Cutting Board Ends (2)	¾" x 1¼" x 12¼"
22	Cutting Board Slides (2)	2" x 1¾" x 32¾"
23	Towel Rack Sides (2)	¾" x 4" x 9"
24	Towel Rack Handle (1)	1¼" Dia. dowel
25	Corian Top (1)	½" x 15" x 32¾"
26	Bottle Opener (1)	Solid brass
27	Door Rails (4)	¾" x 2" x 11¾"
28	Door Stiles (3)	¾" x 2" x 26"
29	Door Lip Stile (1)	¾" x 2⅜" x 26"
30	Middle Door Panels (2)	¾" x 2½" x 21½"
31	Outer Door Panels (4)	¾" x 4⅞" x 21½"
32	Strap Hinges (4)	9" Forged Iron
33	Door Latch (1)	Forged Iron
34	Magnetic Catch (1)	5/16" x 2" x 13/16"
35	Door Knobs (2)	1⅜" Dia. Forged Iron
36	Utensil Hooks (4)	Forged Iron

Door Stiles *(Top View)*

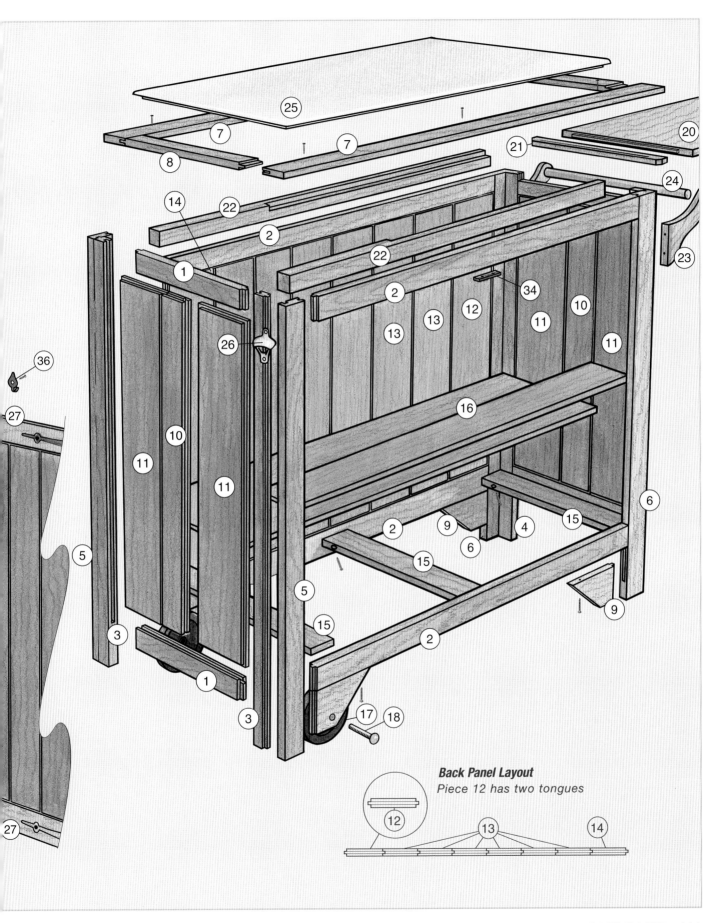

Back Panel Layout
Piece 12 has two tongues

tongues (a tight fit is essential here). While you're cutting tongues in the frame pieces, you can also cut them on the leg braces (pieces 9). The tongues and grooves on the top frame are 1" long, so make these cuts in several passes.

Milling the Redwood Panels

Stick with your 1/4" 'straight bit to create the grooves and tongues on the redwood panels (pieces 10 through 14, 30 and 31). Since 3/4" nominal redwood comes in various thicknesses, adjust your router table's

Figure 3: Use a pocket hole jig to create the hidden pilot holes in the three stretcher pieces.

fence accordingly to make certain that you're centering the grooves in your stock.

Check the *Technical Drawings* to determine where the tongues and grooves are cut. Just like you did on the frame pieces, start with the grooves and test your setups on scraps of the same thickness. As these won't be glued together, a loose fit is appropriate. Start milling the edges (see *Figure 2*), and then, without changing your setup, move on to the tops and bottoms of the panel pieces, which also have to fit into a frame. Finish the milling process on the redwood panels by chucking a 90° V-groove bit in your router to cut the decorative chamfers on all sides of the panel faces, as shown in the *Figure 2* inset and also on the *Technical Drawings*.

WORKING WITH CORIAN®

Corian® is the most popular brand name of a family of products called solid surface materials - plastics with color patterns that permeate the material. Corian usually comes in 1/4", 1/2" and 3/4" thicknesses. Originally, it was used just for countertops. But innovative fabricators have found many new uses for Corian: from shower surrounds and plaques to cutting boards and wall panels.

Carbide bits are essential when routing Corian, which is three times as dense as most hardwoods.

Corian is relatively easy to work. Standard woodshop equipment is quite adequate, but to provide quality work, you must equip your machines with carbide blades or bits. Sharp cutters are essential to prevent chatter and surface irregularities because Corian is three times as dense as most hardwoods.

Cutting straight lines in Corian is best done with a router. If you use a table saw, the cut will have kerf marks that will have to be removed with a router anyway, so you may as well use the right tool to begin with.

Also, when using a router and a straightedge, the tool moves across the surface of the material. A table saw, on the other hand, requires that you push the entire surface of the workpiece across the tabletop, which makes it prone to scratches.

Wearing protective gear is a must with Corian and similar products. Although the dust is chemically non-toxic, it can be pervasive and constitutes a mechanical nuisance. Eye protection is also recommended by the DuPont Corporation,

which manufactures Corian. The product, though extremely durable, is somewhat brittle, so particles can fly under certain circumstances. It's also heavy, so use proper lifting techniques. And that density prompts one more piece of advice: When routing a decorative edge, or using a router to cut Corian, make several passes rather than trying to remove all the waste in a single pass. This is easier on your tools and improves the quality of the cut.

Achieving a matte finish on Corian is also easy. Start sanding with 180-grit paper and work your way through 400-grit. Use a silicon carbide open-coat paper, and change papers often as the fine dust tends to clog even open coats rather quickly. Wash off the excess dust with cold water, and buff with a green Scotchbrite® pad.

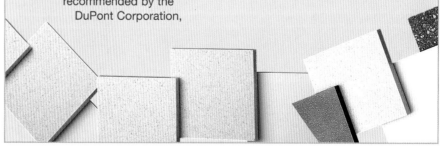

Assemble the Frames and Panels

After you've milled all the frame and panel pieces, it's time to glue and clamp each frame and panel assembly together. Before you do, rip one of the end rails (pieces 1) to 1⅛", and remember that one stile on one of the doors (piece 29) is wider than the others. Spread your glue sparingly and don't glue the redwood panels to each other or to the frames - they float freely. Make sure each panel is square by measuring diagonally.

After the glue has dried in each sub frame, dry-fit the four frames that create the cart's carcass (where pieces 3 and 5 and 6 and 4 meet). If everything fits, apply your glue to the mating tongues and grooves and use web clamps to hold them together. You may need a couple of extra hands for this step, but polyurethane glue has a long open time, so there's no rush.

Cutting Rabbets on the Doors

There are two last milling steps on the doors, after they've been assembled. The doors are offset, so rabbets must be cut on their inside edges, and a lip must be cut on one door where they overlap. These two steps are handled on the router table with a 1/2" straight bit, following the dimensions shown in the *Technical Drawings*. Cut the rabbet around the inside edge of all the rails

Figure 4: After rounding over the top edge of the Corian with a 1/4" roundover bit, create a rabbet in the bottom edge with a straight bit.

and stiles except the wide lip stile (piece 29), which gets a rabbet on the outside edge.

Making the Bottom

Stretchers (pieces 15) are installed between the lower front and back rails to support the redwood bottom boards (pieces 16). If you'd prefer not to see any screws or screw hole plugs on the cart's exterior, you can use a pocket hole jig to drill screw holes diagonally through the sides of the stretchers and into the rails (see *Figure 3*).

After the bottom redwood boards are cut to size, set them loosely in place. It will make cleanup easier; if charcoal spills, just lift out the boards and brush them off.

This is also a good time to glue and screw the braces to the legs below the lower rails. Before you attach them, drill holes (see *Technical Drawings* for locations) for the carriage bolts that serve as axles for the wheels (pieces 17 through 19).

Cutting Board

This cart includes a reversible cutting board that pulls out for clean up in the kitchen sink. Create the panel (piece 20) by gluing up pieces of white oak. While the glue is drying, rout a 1/4"-wide by 3/8"-deep stopped groove (see the *Technical Drawings*) in each cutting board end (pieces 21). After the glue has dried in the panel, route a corresponding tongue on each of its ends.

Assemble the cutting board, using screws instead of glue to allow for the expansion and contraction you'll surely get with this outdoor piece of furniture. You'll find the oversized screw hole locations and dimensions on the *Technical Drawings*. Wrap up by covering the screws with plugs.

With the cutting board panel assembled, use a 90° V-groove bit to route finger pulls on both sides of both ends. Finish the cutting board by drilling a 1/8" drain hole through the middle of each finger pull.

The cutting board is held in the cart by two oak slides (pieces 22) that have stopped

rabbets cut in them (see the *Technical Drawings*). After the rabbets are cut, simply glue and clamp the slides to the carcass.

Towel Rack/Handle

Copy the towel rack sides (pieces 23) from the Full-size Pattern and cut them out on your band saw. Clean up the saw marks with a drum sander. (See page 54 for a drum sanding jig that attaches to your drill press.)

After you have shaped the sides, use a Forstner bit to cut 1¼" holes (see the Full-size Pattern for all locations) that will hold the handle (piece 24). Attach the sides to the frame stiles with screws and glue, making sure the cutting board has enough room to slide out.

The Corian Top

Screw the top frame you built earlier to the cutting board slides now. This top frame will hold the Corian panel (piece 25). There are two milling steps involving the Corian: Rounding the top edge with a 1/4" roundover bit and creating a rabbet on the bottom edge (see *Figure 4*) to hide the screws in the top frame. If you've never used Corian, be sure to follow the tips described in "Working With Corian" on the preceding page. It's not the same as wood.

We used Olympic WaterGuard to seal this project. It's a waterproofing sealant that resists mildew growth and blocks the sun's ultra-violet rays. Apply three coats to everything but the cutting board, sanding lightly between coats. Give the cutting board a couple liberal coats of salad bowl finish since it comes in contact with food. Paint the carriage bolt heads with black enamel so they match the forged iron hardware.

After the finish dries, attach the bottle opener, hinges, door latch, magnetic catch, knobs and utensil hooks (pieces 32 through 36). To keep charcoal dry, apply silicone caulking around the top frame before setting down the Corian top. Then start getting ready for that next big cookout!

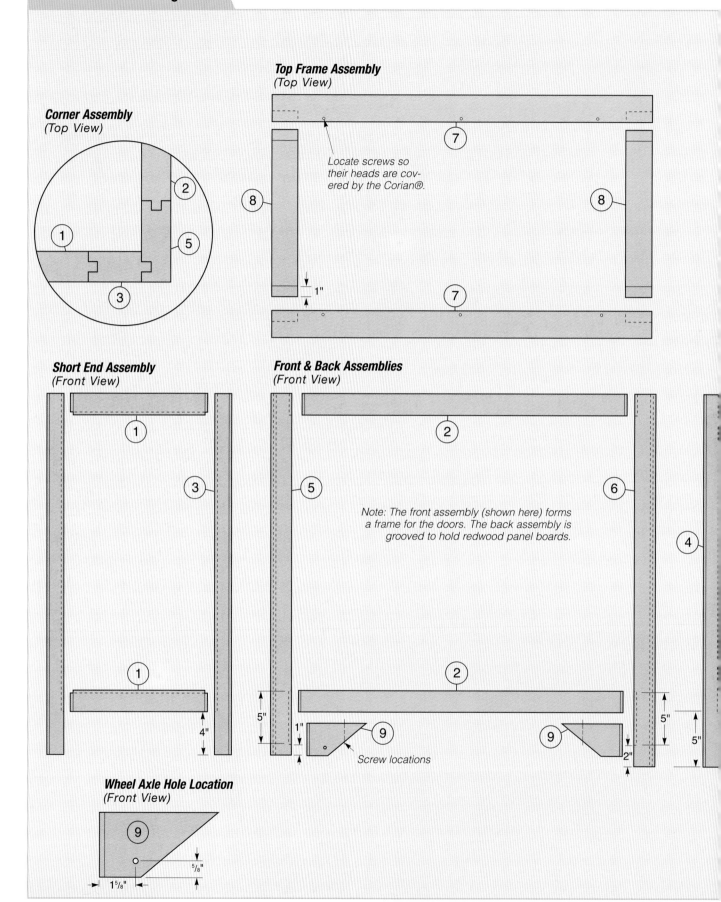

Corner Assembly
(Top View)

Top Frame Assembly
(Top View)

Locate screws so
their heads are cov-
ered by the Corian®.

1"

Short End Assembly
(Front View)

Front & Back Assemblies
(Front View)

Note: The front assembly (shown here) forms
a frame for the doors. The back assembly is
grooved to hold redwood panel boards.

4"

5"

1"

5"

5"

2"

Screw locations

Wheel Axle Hole Location
(Front View)

⁵⁄₈"

1⁵⁄₈"

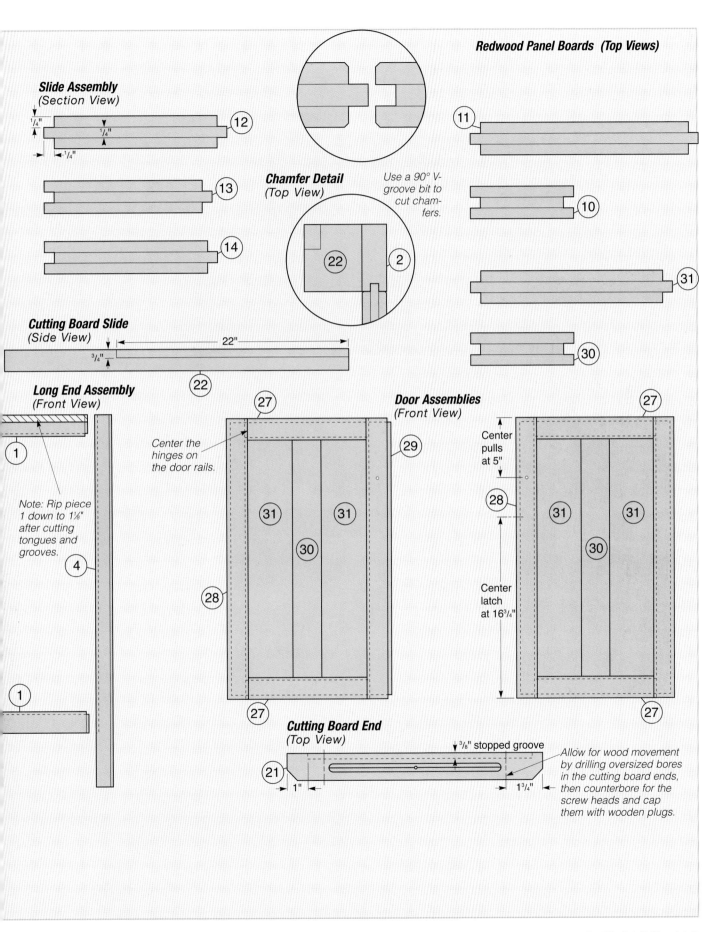

Redwood Panel Boards (Top Views)

Slide Assembly
(Section View)

¼"
¼"
¼"

12

13

14

Use a 90° V-groove bit to cut chamfers.

11

10

31

30

Chamfer Detail
(Top View)

22

2

Cutting Board Slide
(Side View)

22"

¾"

22

Long End Assembly
(Front View)

1

Note: Rip piece 1 down to 1⅛" after cutting tongues and grooves.

4

1

27

Center the hinges on the door rails.

29

31

31

30

28

27

Door Assemblies
(Front View)

27

Center pulls at 5"

28

31

31

30

Center latch at 16¾"

27

Cutting Board End
(Top View)

⅜" stopped groove

21

1"

1¾"

Allow for wood movement by drilling oversized bores in the cutting board ends, then counterbore for the screw heads and cap them with wooden plugs.

A Portable Folding Bench for Two

I magine this scenario: Your team has just scored its twen-ty-seventh run and it's still the bottom of the sixth. Most of the fans have been sitting on damp grass for over two hours already. No, this isn't a bad day in the majors — it's infinitely worse: We're parents at Tuesday night T-ball, and it's a double header.

Actually, as every parent really knows, T-ball is great fun. In fact, the only true downside to a long evening of spectating is those horrible chairs — you know the ones — flimsy nylon contraptions that fold up, usually while you're still in them! What we need is a comfortable bench that can hold two weary parents and still fit in the trunk after the game. Well, you're in luck, because that's exactly what this project is — a light-weight, strong, weather-resistant bench that, when folded and stored, protrudes a mere 3" from the garage wall or trunk floor.

The inspiration for this bench came from a similar design that dates from the early 1940s. It was made of weather-resist-ant white oak, so that's the species we're using for this project.

Building the Seat

The best way to get started on this project is to cut all the parts to the sizes given in the *Material List* on page 149, then begin the milling process by working on the seat subassembly. The two seat supports (pieces 1) are shaped pieces, and their pro-file can be found in the *drawings* on page 151. Cut them to shape on your band saw, then clean up the kerf marks with a drum sander in the drill press.

Stay at the drill press to bore holes for the pivot hinges (pieces 2) and the dowel stretcher (piece 3) at the locations given on the *drawings*, noting the holes for the hinges step down from 1" in diameter to 1/2", requiring a change of bits (see *Figure 1*). Now turn your attention to the seat slats (pieces 4). Four of the five slats are simply rounded over on their top edges with a 1/4"-radius router bit, then screwed in place (see the *drawings* for locations and spacing).

Counterbore for the short screws (pieces 5) with a 3/8" Forstner bit: These will later be filled with oak plugs (pieces 6), to protect your family from sun-heated screw heads. Drive the screws home, but don't use any glue yet. You'll remove the slats during the assembly process.

The fifth and middle slat is rabbeted on each end (prior to rounding over the top edges) so the back legs have room to pivot (see *drawings* on page 149). You can cut

Figure 1: The holes in the seat supports for the pivot hinges are drilled in two stages, changing from a 1" bit to a 1/2" bit.

Figure 2: Various elements of the back leg assembly are rounded over with a 1/4"-radius router bit. These cuts are stopped.

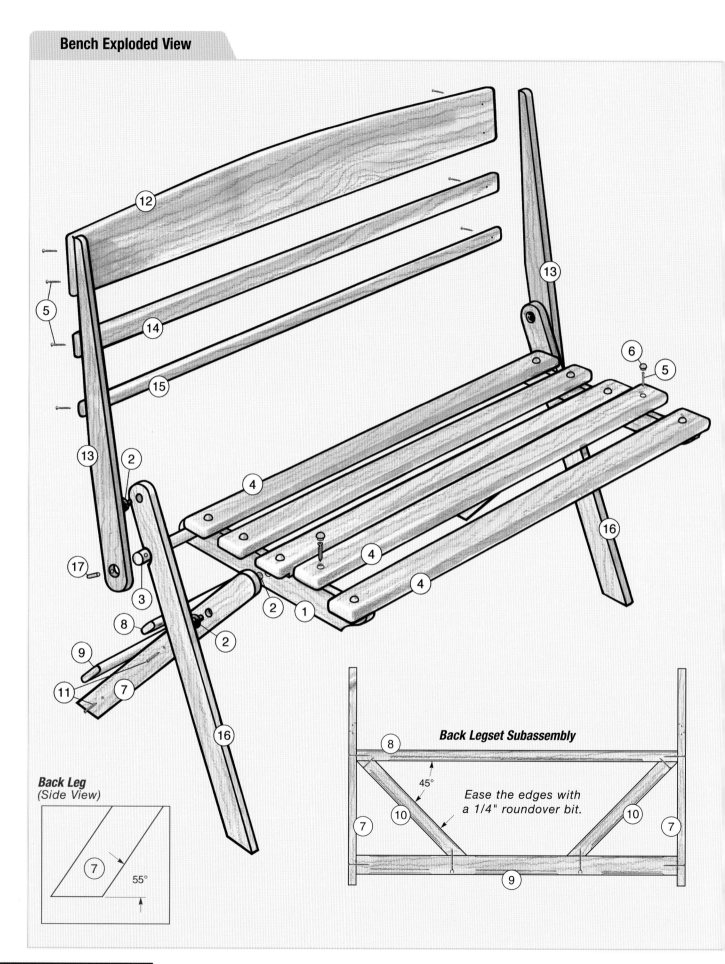

Back Leg
(Side View)

55°

Back Legset Subassembly

45°

*Ease the edges with
a 1/4" roundover bit.*

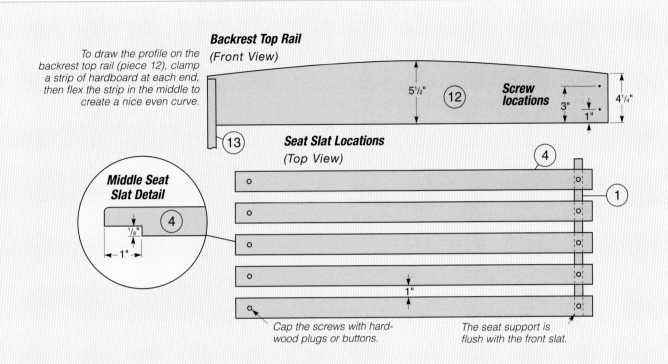

Backrest Top Rail
(Front View)

To draw the profile on the backrest top rail (piece 12), clamp a strip of hardboard at each end, then flex the strip in the middle to create a nice even curve.

5¹⁄₂"

(12)

Screw locations

3"

1"

4¹⁄₄"

(13)

Seat Slat Locations
(Top View)

(4)

(1)

Middle Seat Slat Detail

(4)

¹⁄₈"

1"

1"

Cap the screws with hard-wood plugs or buttons.

The seat support is flush with the front slat.

Use a weather-resistant adhesive like Gorilla Glue or Titebond II when gluing up this subassembly.

MATERIAL LIST

		T x W x L
1	Seat Supports (2)	³⁄₄" x 2" x 13³⁄₄"
2	Pivot Hinges Pair (3)	*Weatherproof*
3	White Oak Stretcher (1)	1" x 36" *Dowel*
4	Seat Slats (5)	³⁄₄" x 1³⁄₄" x 32"
5	Short Screws (20)	#8 x 1¹⁄₂"
6	White Oak Plugs (10)	³⁄₈"
7	Back Legs (2)	³⁄₄" x 2" x 20¹⁄₈"
8	Back Legset Top Rail (1)	³⁄₄" x 1" x 30¹⁄₈"
9	Back Legset Bottom Rail (1)	³⁄₄" x 1³⁄₄" x 30¹⁄₂"
10	Diagonal Braces (2)	³⁄₄" x 1¹⁄₄" x 13⁵⁄₈"
11	Long Screws (6)	#8 x 2¹⁄₂"
12	Backrest Top Rail (1)	³⁄₄" x 5¹⁄₂" x 35⁷⁄₈"
13	Backrest Stiles (2)	³⁄₄" x 2" x 22"
14	Backrest Middle Rail (1)	³⁄₄" x 1¹⁄₄" x 35⁷⁄₈"
15	Backrest Bottom Rail (1)	³⁄₄" x ³⁄₄" x 35⁷⁄₈"
16	Front Legs (2)	³⁄₄" x 2" x 23³⁄₈"
17	Retainer Pins (2)	¹⁄₄" x 1" *Dowels*

these rabbets on your table saw with a dado head, using the miter gauge to keep the cuts square to the end of the slat. Now secure this final slat to the seat supports with the same screws.

Making the Back Leg Subassembly

This subassembly is made up of the two back legs (pieces 7), two rails (pieces 8 and 9) and a couple of diagonal braces (pieces 10). Create a radius on the top of each leg with your band saw (see *Elevation Drawings*, page 151) and sand it smooth. Cut the 55° miter on the bottom of each leg using a table saw with the miter gauge set at 35°. A similar setup can be used to create

Figure 3: *Installing the weather-resistant pivot hinges is a simple matter of lining up the two sides of each hinge and bolting them together.*

the 45° miters on both ends of the braces.

Drill 1/8" pilot holes through the bottom rail (locations are on the *drawings*), then counterbore for the heads of the long screws (pieces 11). Dry-fit the braces to the bottom rail and extend the pilot holes with a 3/32" bit. Apply Titebond® II or a similar water-resistant glue to the joint and drive the screws home.

Attach the top rail to the braces in much the same fashion, only this time use the short screws. Be careful that your pilot holes follow the *drawings* exactly, as there is little room for error here. Now drill countersunk pilot holes through the legs and glue and screw them to the rails. Make sure this subassembly is perfectly flat, and set it

aside to dry. Once the glue has dried, round over all the areas shown on the *drawings* using a 1/4" roundover bit in your router table, as shown in *Figure 2* on page 147.

Assembling the Backrest

Cut the profile on the top edge of the backrest's top rail (piece 12) according to the *Backrest Top Detail Drawing*, page 149, then sand it smooth. Round over both the top and bottom edges with the same 1/4" router bit you used on the seat and legs earlier, then drill 1/8" pilot holes at the locations shown on the *drawings*. Countersink these holes on the rear face of the top rail, then turn your attention to the two backrest stiles (pieces 13). These are also shaped pieces, and their profiles can be found on the *drawings*. Cut them on the band saw, round over the areas indicated (use the 1/4"-radius bit), and then break all the other edges with sandpaper. Use the pattern to locate the holes for the dowel and pivot hinges and drill them on your drill press. Be aware of the stepped nature of the pivot hinge holes as well as which side is drilled with the larger bit (see *sidebar*, this page).

Clamp the top rail to the stiles, then extend the pilot holes with a 3/32" bit, apply glue and drive the screws in snug.

At this time you can also round over the two lower rails (pieces 14 and 15) and drill countersunk pilot holes in them. But don't attach them to the uprights yet — you'll see why during the next assembly step.

Moving to the Front Legs

The front legs (pieces 16) are simply cut to shape on your band saw and sanded (see the *Elevations* on page 151). Miter their bottom ends on the table saw. You'll have to drill each leg in two locations for the pivot hinges (refer to the *drawings* for locations), then you're ready to try a dry assembly on the whole project. The pivot hinges are the key to this assembly process, so let's take a closer look at them.

INSTALLING PIVOT HINGES

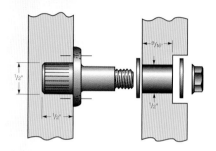

Install the main, knurled section of the hinge (the piece on the left) into a stopped boring in the first piece of wood. Slide on a washer and the plastic sleeve, then insert the threaded end into the 1/2"-diameter boring in the second piece of wood. Secure it with a second washer and a nut, both of which are set into a larger counterbore to keep them below the surface of the wood.

Installing the Pivot Hinges

The drawing of the pivot hinge (above) gives you a good idea of how this inexpensive but wonderful piece of weather-resistant hardware works. One end is fixed in place by a combination of knurled teeth and a pair of screws. The other end is threaded, allowing you to secure the second (moving) piece of wood to the fixed piece with a nut. A sleeve placed over the middle of the hinge ensures you don't overtighten the nut, and it also prevents any friction buildup.

With the holes for your hinges already drilled at the locations given in the *Elevations*, you can go ahead and secure all

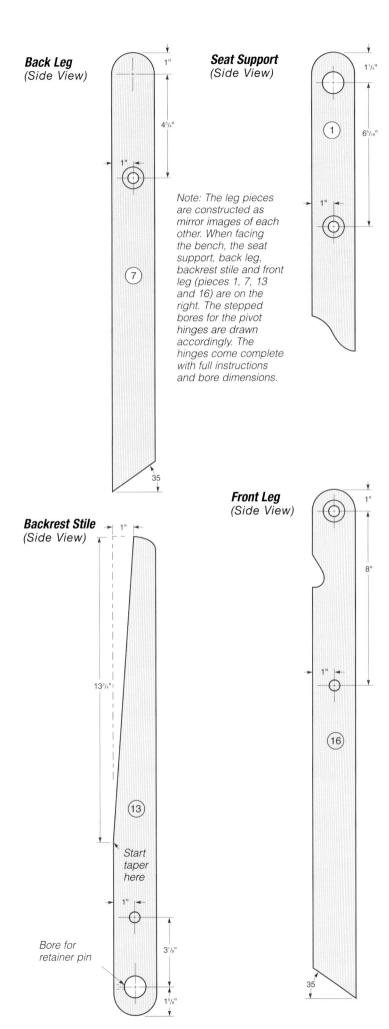

Back Leg
(Side View)

1"

4³/₄"

1"

⑦

35

Seat Support
(Side View)

1¹/₄"

①

6⁵/₁₆"

1"

Note: The leg pieces are constructed as mirror images of each other. When facing the bench, the seat support, back leg, backrest stile and front leg (pieces 1, 7, 13 and 16) are on the right. The stepped bores for the pivot hinges are drawn accordingly. The hinges come complete with full instructions and bore dimensions.

Backrest Stile
(Side View)

1"

13³/₄"

⑬

Start taper here

1"

Bore for retainer pin

3¹/₈"

1⁵/₈"

Front Leg
(Side View)

1"

8"

1"

⑯

35

the knurled ends of the hinges in place. Predrill for the screws that come with the hinges to avoid splitting, and locate these screws so they aren't exactly in line with the grain of the wood.

You have already drilled four holes for the stretcher (piece 3), one hole in each seat support and another in each of the backrest stiles. Now chuck a sanding drum in your portable drill and enlarge these holes slightly — enough so the dowel passes freely through them without much play.

Slip the dowel through the holes in the seat supports, then attach the backrest in the same manner. Secure the stretcher in the backrest uprights with retainer pins (pieces 17), glued into holes drilled through both pieces. Attach the back leg assembly next (temporarily remove the screws in the seats slats to do this), then install the spacers, nuts and washers that come with the hinges.

Wrapping Up Construction

Apply waterproof glue to the seat slats and drive the screws home for the last time. Glue oak plugs into the screw counterbores. We used button plugs with domed tops to make sure the rain runs off. Measure diagonally in both directions to verify that the seat is square before the glue dries, and tweak it if it's not. Slip the front legs in place next, then install the spacers, washers and nuts and fold the bench into its closed position.

The last step in assembly is to install the two lower rails of the backrest — the ones you held aside awhile back. The idea is to ensure that the backrest rails fit neatly on either side of the front seat slat when the bench is folded. Instead of relying on the pattern, simply fold the backrest down and position the rails on either side of the front slat. Once they're positioned, drill the pilot holes and countersinks and attach the rails to the stiles with the short screws.

Applying Finish

We wanted this bench to last at least as long as the original — that one was built around World War II — so we sprayed it with exterior polyurethane. With all its slat nooks and narrow parts, this project really lends itself to spraying rather than brushing. If you don't own spray equipment, a couple of aerosol cans will do a respectable job. To avoid exposure to the fumes, spray the bench outside. After all, that's where this handy, lightweight folding bench belongs.

Classic Kitchen Island

itchen islands are just wonderful — just ask editor
Rob Johnstone, owner of this handsome project. It
has a counter-height work surface where you can also
eat, featuring ample storage as well as being darn good
to look at. This project is reminiscent of an old-fashioned
butcher's table, but it's a lot easier to build because the
top is a slick, built-up assembly rather than a heavy chunk
of hard maple.

*The legs are a glued-up hollow construction. Because the plan was to paint the base, we used
yellow poplar, a stable wood that accepts paint well.*

Wrap-around Top

To achieve the butcher block look and
strength, Rob began by cutting two pieces
of birch plywood (pieces 1) and glued and
screwed them together to form the core.
Next, he selected attractively figured hard
maple lumber to glue up for the top (piece
2). Even though Rob purchased 3/4" S-4-S
lumber, he still took the time to make sure
the edges were dead straight with a pass on
the jointer. After Rob glued up the top, he
took it to a cabinet shop to have it sanded
smooth and flat on a wide belt sander. You
can flatten it yourself with a plane or hand-
held belt sander ... but he was in a hurry.

Once the top is flat, smooth and
trimmed to size, glue the top edges (pieces
3) in place, which provides an illusion of
thickness. Add to the illusion by making the
end caps (pieces 4). Cut them to size and
then plow a stopped groove on their inside
faces (as shown in the *drawings* on page
155). Now slice biscuit slots into the top to
match the grooves you just plowed. The biscuits must not stick out farther than the
depth of the endcap grooves, or you'll have
a big problem. Glue the biscuits in place,
and make sure there are no excess glue
drops to harden and get in the way. Put the
top onto the plywood core: there needs to
be a gap of at least 3/16" between the core
and the sides of the top, but the biscuited

Base Exploded View

MATERIAL LIST—*TOP ASSEMBLY*

		T x W x L
1	Core (2)	¾" x 40⅛" x 52½"
2	Top (1)	¾" x 40½" x 52½"
3	Top Edges (2)	¾" x 2¼" x 52½"
4	End Caps (2)	¾" x 2¼" x 42"

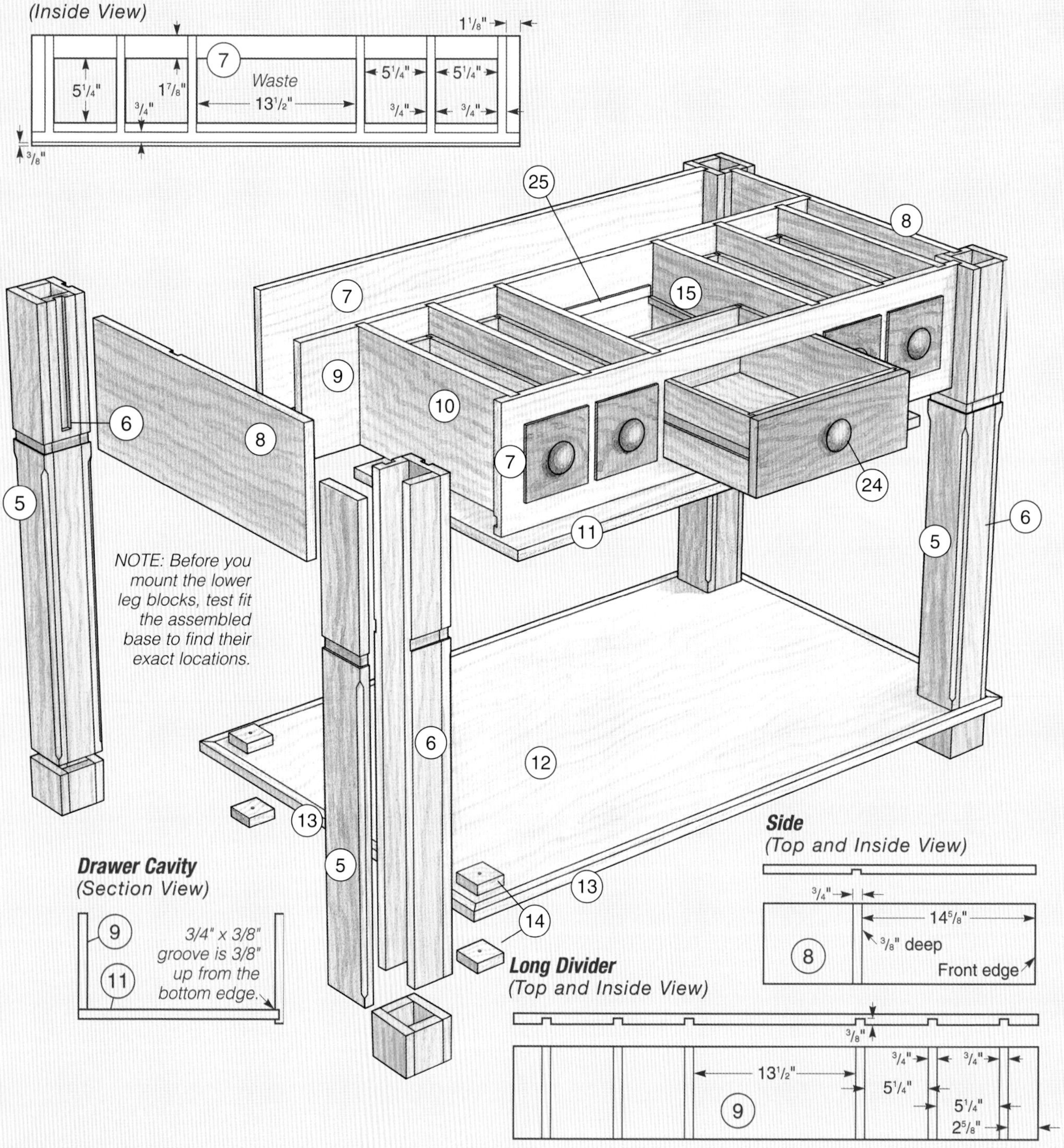

Front
(Inside View)
1 1/8"
5 1/4"
1 7/8"
3/4"
Waste
13 1/2"
5 1/4"
5 1/4"
3/4"
3/4"
3/8"
NOTE: Before you mount the lower leg blocks, test fit the assembled base to find their exact locations.
Drawer Cavity
(Section View)
3/4" x 3/8" groove is 3/8" up from the bottom edge.
Long Divider
(Top and Inside View)
Side
(Top and Inside View)
3/4"
14 5/8"
3/8" deep
Front edge
3/8"
13 1/2"
3/4"
3/4"
5 1/4"
5 1/4"
2 5/8"

ends of the top must match the core exactly. Put the endcaps onto the top with the biscuits nestled in their grooves. DO NOT GLUE THIS PIECE ON! Drill counterbored screw holes through the endcaps and screw them to the core. This allows the laminated top to expand and contract with seasonal humidity without fracturing. Plug the screw holes, sand the top smooth, and set it aside for a bit.

The Basic Base

There is nothing tricky about constructing the base unit. Begin by creating the legs from the staves and fillers (pieces 5 and 6). Cut them to size, then glue and clamp together. Their hollow construction will come in handy later. Once the glue has cured, sand them smooth and trim them exactly to length on the table saw. Go ahead and cut off the feet, and set them aside. Now use the table saw to reveal the little decorative dado around the barrel of the leg. (See the *Elevation Drawing on the next page* for these details.) Use a router in a router table to plow the grooves into the upper faces of the legs. Square up the ends of the grooves so they are ready for the front, back and sides

(pieces 7 and 8). Finally, use your router and a large chamfering bit to form the decorative leg bevels.

Cut the remaining sheet stock parts (pieces 9, 10, 11 and 12) to size. There are a number of dadoes and grooves to be cut into these pieces. Form them all on the table saw with a dado head installed. Again, the *Elevation Drawings* will specify the details.

Cut openings for the drawers in the face of the front after you form the dadoes and groove in its back face. Miter the shelf trim (piece 13) around the shelf (glue and finish nail it securely), and cut the leg blocks (pieces 14) and drawer slides (pieces 15) to size, but set them aside for the time being.

Now it's time to assemble the base. Rob glued and clamped it together on his work table with the legs pointed up in the air. That helped him align the upper edges of all the dividers, front, back and sides evenly. If you plan to paint this unit as Rob did, a finish nail here and there is no cause for worry. You might want to hold off on attaching the feet until you get it into your kitchen: that way it will clear a 30" door. (Rob found this out the hard way!) Once the glue has cured, go ahead and glue the drawer slides in place to complete the base assembly.

MATERIAL LIST—*BASE ASSEMBLY*

		T x W x L
5	Leg Staves (8)	¾" x 3¾" x 33"
6	Leg Fillers (8)	¾" x 2¼" x 33"
7	Front and Back (2)	¾" x 9" x 41¼"
8	Sides (2)	¾" x 9" x 23¼"
9	Long Divider (1)	¾" x 7⅞" x 44¼"
10	Short Dividers (6)	¾" x 8¼" x 16½"
11	Bottom (1)	¾" x 16⅞" x 39"
12	Shelf (1)	¾" x 30" x 48"
13	Shelf Trim (1)	¾" x ¾" x 170"
14	Leg Blocks (12)	¾" x 2¼" x 2¼"
15	Drawer Slides (10)	⅜" x ¾" x 16½"

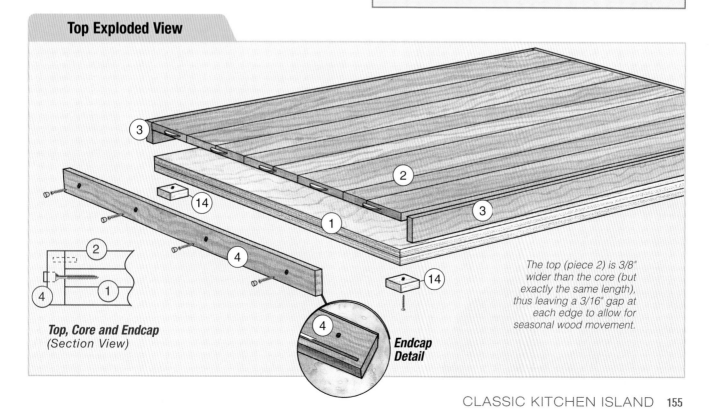

Top Exploded View

Top, Core and Endcap
(Section View)

Endcap Detail

The top (piece 2) is 3/8" wider than the core (but exactly the same length), thus leaving a 3/16" gap at each edge to allow for seasonal wood movement.

MATERIAL LIST—*DRAWERS*

		T x W x L
16	Drawer Sides (8)	1/2" x 5 1/4" x 15 3/4"
17	Drawer Fronts and Backs (8)	1/2" x 5 1/4" x 4 3/4"
18	Drawer Bottoms (4)	1/4" x 4 3/4" x 15 1/4"
19	Drawer Faces (4)	3/4" x 5 1/4" x 5 1/4"
20	Large Drawer Sides (2)	1/2" x 5 1/4" x 15 3/4"
21	Large Drawer Front and Back (2)	1/2" x 5 1/4" x 13 1/4"
22	Large Drawer Bottom (1)	1/4" x 13 1/2" x 15 1/4"
23	Large Drawer Face (1)	3/4 x 5 1/4" x 13 1/2"
24	Drawer Pulls (5)	2" Dia.
25	Spacers (5)	Trim to fit
26	Baskets (2)	Wicker, optional

Leg Block Locations
(Bottom View, Core)

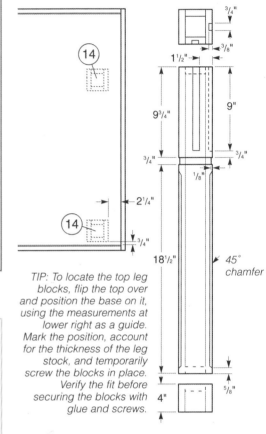

TIP: To locate the top leg blocks, flip the top over and position the base on it, using the measurements at lower right as a guide. Mark the position, account for the thickness of the leg stock, and temporarily screw the blocks in place. Verify the fit before securing the blocks with glue and screws.

Drawer Exploded View

Drawer Slide Locations

The 3/4" grooves for the slides are 3/16" deep, centered on the drawers and dividers.

Drawer Corner Detail

If you choose to use hanging wicker baskets, you may need to re-machine their hangers to match the inset drawing at right.

Remove

The Drawers and Last Details

The simple corner joints on these drawers call for a bit of production woodworking. Rob machined all the drawer parts (pieces 16 through 23) at once and took advantage of each setup on the table saw to do all similar pieces at the same time. Dry-fit the drawers to test their joinery and to see how they fit into the base. When you're satisfied, glue and clamp them up, then mount the drawer pulls (pieces 24) to the drawer faces before you mount the faces to the drawers with screws.

With drawer construction behind you, sand them smooth and put two coats of clear finish on the drawers, inside and out.

Finishing Up

Use the drawer spacers (pieces 25) to adjust the drawer registration. Rob painted the base unit with white oil-based enamel so it would be easy to clean. As for the top, sand it to 600 grit, raise the grain with water and sand again with 600. Follow that up with several coats of butcher block oil.

Move the island to where you want to use it before you attach the top and feet (see notes on *Elevation Drawing*). Apply construction adhesive around the top of the legs to secure the top.

Add some sliding baskets to store spuds and onions down below, if you like. With that done, the only thing left is to screw the legs to the floor and get ready to start cooking. This project will delight your guests, no matter how good a chef you are.

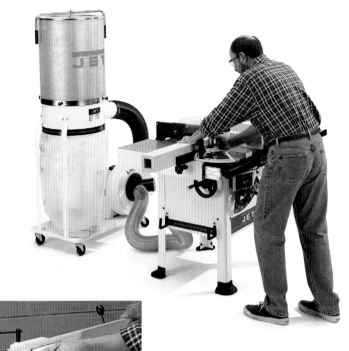

Form the island's feet by cutting them off the glued-up legs. Most of the machining on this project can be completed on a good table saw.

Before laminating the top, establish straight, square edges by jointing the hard maple stock.

Quick Tip

Table Saw Extension

After many years of using a radial arm saw, one reader wrote in to tell us the immediate weakness of table saws when he finally bought one: whatever he sawed went off the end of the table onto the floor. His answer was to make a sliding 24" x 24" plywood extension table attached to square aluminum tubing, as shown in the sketch here. When it's not in use, this outfeed table slides out of it's telescopic tubes and can be hung on a wall. For sawing heavy or extra-long stock, you may need to put a support under the table to prevent the tubing from bending. For greater rigidity, buy thicker-walled aluminum tubing, or switch to steel tubing instead.

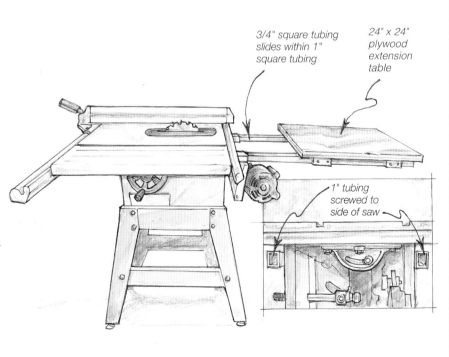

3/4" square tubing slides within 1" square tubing

24" x 24" plywood extension table

1" tubing screwed to side of saw

Barbecue Cart

Full size pattern

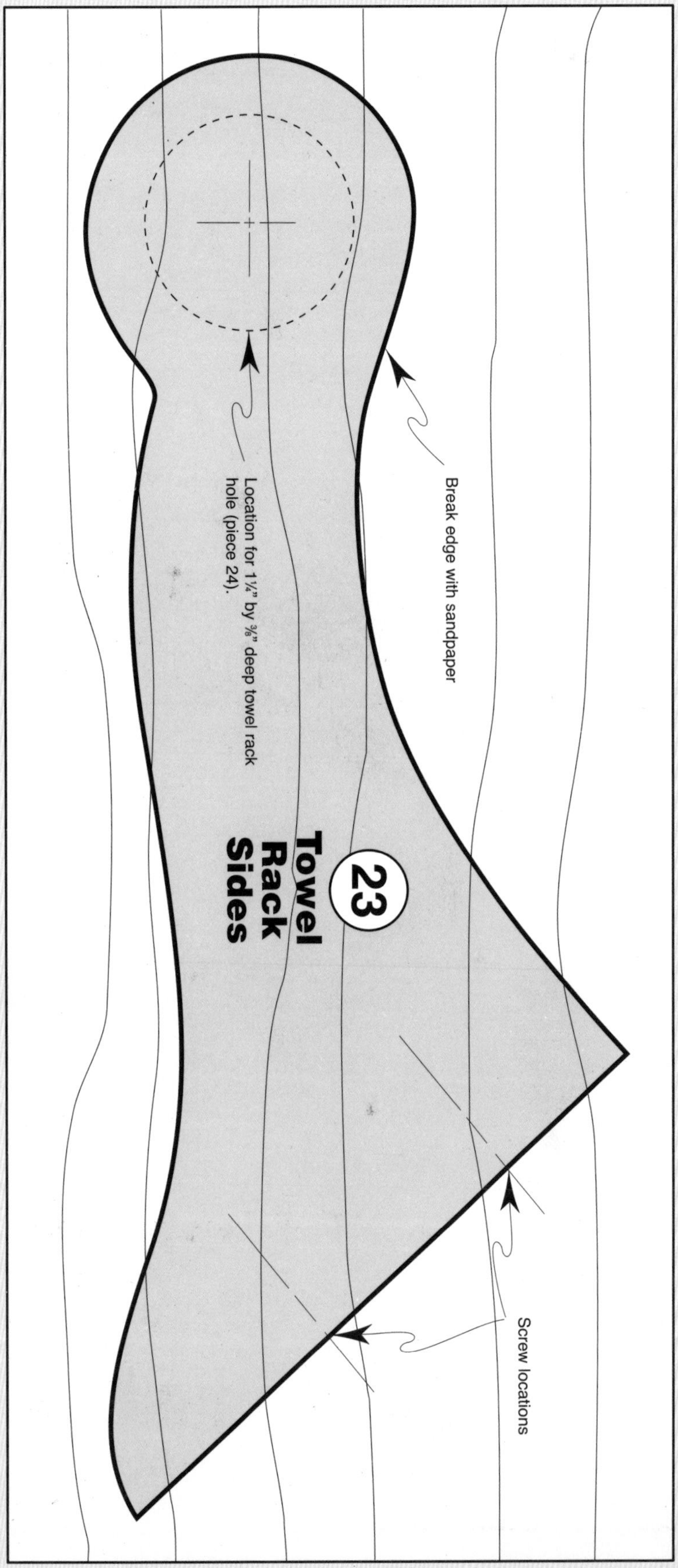

Location for 1½" by ⅜" deep towel rack hole (piece 24).

Break edge with sandpaper

Towel Rack Sides

(23)

Screw locations

Sharpening Station

Full size pattern

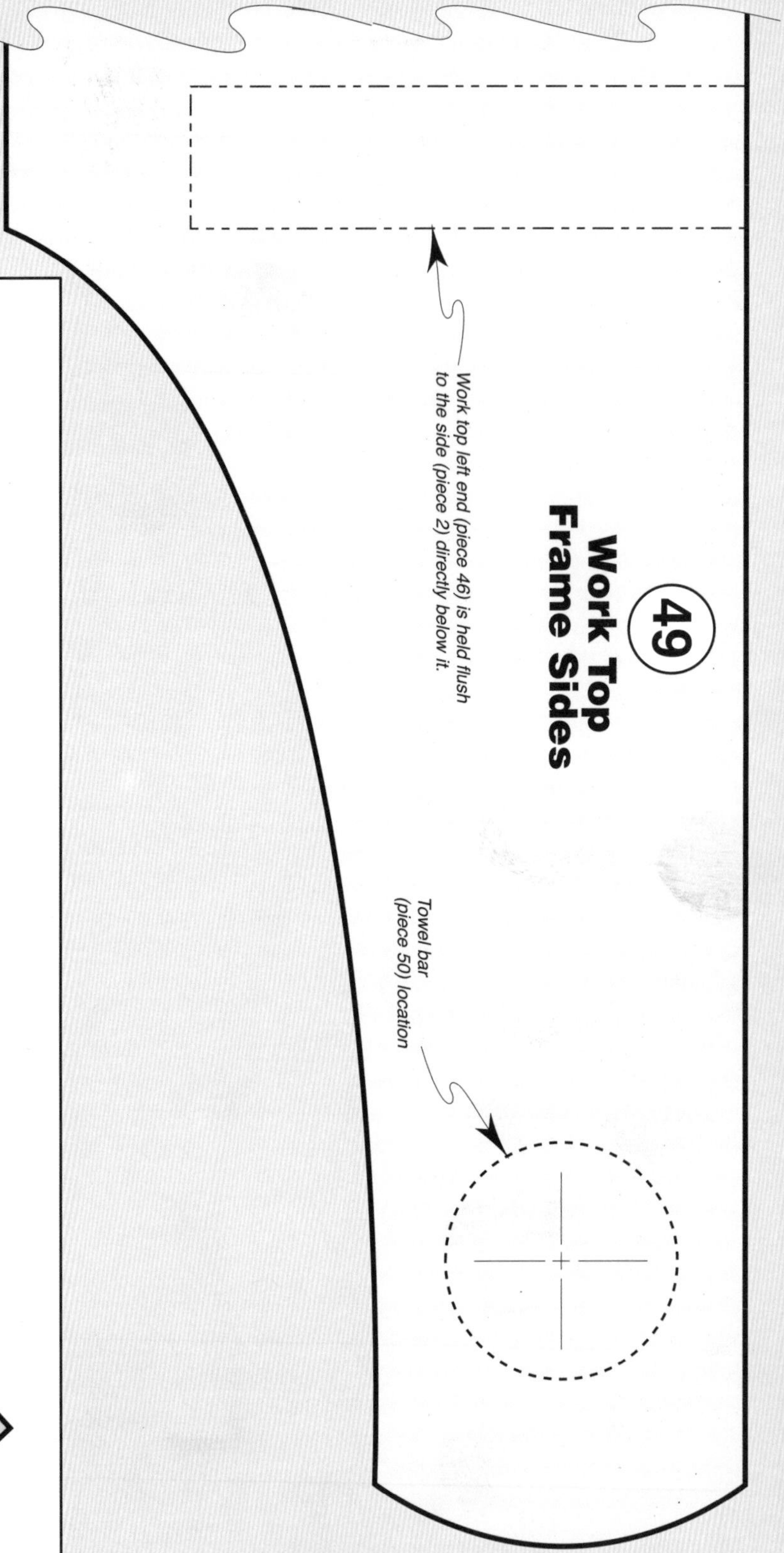

Work top left end (piece 46) is held flush to the side (piece 2) directly below it.

Work Top Frame Sides

(49)

Towel bar (piece 50) location